IMAGES
of America

NORTH CAROLINA SKI RESORTS

On the Cover: Pausing near the top of Sugar Mountain, this young lady is likely Hope Martin—niece of founder Tom Brigham. Here, she poses with a friend about 1968, as they admire the sweeping, snowcapped vistas of North Carolina, Virginia, and Tennessee. (Photograph by Bob Webb; courtesy of Al Traver Collection.)

IMAGES
of America

North Carolina Ski Resorts

Donna Gayle Akers

ARCADIA
PUBLISHING

ISBN 978-1-4671-2256-6

Published by Arcadia Publishing
Charleston, South Carolina

Printed in the United States of America

Library of Congress Control Number: 2014938391

For all general information, please contact Arcadia Publishing:
Telephone 843-853-2070
Fax 843-853-0044
E-mail sales@arcadiapublishing.com
For customer service and orders:
Toll-Free 1-888-313-2665

Visit us on the Internet at www.arcadiapublishing.com

To the brave visionaries who believed that skiing could succeed in Dixie, and to the staff members who kept these resorts open.

Contents

ACKNOWLEDGMENTS

Several people provided information, assistance, and photographs for this book, and it could not have come together without their enthusiasm, patience, and encouragement. Specifically, I would like to thank Gil Adams, Chris Bates, the Blowing Rock Art & History Museum, James Brooks, Tammy Brown, Greta Browning, Cataloochee Ranch Collection, Mary Coker, Jim Cottrell, Lennie Cottom, Hawksnest Snowtubing and Zipline, Hound Ears Collection, Kim Jochl, Randy Johnson, Cindy Keller, Katie McAlpin Owens from Arcadia Publishing, Ann Isles, Kent Moberg, Brad Moretz, Reba and Grady Moretz, Fred Pfohl, Jason Reagan, skisoutheast.com, Judy Coker Sutton, Rick Stargill, Alison Teague, Dedy Trever, and the W.R. Eury Appalachian Collection at Appalachian State University.

Introduction

The history of the ski industry in North Carolina has its roots in the vision of community leaders who wanted to supplement the economies of their rural mountain communities by attracting tourists during the winter months. Tourism had been increasing since the Civil War, when many lowland families had sent their kinfolk up to the mountains for safety. From the 19th century on, the residents of the warmer flatlands began to summer in the mountains—looking for relief from the oppressive heat, mosquitoes, and diseases of the summer months. Grand hotels—such as the Greene Park Inn in Blowing Rock, the Old Edwards Inn in Highlands, the High Hampton Inn in Cashiers, and the Grove Park Inn in Asheville—and healing springs resorts in the mountains of North Carolina still provide visitors with fine accommodations, recreation, and health improvements. Areas such as Blowing Rock, Highlands, Cashiers, and Asheville developed into summer resort communities that promised relaxation, recreation, and salubrious results. Visitors to the area were said to "summer" in the mountains, but, in the late 1800s, the tourists' goals shifted more from health to recreation. As a result, these communities began to promote the natural beauty of the area as a major draw.

Despite this, community leaders in these areas knew that creating a year-round tourist economy would be even more beneficial. Improved roads and transportation enabled easier access to the mountains, drawing greater numbers of visitors. As snowmaking technology improved, neighboring southeastern states built ski areas, and Southerners became more interested in the sport, these communities found the winter tourism activity that they had been missing.

Very little organized, recreational skiing took place in North Carolina prior to the 1960s, although students from Lees-McRae College, in Banner Elk, are reported to have made skis in the 1930s and skied around small hills near campus. Using skis made in the college shop, these brave students slid down the hills and formed a ski club. During the Great Depression, skiers were photographed by Works Progress Administration photographers in the Banner Elk area, lending credence to this claim.

According to Randy Johnson—author of *Southern Snow: The Winter Guide to Dixie*—a group of investors planned to build a ski slope on Roan Mountain, near Spruce Pine, North Carolina, as early as 1951. This would have been the first resort south of the Mason-Dixon Line, but it was never developed. Instead, the earliest recorded ski area in North Carolina was the Mount Mitchell Ski Club, which was founded in 1954 by E.M. Carr, Robert Beard, and other investors. Although the 6,684-foot-tall Mount Mitchell was—and still is—a state park, the group obtained permission to clear an area for a ski slope. In 1957, a small 100-by-500-foot slope was cut into the forest for cross-country skiers to use. There were problems with reaching the site, however, as the mountain was accessed via the Blue Ridge Parkway, which is often obstructed by snow during the winter months. This kept the mountain ski area from growing, so it was shut down.

The South faced many challenges in the development of its ski resorts, including unpredictable winter weather, the development of snowmaking technology, and convincing Southern residents to try skiing. The South's first ski area was located at Virginia's Homestead resort, which was developed in the winter of 1959–1960. Southerners were becoming aware of skiing, as ski resorts in neighboring Virginia and West Virginia were proving that—with the help of snowmaking equipment—one could ski in the land of Dixie. As a result, developers and investors began to study the possibilities of creating southern ski areas.

Due to deep, regular snowfall in the mid-to-late 1960s, improvements in snowmaking technology, and the increasing interest in skiing among Southerners, the mountainous areas south of the Mason-Dixon Line began to look like prime locations for ski areas. This was especially true after record snowfalls resulted in the National Guard organizing helicopter food drops to snowbound mountaineers. Following these deep snows, families from the flatlands would drive up to the mountains to see the snow and sled down hillsides. As an example, over 83 inches of snow reportedly fell in the Boone area during the winter of 1960. As a result, the Boone Chamber of Commerce began to study winter tourism avenues. Later, in the winter of 1961–1962, the Cataloochee ski resort was built in Maggie Valley, North Carolina, as was the Ober Gatlinburg resort in Tennessee, both of which introduced more Southerners to the sport.

The town of Banner Elk can also claim to have provided the area's first lift-served skiing in 1964, serving a small bowl on land owned by Auburn and Nelta Andrews. Dr. Charles Wiley installed a tow, sold shares to local doctors, and utilized a Jeep to power the lift. Eventually, larger ski areas proved more attractive and challenging, and this area closed. However, the old equipment is still sitting in the field.

Snowmaking has come a long way over the decades and is key to the success of these southern resorts—allowing the resorts to open earlier, extend the season, and offer better quality and more controlled amounts of snow for the sport. In fact, the southern ski areas were the world's first resorts to depend solely on snowmaking. Although the identity of the inventor of the snowmaking process is debatable, it is believed that Wayne Pierce—a Northeastern skier—had skied on crushed ice on the slopes at Mohawk Mountain, Connecticut, which was laid on the slope by owner Walt Schoenknecht. The owner of Larchmont Engineering visited Mohawk to see Pierce's snowmaking and ended up buying the patent—making the concept of mixing pressurized air and water inside a snow gun into a reality by the mid-1950s. Another claim has been made that the first snowmaking process was developed by Joseph Tropeano, who used compressed air and water propelled from a gun to create a mist that protected orange groves during freezing weather. When Tropeano tested his system in Massachusetts, it resulted in snow—which surprised everyone. Larchmont investigated this process as well and began to produce and sell these early snowmakers to ski resorts in 1951.

Snowmaking technology continued to improve and develop, and today, these systems are able to provide all of the snow cover needed for skiing in North Carolina, though natural snow is always welcomed. Grooming has become more high tech as well, and resorts have invested in expensive machines to shape the snow and create terrain parks that challenge experienced skiers and accommodate snowboarders.

According to Randy Johnson, the next step in the development of the North Carolina ski industry came when Tom "Doc" Brigham visited the region and shared his research on the potential for skiing in the area. Tom Brigham was a New Englander living in Alabama, where he had a successful dental practice. Possessing a Northerner's skiing interest and having read about the new snowmaking technology in *Reader's Digest*, Brigham noted ski areas springing up in adjoining Virginia and decided that they might work in North Carolina, too. He studied the mountains and their weather patterns, accumulating the research needed to convince investors that skiing could work in the state. He is now acknowledged as the "Father of Southern Skiing."

The history of each North Carolina resort will be discussed throughout this text—their stories accompanied by historic images taken from the collections of dedicated locals. Many of these resorts still exist today, including Cataloochee Ranch and Ski Area (opened in 1961), Appalachian Ski Mountain (opened as Blowing Rock Ski Lodge in 1962), Ski Sapphire Valley (1964), Beech Mountain Resort (1967), Sugar Mountain Resort (1969), and Wolf Ridge Resort (1970). Several other ski areas were opened in the state, but have since been closed for various reasons. These "lost" ski areas include Hound Ears (opened in 1964–1965), High Meadows (1966), Mill Ridge (1970), Hawksnest (opened as the Seven Devils Ski Area in 1966), and Ski Skaly (1980). Most of these resorts were built as components of residential real estate developments, which provided recreational amenities to residents and lodging for vacationers.

Although these ski resorts were profitable in their early years, the real estate slump in the 1970s caused many of these partnerships to go bankrupt. Problems with financial management were an issue with several of the resorts as well. It is amazing that the six extant ski areas have managed to expand, improve, and still remain popular and profitable in spite of their difficulties and the number ownership changes.

Selling skiing in North Carolina faced two major challenges: combating the negative stereotypes of the region and introducing Southerners to skiing. National publications may have featured jokes about southern ski slopes being covered with grits instead of snow, but the perseverance and skill of the resort marketing teams allowed them to succeed and be taken seriously as ski destinations. Fortunately, the media eventually realized how popular the southern ski resorts had become, thanks to both their contribution to local economies and the testimonials of thousands of people who lived nearby.

In an astute marketing ploy, several ski resort managers put together ski shows, employing an Astroturf or plastic-pellet covered ski slope that they took to stores, shopping centers, and trade shows. The ski resorts also featured races and special events and partnered with hotels to offer ski travel packages. Jim Cottrell and Jack Lester were responsible for fostering skiing as a credited college course and also sponsored college classes at Appalachian Ski Mountain through the French-Swiss Ski College. In 1969, the Snow Carnival of the South was formed to draw skiers to Watauga and Avery Counties, which led to other competitions being held at the region's ski resort. North Carolina governor Robert Scott even lauded the Snow Carnival of the South and ski industry as helping to establish the state as a year-round vacationland. In 1972, the High Country's resorts had a special visit by three-time Olympic gold medalist Jean-Claude Killy. His visit coincided with the premiere of his first feature film, *Snow Job*, and enhanced the reputation of these resorts by earning them international media coverage. In 1976, the first North Carolina Winter Special Olympics were held at Appalachian Ski Mountain—an event that is still hosted there today. All of these tactics served to focus attention and media on the ski areas and helped to educate Southerners about skiing.

According to Randy Johnson, the Southeastern Ski Areas Association was first organized in 1964, helping to build a coalition from the South's disparate ski resorts and establishing a dependable reporting system for ski conditions. In 1977, North Carolina formed a ski area association and, in 1981, helped to pass the South's first skier safety act. In addition, ski clubs formed across the Southeast, and these groups made regular group trips that helped to sustain the ski areas. In fact, the Atlanta Ski Club was so determined to learn to ski prior to visiting the resort that members took their first lessons on sawdust.

Another reason for the success of these resorts is the high caliber of instruction offered to skiers. Initially, Austrians and other Europeans were imported to teach, as they had the needed accreditations, but, eventually, Dick Heckman at Cataloochee started teaching and joined the Professional Ski Instructors of America (PSIA). At first, native North Carolina ski instructors had to drive up to New England for training, but that is no longer necessary today. Additionally, there is French-Swiss Ski College—an independent school formed at Appalachian Ski Mountain by Jim Cottrell. Over the years, it has raised the standards for teaching and has attracted many high-quality teachers. Today, each of the resorts provides lessons by accredited teachers, and they have, together, taught thousands of guests how to conquer the slopes.

The National Ski Patrol has made ski safety a priority as well, and it was the first national ski organization in the South. Keith Argow became a patrol examiner and helped to develop a training regimen for local ski patrol members. Other patrollers who were important in the early development included Dave and Lynn Dillard, Carl Lathrop, Eric DeGroat, Roger Bollinger, and Jack Britt.

Over the years, the ski resorts have had a major positive impact to the local economies—contributing through occupancy taxes, as well as lodging and retail sales. This impact is most directly shown during ski season, from mid-November through early March. An economic impact study of the 2009–2010 ski season—conducted by RRC Associates—estimated that the gross lodging revenues collected during ski season provide a large percentage of total tax revenue: 82 percent for the Village of Sugar Mountain, 53 percent for Banner Elk, 73 percent for Beech Mountain, 36.5 percent for Watauga County, 25.7 percent for Blowing Rock, 21.4 percent for Haywood County, and 46.7 percent for Madison County. According to this study, the North Carolina ski industry provided over 96 year-round jobs and 1,557 seasonal jobs during the 2009–2010 season. According to the report, the industry also generated over $32 million in gross revenue through the sales of lift tickets, equipment and lessons, retail items, and food and drink. Additionally, 52 percent of visitors to the six ski areas came from North Carolina, while the remaining 48 percent were from other areas.

Although the forecast is snowy, the future of this industry is certainly bright. Interest in skiing does not seem to be waning, and the local governments depend on the winter tourism the ski resorts bring. All six of the state's ski areas are planning for the 21st century and are prepared to change with the times. Just as snowboarding changed the dynamic of ski areas, other changes may occur, and these tough, underdog southern resorts have already proven that they can handle themselves.

Being the leader in southeastern skiing is an important boon for the state of North Carolina. We may not ski on grits, but we have the grit and determination to make ski resorts a part of our history *and* our future.

One

Cataloochee Ski Area

Cataloochee is derived from a Cherokee word meaning "wave upon wave"—an apt description of the lofty mountains surrounding this area in Haywood County, above Maggie Valley, North Carolina. Tom Alexander—a former park ranger and forester—and his wife, Judith, first opened a tourist camp on the site during the Great Depression, catering to those who wanted to fish and camp in the woods. This was successful, and in 1939, the Alexanders opened Cataloochee Ranch on Fie Top—offering a lodge and cabins, as well as horseback riding, hiking, and fishing. Cataloochee Ranch was also a working sheep and cattle farm, and it provided much-needed jobs for local residents.

As early as the 1940s, the Alexanders and their ranch hands made skis from scrap lumber and harness straps. Tom began to believe that winter skiing on the ranch might help to provide winter work for his employees and attract more guests. The Alexanders studied the local climate and visited several New England ski resorts to observe the business and the new snowmaking technologies. They opened the ski resort in 1961, with a 1,000-foot slope, a 300-foot beginner area, and only three inches of natural snow. Converting the old barn into a ski lodge, the Alexanders purchased equipment and hired a ski instructor from Austria. Due to the family's hard work, the resort was immediately popular and profitable in its first year.

In 1968, the slopes were moved to a nearby mountain that was more conducive to snowmaking. The Alexanders also built a new lodge, expanded snowmaking capacity, and installed a chairlift on Moody Top. Richard Coker Jr., the Alexanders' son-in-law, helped introduce telemark (or cross-country downhill) skiing to the South. Additionally, the Cataloochee Ski Patrol provided early training for subsequent ski patrols around the state. New trails were added over the years, and the resort always seemed to attract more visitors.

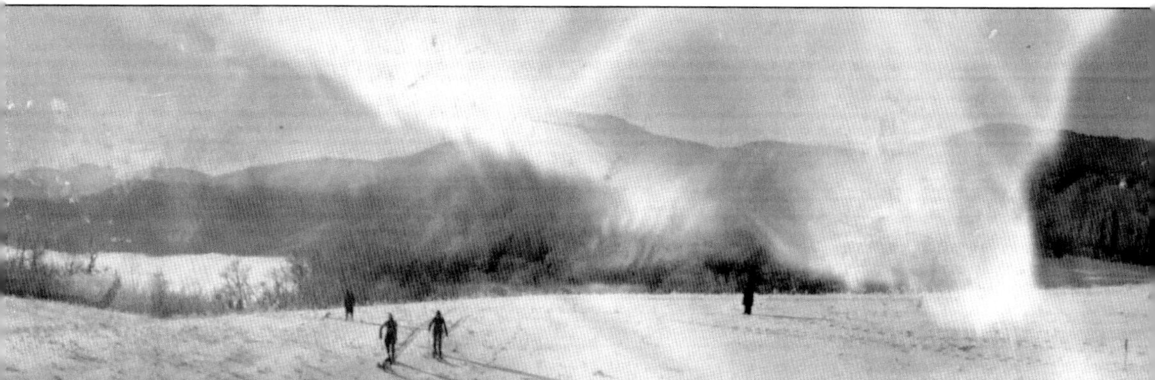

This c. 1940 photograph shows Alexander family members and ranch employees using their homemade skis—made from scrap lumber and harness straps—to cross a pasture in a deep snow. This same pasture was later the location of the resort's first ski slope. When Tom lost his timber industry job during the Depression, he was given the company's camping equipment as his final salary, but he had an idea for how to use it to earn a living. In 1929, he and his wife, Judy, started a tourist business for camping and fishing, and in 1933, they opened a permanent ranch on a farm at the bottom of the Cataloochee Valley, which they leased from the National Park Service. Due to the ranch's success, the Alexanders purchased acreage on Fie Top from Verlin Campbell, the "potato king" of Haywood County, in 1938 and opened the site to visitors in 1939. Tom and Judy Alexander were intent on building the ranch's reputation as a getaway for visitors by offering fishing, horseback riding, and camping trips. The Plott Balsam mountain range—named for the balsam stands that grow at its higher elevations—looms in the background of this photograph. (Courtesy of Cataloochee Ranch Collection.)

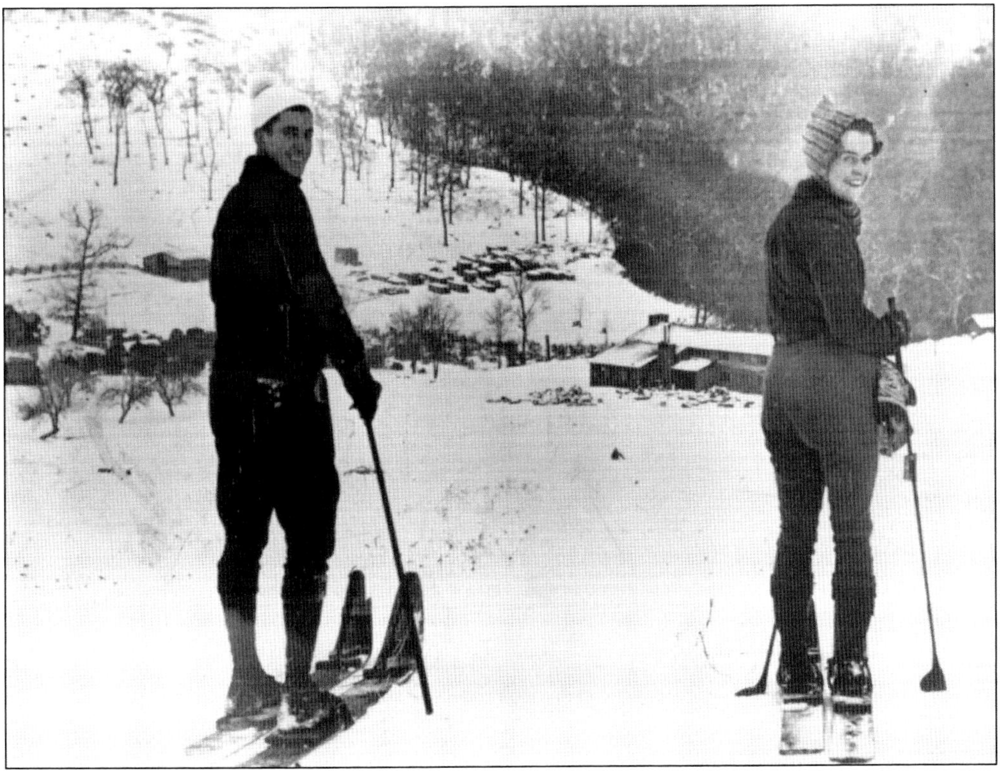

In this c. 1940 photograph, Judy Alexander (right), cofounder of the ranch and resort, stands on her homemade skis looking toward Moody Top Mountain. Judy Alexander worked alongside her husband to build Cataloochee's reputation as a recreational escape. Note the stumps left behind from logging and the original farm buildings, many of which were saved and utilized as part of the ranch and ski resort. (Courtesy of Cataloochee Ranch Collection.)

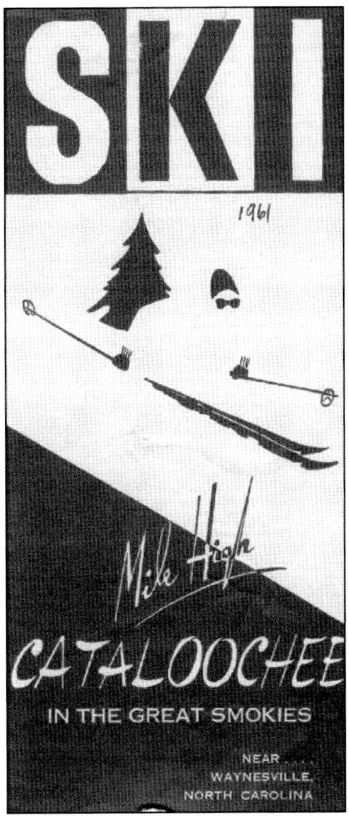

The Alexander family's astute marketing skills produced this ski brochure in 1961, which publicized their new ski area and built on the ranch's popularity. It reads, "At Cataloochee, long-famed as a summer resort, skiing is now a reality. Cataloochee is the highest and southernmost developed ski area in eastern America at 5000 ft.; a truly Alpine feeling pervades this winterland in the Great Smokies." (Courtesy of Cataloochee Ranch Collection.)

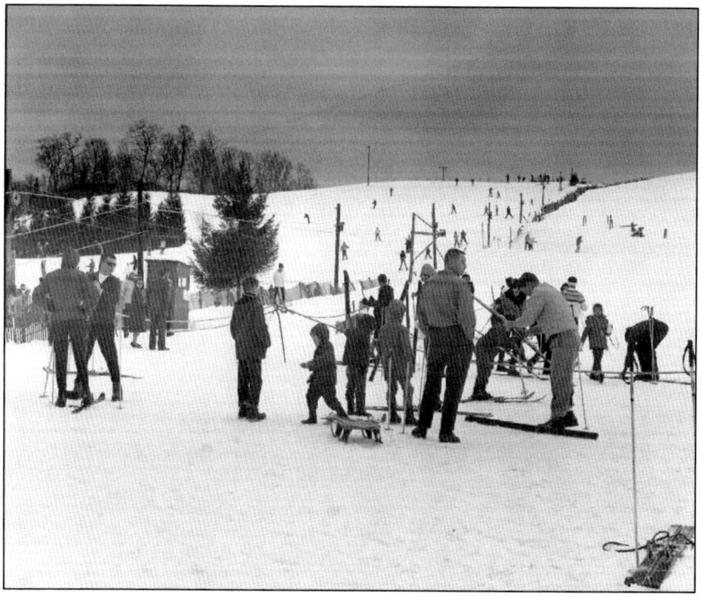

Cataloochee's original ski area was immediately successful when it opened in 1961, as shown in this photograph of a busy day around 1964. A simple rope tow pulled skiers up the 1,000-foot-long slope. Note that the early bindings on the skis in the right foreground were merely straps to secure to one's boots. A youngster in the front of the image has decided to sled instead. (Courtesy of Cataloochee Ranch Collection.)

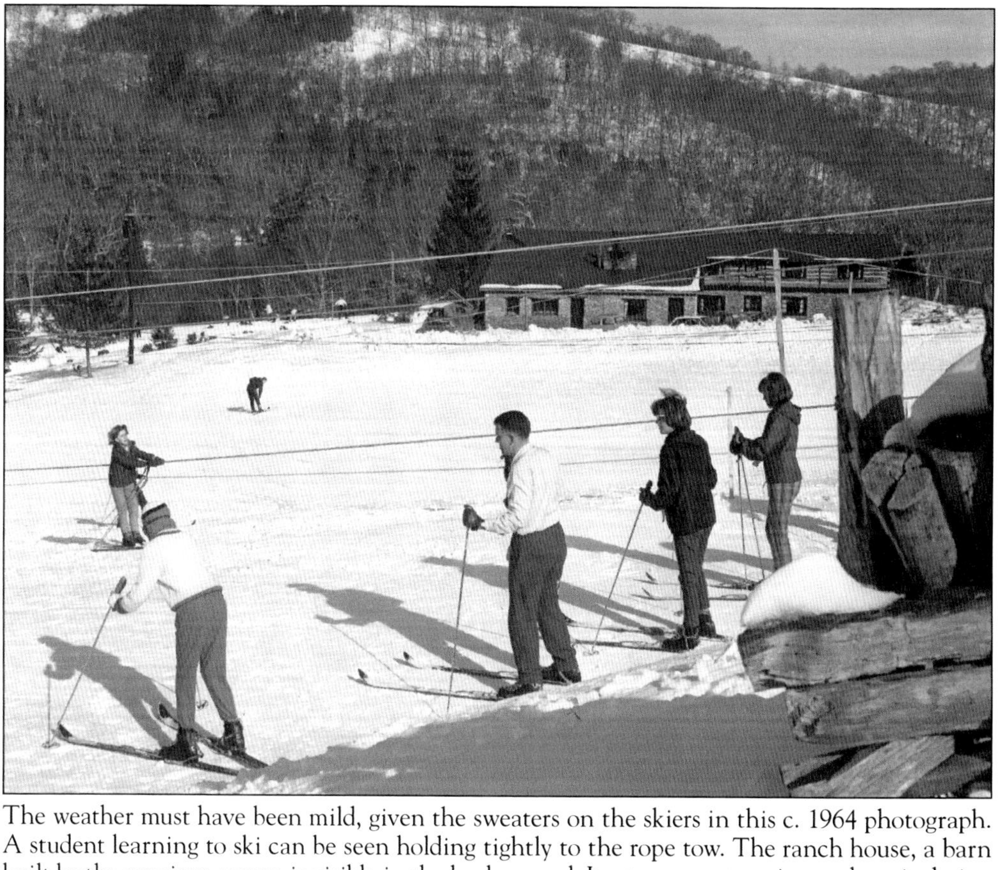

The weather must have been mild, given the sweaters on the skiers in this c. 1964 photograph. A student learning to ski can be seen holding tightly to the rope tow. The ranch house, a barn built by the previous owner, is visible in the background. Its stone construction and rustic design complimented the ranch atmosphere, and meals were served family style at large tables in front of the fireplace. (Courtesy of Cataloochee Ranch Collection.)

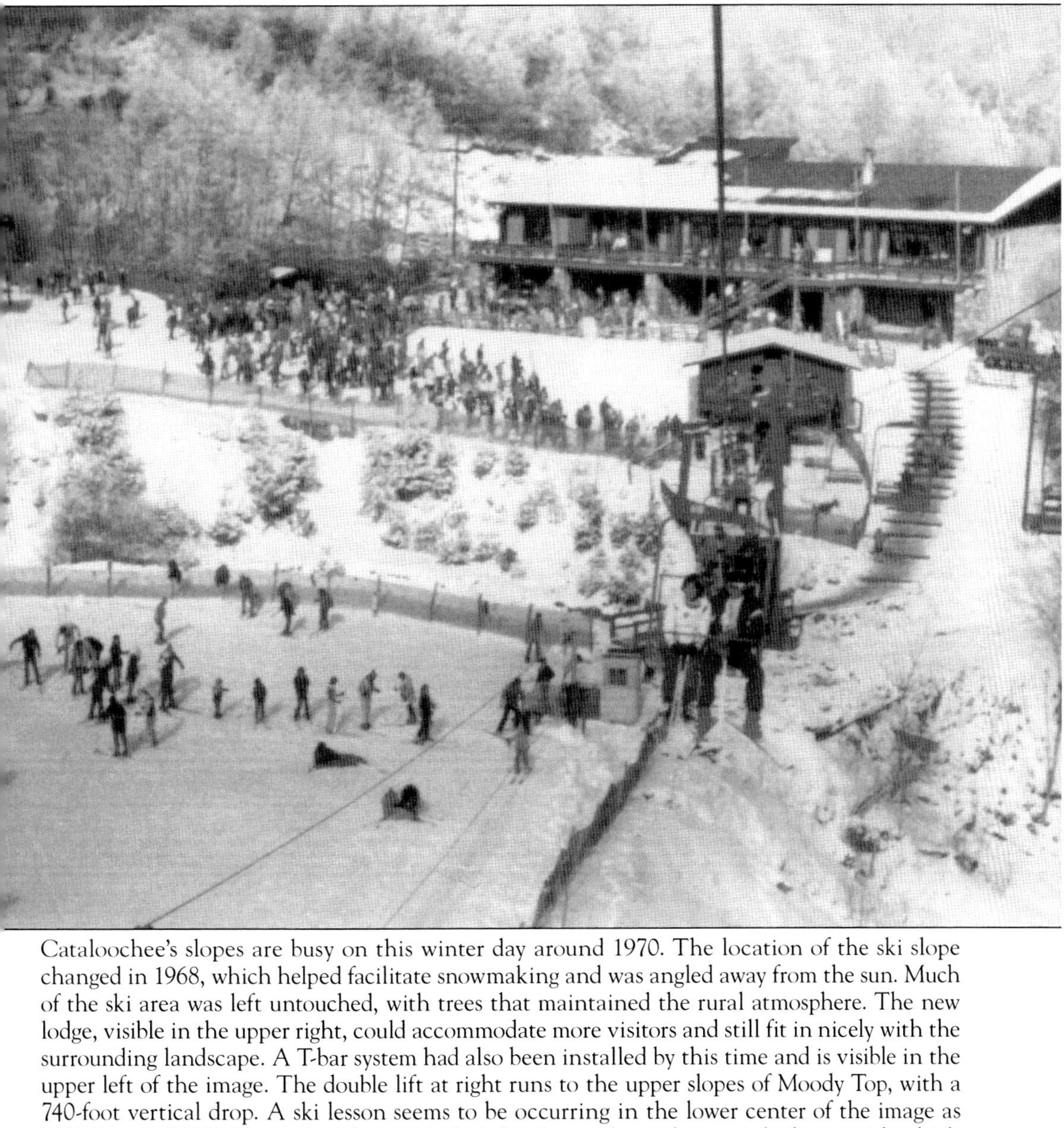

Cataloochee's slopes are busy on this winter day around 1970. The location of the ski slope changed in 1968, which helped facilitate snowmaking and was angled away from the sun. Much of the ski area was left untouched, with trees that maintained the rural atmosphere. The new lodge, visible in the upper right, could accommodate more visitors and still fit in nicely with the surrounding landscape. A T-bar system had also been installed by this time and is visible in the upper left of the image. The double lift at right runs to the upper slopes of Moody Top, with a 740-foot vertical drop. A ski lesson seems to be occurring in the lower center of the image as well. Tom and Judy Alexander, along with their family members, always worked to provide a high caliber of customer service that set them apart from other resorts. In fact, Cataloochee Ranch was recommended as a year-round resort in *Southern Living* magazine in the 1970s. (Courtesy of Cataloochee Ranch Collection.)

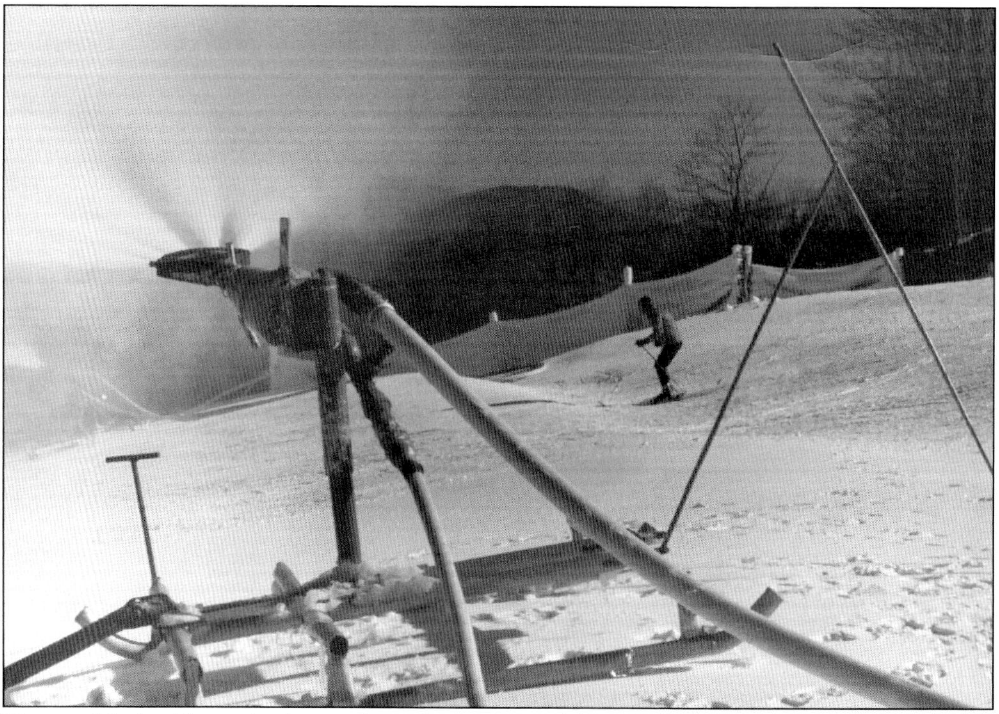

Tom and Judy Alexander knew their ski resort could not provide consistent snow without snowmaking equipment. Tom Aumen, who married into the Alexander family, built the pictured snow gun. The device worked well until the family needed to provide snow to a greater area, driving them to invest in more snowmaking equipment from national distributors. Since snow levels were unpredictable on the southern slopes, relying on snowmaking technology was the only way to stay open all winter. (Courtesy of Cataloochee Ranch Collection.)

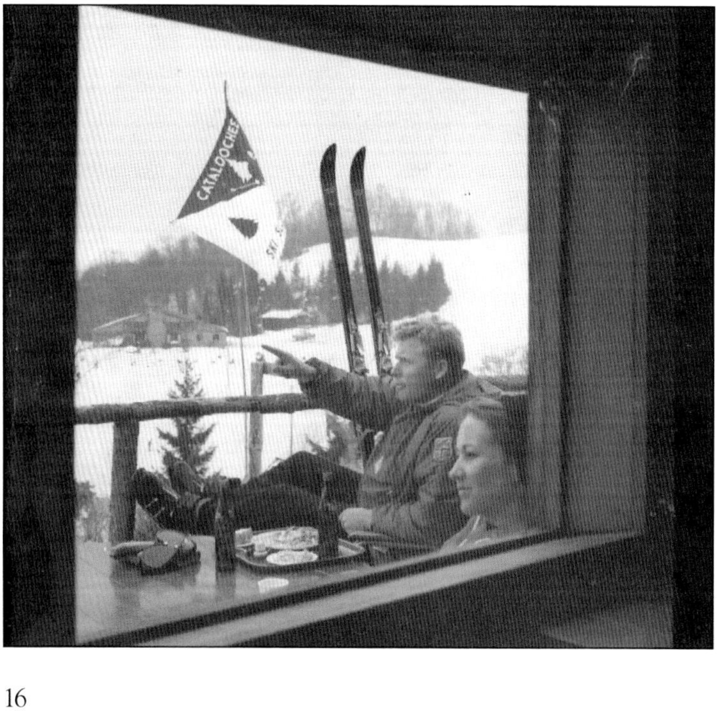

In this c. 1963 photograph, two skiers eat a meal at the ranch house while enjoying the view. A flag advertising the ski school—at which this man may be an instructor—flaps in the wind on this cold day at the slopes. (Courtesy of Cataloochee Ranch Collection.)

This trail map from about 1968 showcases the new, expanded slope area, with its vertical drop of 740 feet. It shows that the resort included a T-bar, with a capacity of 1,200 riders per hour; a beginners' slope, which was 1,000 feet in length; an intermediate slope; a double chairlift, with a capacity of 1,000 riders per hour; and an advanced slope, which was 3,600 feet in length. The area marked for "potential expansion" was later developed into additional slopes (Courtesy of Cataloochee Ranch Collection.)

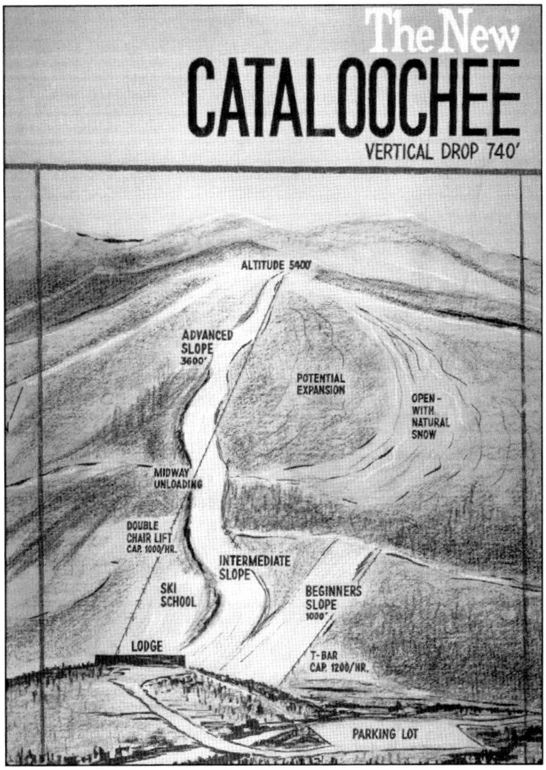

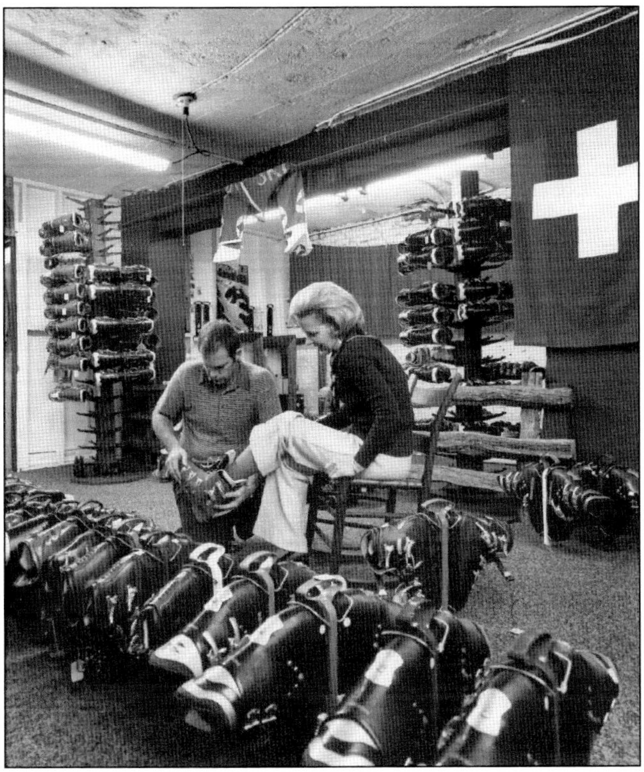

The Alexanders knew that the Atlanta Ski Club was an active one, so—seeing an expanding market—they set up a Cataloochee ski shop in Davison's department store in Atlanta. Davison's first opened its doors in 1891, and in 1927, a large, still extant, store on Peachtree Street was built. Expert staff could fit a customer in boots, skis, and outerwear so they would be ready to hit the slopes when they arrived in the mountains. (Courtesy of Cataloochee Ranch Collection.)

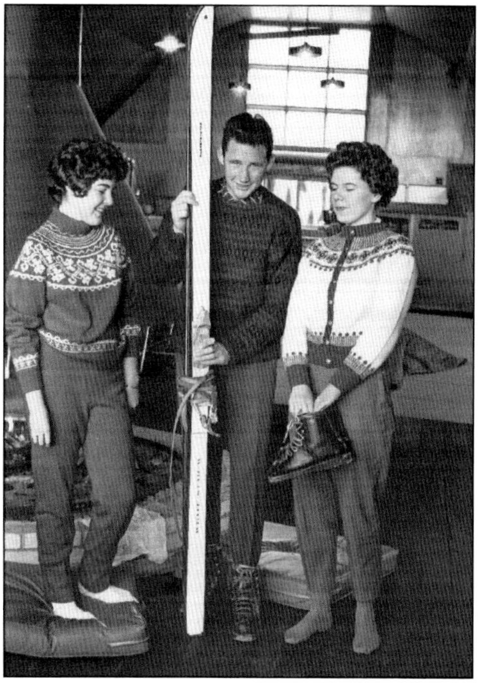

Karl Schoenthaler, an Austrian ski instructor, was brought in during the early days. In this c. 1961 photograph, he shows two female customers skis in the shop at the resort. The skis on display are Kneissl White Stars, which were some of the most sought-after skis in the world in the 1960s. (Courtesy of Cataloochee Ranch Collection.)

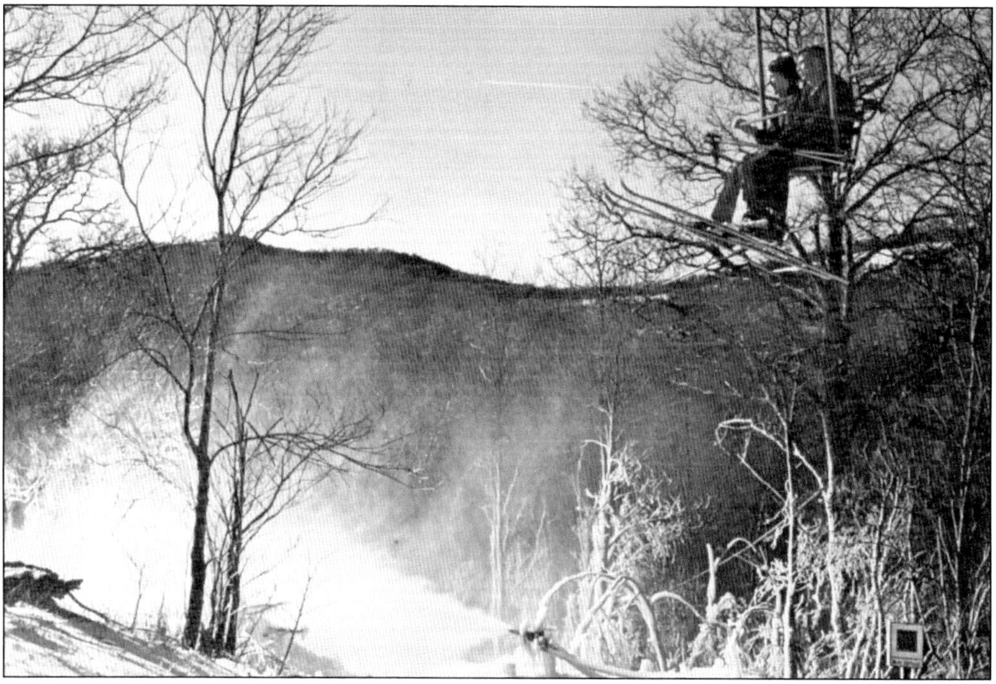

This 1974 postcard from the Cataloochee Ski Area shows the simple double lift transporting skiers up the slopes. The back of the postcard reads, "North Carolina's favorite winter sport is snow skiing, made possible with the advent of below freezing temperatures, modern snow making equipment, and generous amounts of natural snow. Here at Cataloochee Ski Area, skiers enjoy mile long slopes reached by double chair lifts that climb to 5400 feet." (Photograph by Aerial Photography Services; courtesy of Cataloochee Ranch Collection.)

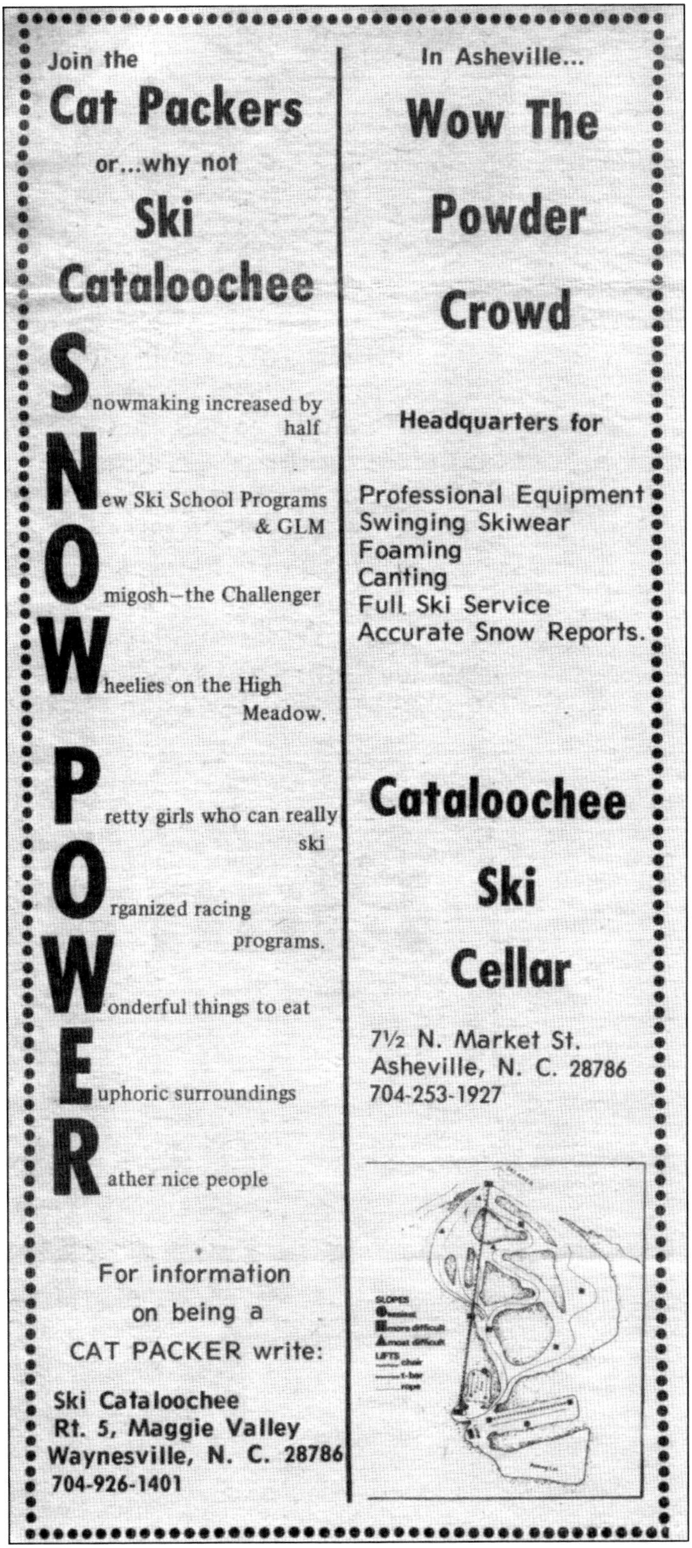

The Alexander family knew promotion was instrumental to the survival of their rural ski lodge. This c. 1970 advertisement for the resort and their store, the Cataloochee Ski Cellar, was published in an Asheville newspaper. The marketing director had coined the phrase "Cat Packer" as a name for Cataloochee skiers. The advertisement describes their increased snowmaking capacity, as well as new ski school programs using the GLM (Graduated Length Method). Since this was one of the earliest ski resorts in North Carolina, marketers had to combat negative views about southern skiing. In the 1960s, news articles called it the "Banana Belt of Skiing" and included jokes about grits covering the slope instead of snow. One photographer even tried to drive some of the ranch's cattle onto the ski slopes to set up a derisive photograph, but Mr. Tom (as he was called) put a stop to it. Advertising in area newspapers, along with their ski shops in Asheville and Atlanta, helped to sell Southern residents on Cataloochee and skiing. (Courtesy of Cataloochee Ranch Collection.)

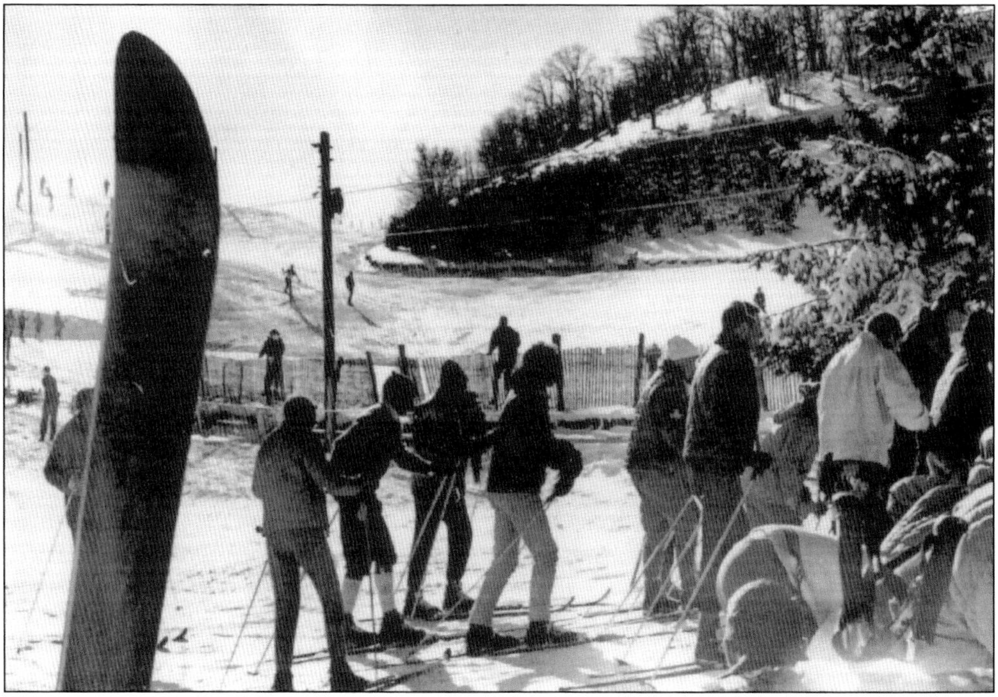

Skiers are lined up for the rope tow in this c. 1965 photograph of the original ski area. Note the alpine-style pants worn by the man in the center. In those days, insulated ski bibs and pants were not common, and skiers often wore their regular pants. (Courtesy of Cataloochee Ranch Collection.)

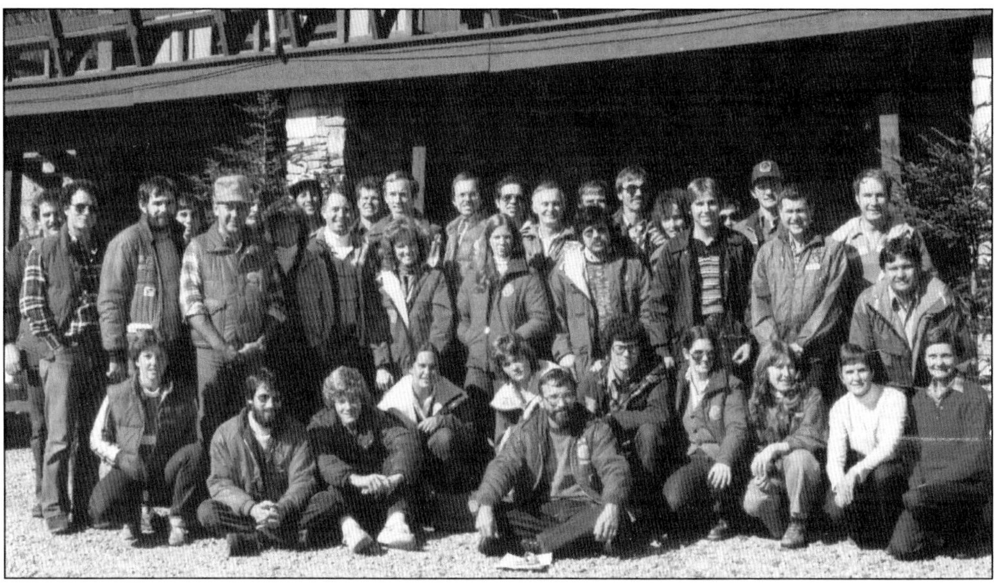

Members of the Cataloochee Ski Patrol are grouped together in this c. 1975 photograph. Ski patrols were mainly volunteer services in the early days, and some patrollers still volunteer their time. Bill and Margie Clinkscales and Karl and Shortie Lathrop organized the first patrol efforts at the resort—outfitting their group with a fiberglass banana boat, splints, and bandages. (Courtesy of Cataloochee Ranch Collection.)

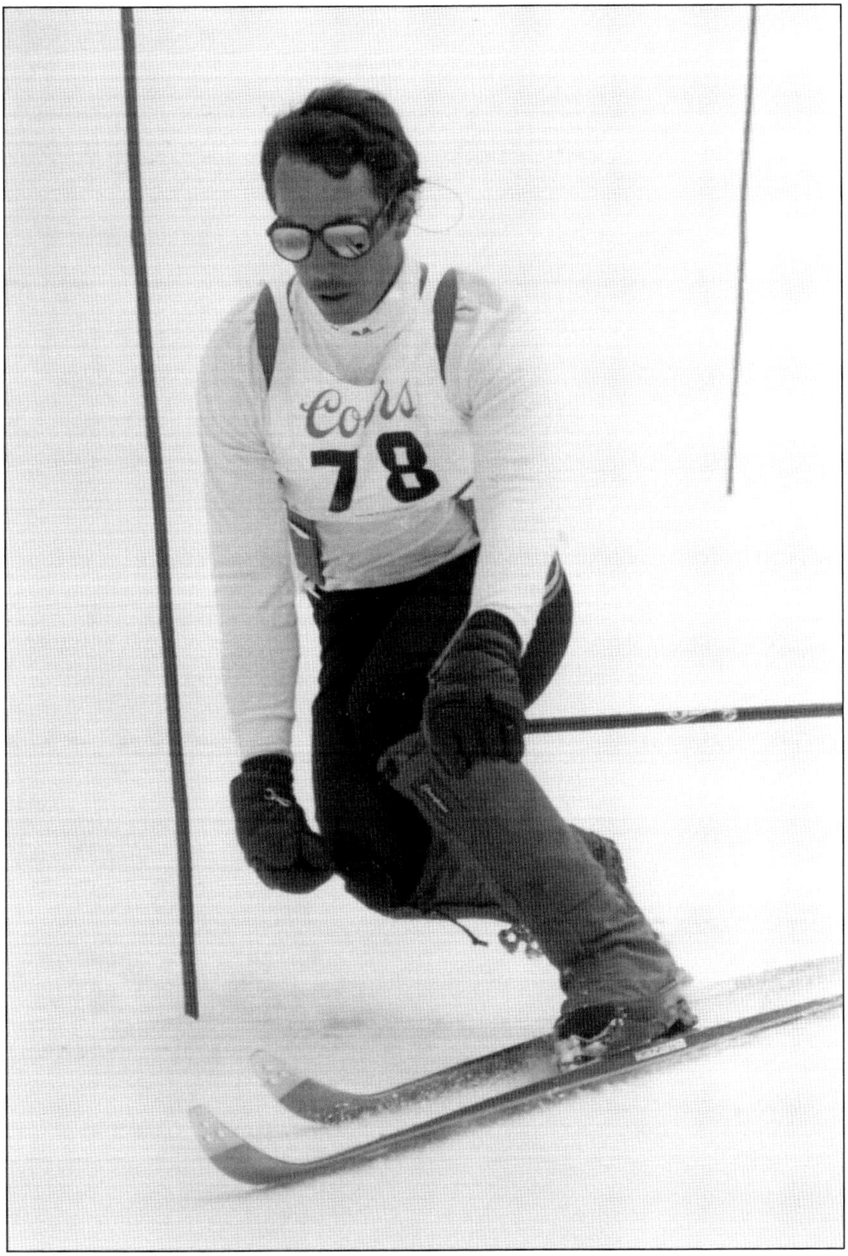

Richard A. Coker Jr., who married Judy Alexander—daughter of Tom and Judy Alexander—became an expert telemark skier and was well known for his telemark turn. Coker is credited with helping to introduce this blend of cross-country and downhill skiing to the South. In fact, Cataloochee sponsored the region's first telemark race, in 1981. Annual telemark races caught on and continued to be held at ski areas in the South. The telemark ski is different because—as with cross-country skis—the boot is only attached at the toe. This allowed the skier to go into a striding position at the end of a turn, and the telemark turn is the term for the movement of the legs past one another. Interest in telemark skiing in the United States waned in the 1940s, but it regained popularity in the 1970s. Telemark skiing still has a following today, with festivals and instruction being offered in certain areas. (Courtesy of Cataloochee Ranch Collection.)

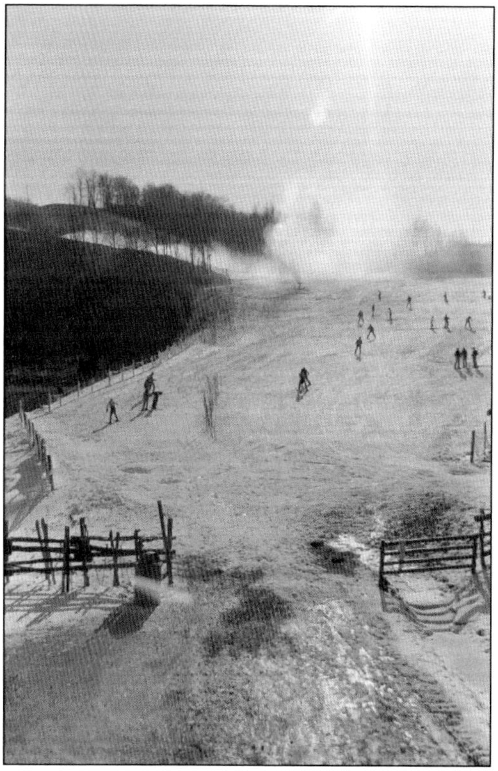

Blowing snow from the snow guns is visible at the top of this c. 1970 image. The lower section of the Omigosh run has plenty of room for the skiers shown schussing down the slope under the bright sun. Obviously, little snow has fallen on the mountain, and the slopes would not be open without the technology of snowmaking. (Courtesy of Cataloochee Ranch Collection.)

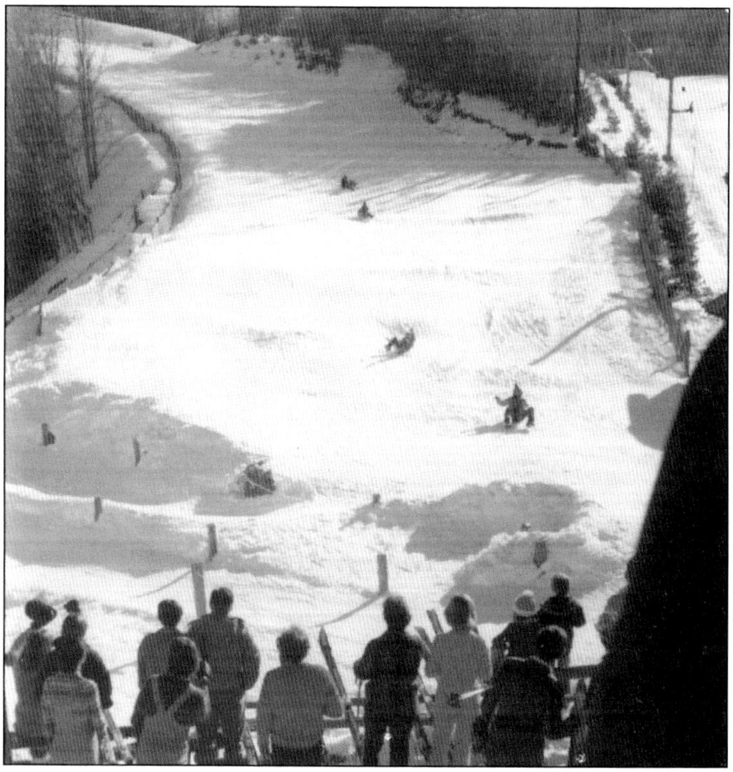

The shovel race became a popular annual event at the slopes, as shown in this c. 1970 photograph. As visiting crowds cheered, lift operators would slide down the slopes on their shovels as part of the Spring Frolic in early March. Special events and festivals were good publicity and brought more skiers to the slopes. (Courtesy of Cataloochee Ranch Collection.)

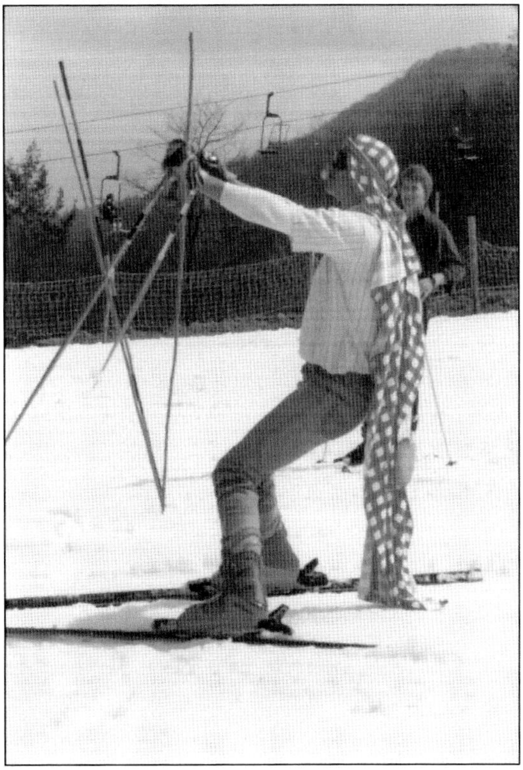

The Spring Frolics, held near the close of the season at Cataloochee, offered several different races and events—including a costume race. The intrepid skier at right seems to be costumed as a sheik. Another popular event was an obstacle course, which had to be accomplished while drinking a certain number of beers. Obviously, wearing garishly patterned pants—as shown below—can only improve your time on the course. The children seem to be amazed at the feat the contestant is about to perform. (Both, courtesy of Cataloochee Ranch Collection.)

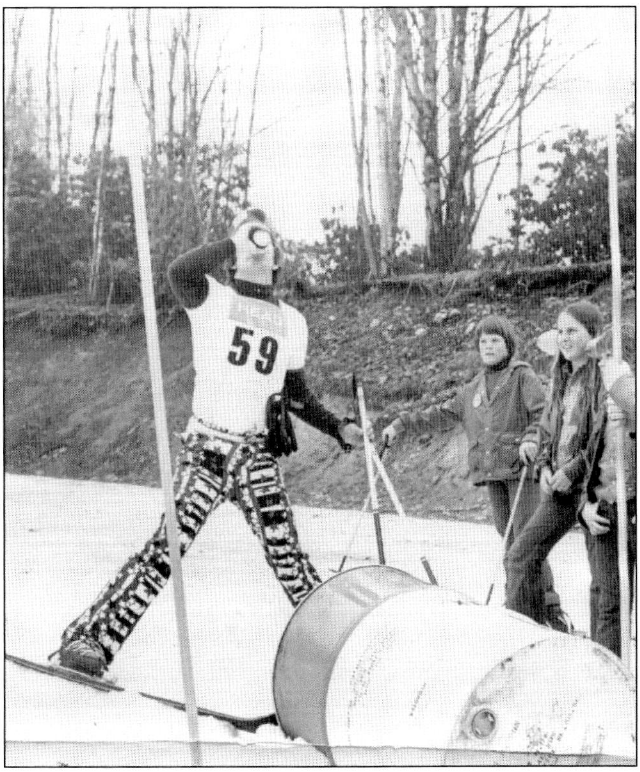

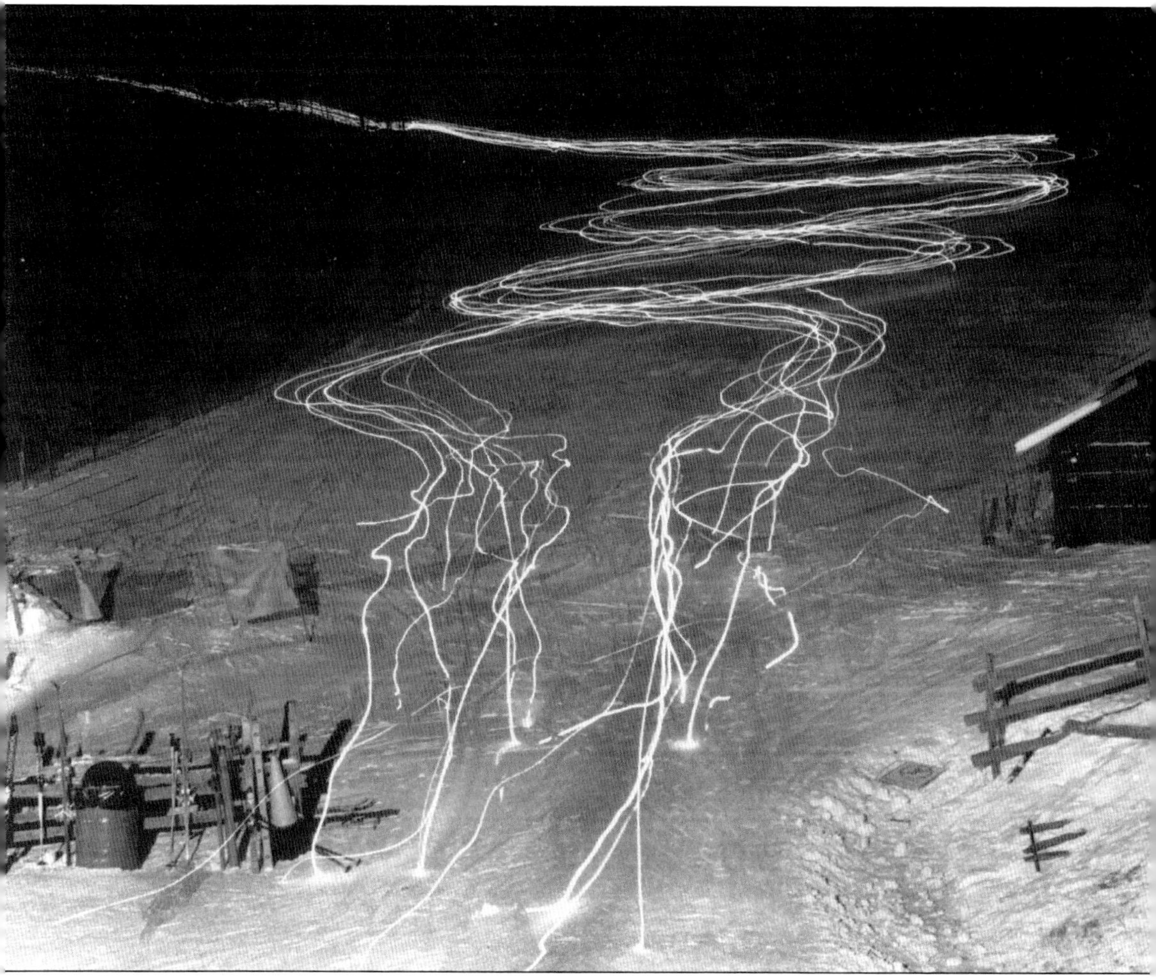

This nighttime torchlight ski parade appears magical on the slopes, as enhanced by time-lapse photography. Cataloochee has added five new trails in the past eight years—and is expected to add more trails in the future—as part of a plan to increase their attendance and compete with larger resorts. Today, the resort boasts 16 trails and areas, three lifts, snowboarding and tubing, and 100-plus snowmaking machines. The ski area takes pride in being one of the first of the state's ski areas to open each year. Without a dependence on real estate sales, this ski area has been able to endure the economic fluctuations that have harmed the larger resorts in Watauga and Avery Counties in the past. Cataloochee Ranch provides a peaceful respite from life's stresses and provides personal customer service that brings families back year after year. Still owned and managed by descendants of the Alexanders, and with more people looking for recreation close to home, the future for this resort looks bright. By offering summer and winter activities, Cataloochee Ranch has grown into a popular southern resort, perhaps even greater than the modest dreams of its brave and determined founders, Tom and Judy Alexander. (Courtesy of Cataloochee Ranch Collection.)

Two

Appalachian Ski Mountain

Appalachian Ski Mountain's story is that of Bill Thalheimer's vision to build the first ski resort in northwestern North Carolina and the Grady Moretz family's purchase and expansion of the resort. M.E. "Bill" Thalheimer, a business owner from Alabama, saw the potential for winter recreation at a time when the local chamber of commerce was already looking for winter tourism avenues. Purchasing land on a mountain near the Blue Ridge Parkway and the village of Blowing Rock, Thalheimer hired the V.L. Moretz & Son Lumber Company to provide building materials. Construction of the resort began in 1961. Known as the Blowing Rock Ski Lodge, it was a public, stock-owned company. Several of the contractors—including Moretz & Son—accepted stocks as partial payment and became active on the board of directors. The lodge opened to huge crowds in the winter of 1962–1963 and included a 12,000-square-foot lodge and just three slopes that were serviced by two rope tows and a T-bar. Thalheimer hired Austrian ski pro Toni Krasovic, who contributed much to the resort's early success. In 1968, financial problems allowed Grady and Reba Moretz, and four other partners, to purchase the resort in foreclosure. Renaming the resort as Appalachian Ski Mountain, the new owners made many improvements, such as replacing rope tows with lifts, lodge additions, improvements to snowmaking, and adding more slopes—all of which were able to make the lodge profitable again. A major ingredient in their success was the 1969–1970 formation of the French-Swiss Ski College by Jim Cottrell and Jack Lester, who developed a new downhill skiing course for credit, which was included at many regional colleges. Thousands of students learned to ski at Appalachian, and it still has a reputation as the best resort for learning how to ski. In 1976, Cottrell arranged for the first North Carolina Special Winter Olympics to be hosted at Appalachian, and this event continues today. The resort continues to change with the times and has installed an outdoor skating arena and created snowboarding terrain. The Moretzs' children successfully manage the resort today, offering skiing for all skill levels without the long and steep mountain drives needed to reach the other High Country resorts.

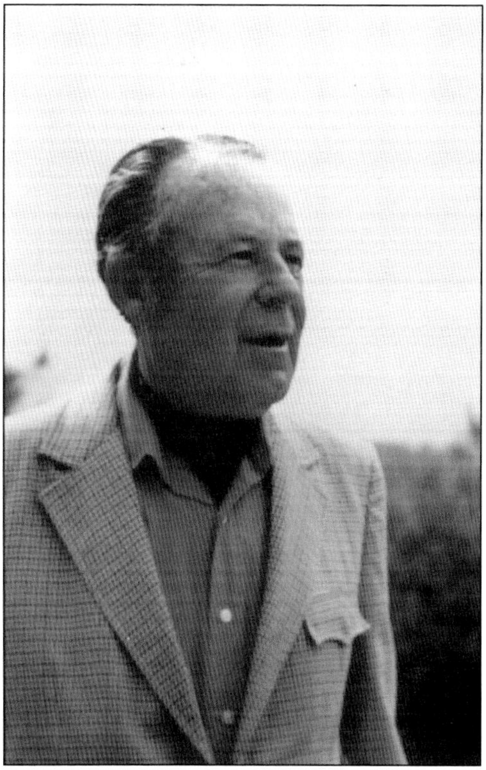

M.E. "Bill" Thalheimer lived in Selma, Alabama, and was the successful owner of a chain of movie theaters and other businesses. When he decided to develop a ski resort in Blowing Rock, his idea was welcomed by the local chamber of commerce, which had been seeking winter tourism opportunities. He formed a public, stock-owned company, which sold shares for $1 each. Although he had never skied before, Thalheimer's dream became a reality when Blowing Rock Ski Lodge opened during the winter of 1962–1963. (Courtesy of the Appalachian Ski Mountain Collection.)

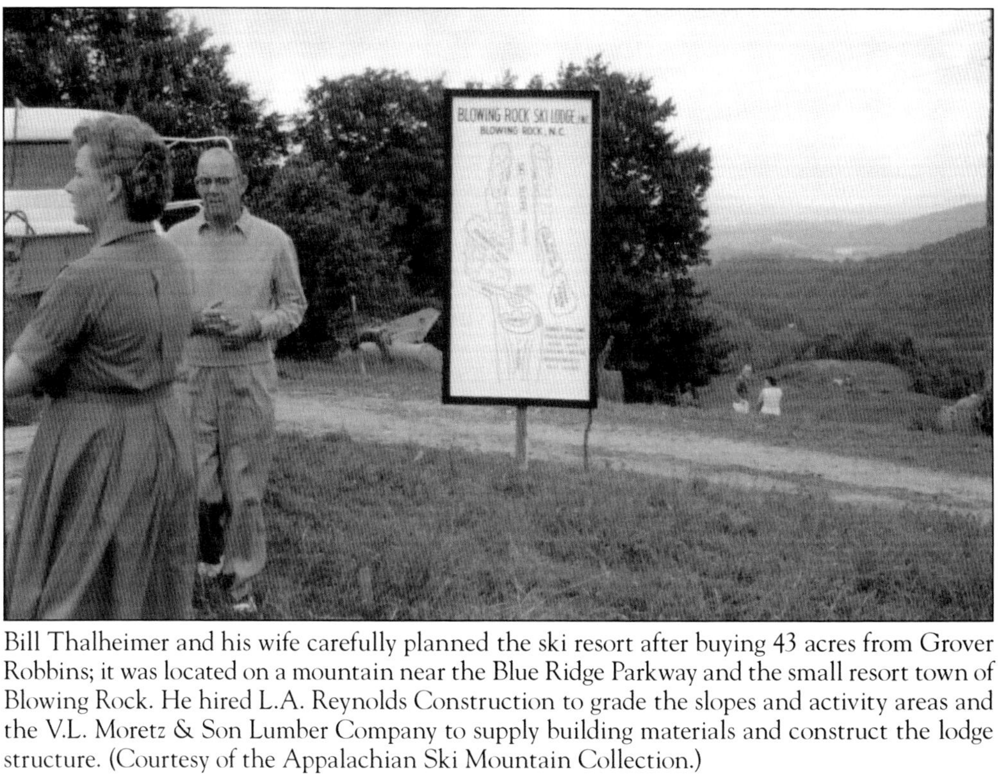

Bill Thalheimer and his wife carefully planned the ski resort after buying 43 acres from Grover Robbins; it was located on a mountain near the Blue Ridge Parkway and the small resort town of Blowing Rock. He hired L.A. Reynolds Construction to grade the slopes and activity areas and the V.L. Moretz & Son Lumber Company to supply building materials and construct the lodge structure. (Courtesy of the Appalachian Ski Mountain Collection.)

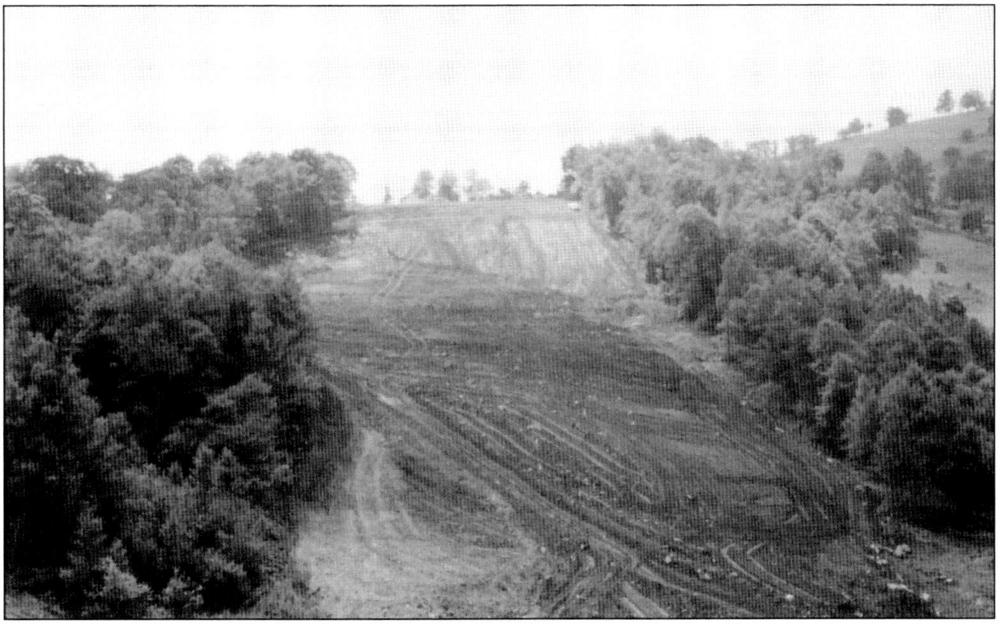

This c. 1961 photograph of the initial grading, done by the L.A. Reynolds Construction Company of Winston-Salem, shows the rocky conditions and the area that became the main slope. Thalheimer was able to convince the contractors to accept stocks in this public company as partial payment for their work, and several of them became board members. (Courtesy of the Appalachian Ski Mountain Collection.)

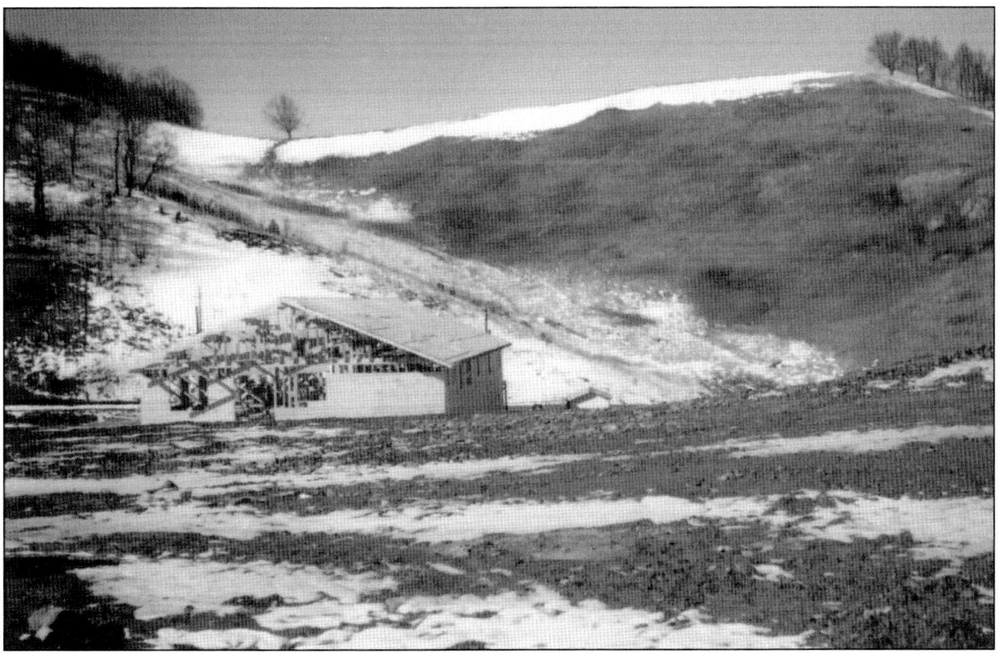

Shown here under construction in 1961, the ski lodge was built of lovely white pine timber, which Moretz & Son had milled with a distinctive wavy edge that gave it a hand-hewn appearance. The first building was 12,000 square feet and provided basic resort services. (Courtesy of the Appalachian Ski Mountain Collection.)

SKI FACTS

- ☆ Altitude—4,000 feet
- ☆ Main Slope—2,000 feet with 350 foot vertical drop
- ☆ Intermediate Slope—700 feet
- ☆ Beginners' Slope—250 feet
- ☆ Lifts and Tows: 2,000-foot T-Bar, 700-foot rope tow, 250-foot rope tow
- ☆ Snow making equipment on all slopes

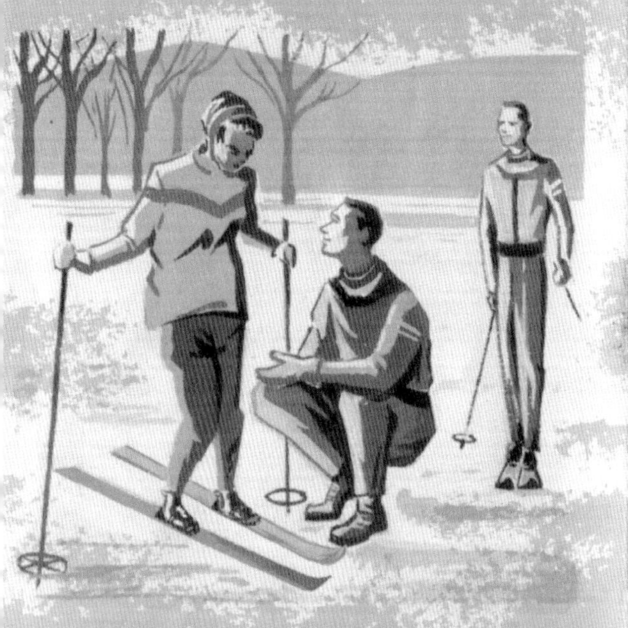

PROFESSIONAL INSTRUCTION

Toni Krasovic's FWSIA-certified ski school offers individual and group lessons. Five instructors are qualified to instruct at any skill level, from beginner to expert. Morning and afternoon sessions daily.

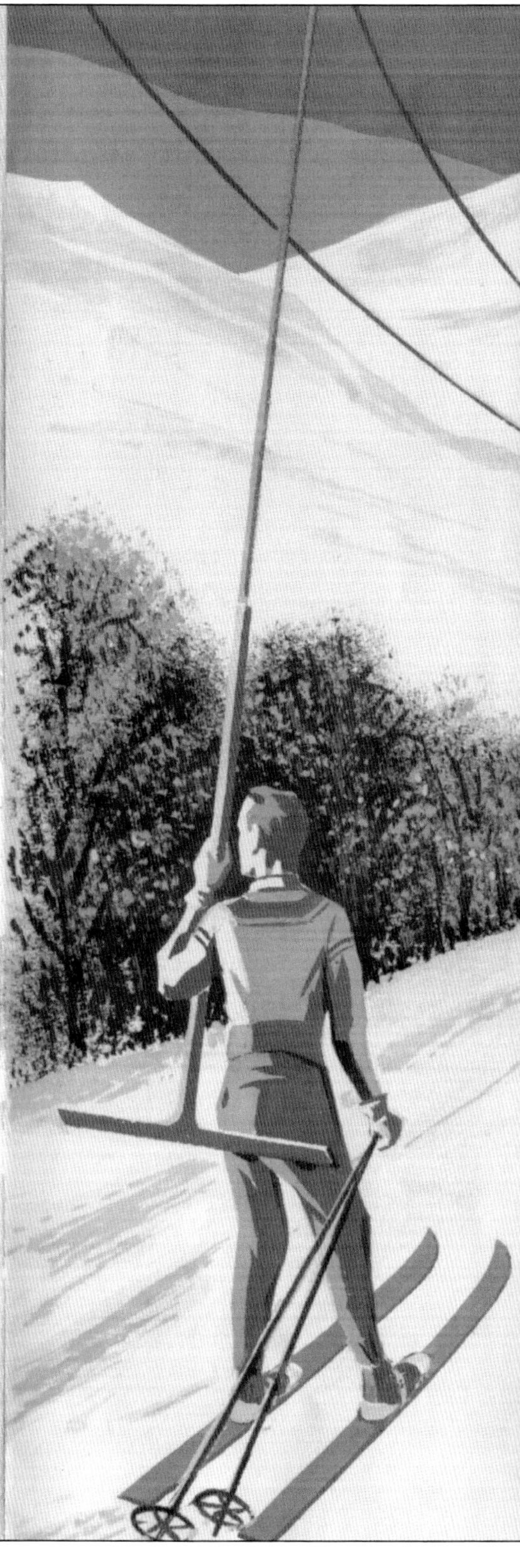

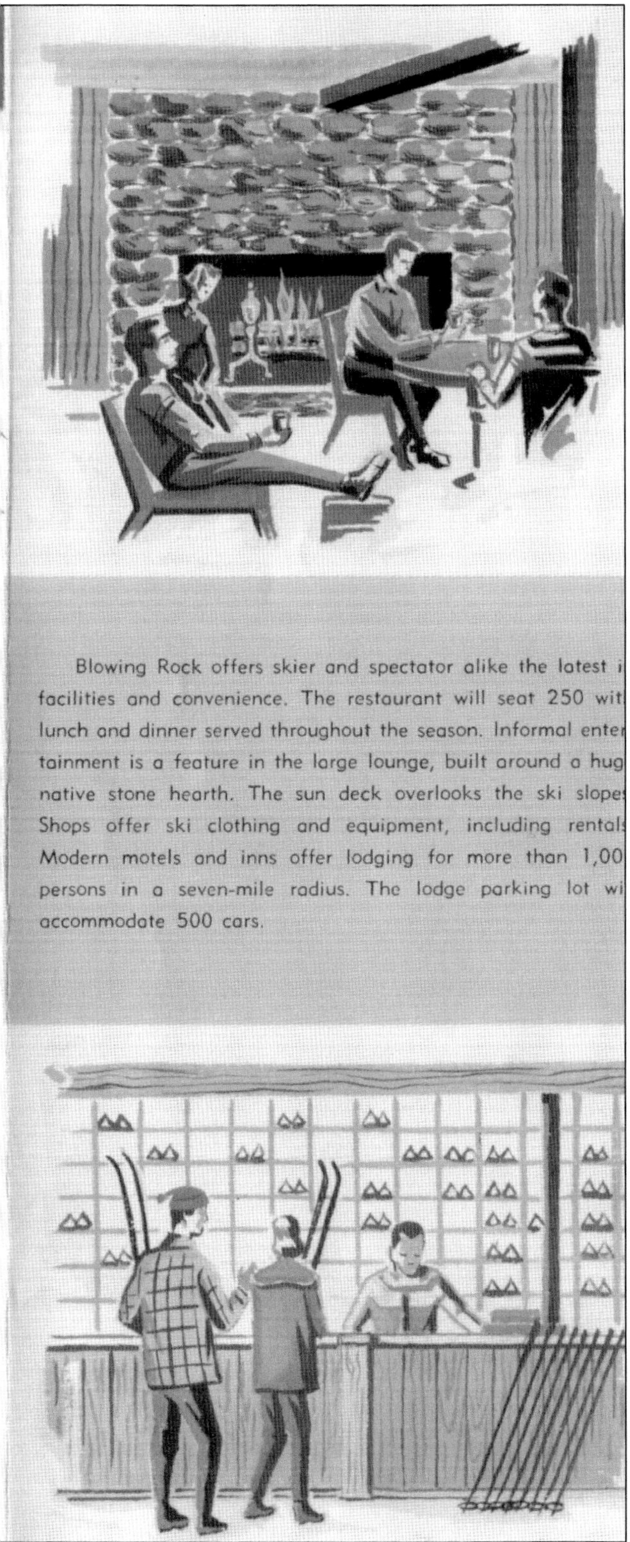
Blowing Rock offers skier and spectator alike the latest i
facilities and convenience. The restaurant will seat 250 wit
lunch and dinner served throughout the season. Informal ente
tainment is a feature in the large lounge, built around a hug
native stone hearth. The sun deck overlooks the ski slope
Shops offer ski clothing and equipment, including rental
Modern motels and inns offer lodging for more than 1,00
persons in a seven-mile radius. The lodge parking lot wi
accommodate 500 cars.

This c. 1963 brochure is titled *The South's Winter and Summer Sports Capitol*—a lofty claim for this new ski resort. Marketing for this new southeastern resort had to be aggressive, though, and provide incentive for Southerners to drive up and try this unknown sport. At this time, Toni Krasovic, the Austrian ski pro hired by Thalheimer, was providing ski lessons. Although the 4,000-foot altitude was not as high as some of the subsequent ski areas in the region, its easy accessibility and beginner-friendly nature have always drawn skiers there—including the rich and famous. This resort has cultivated a family-friendly atmosphere that is still apparent today. (Courtesy of the Appalachian Ski Mountain Collection.)

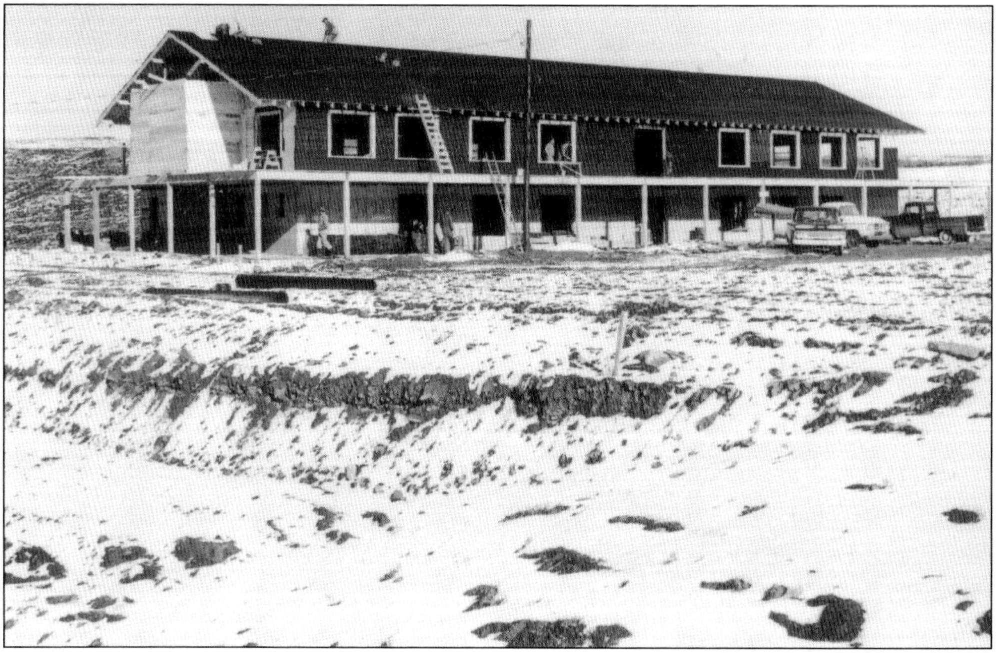

The ski lodge is being built by local workers in these 1961 photographs. Thalheimer wanted it to convey an old-fashioned cabin atmosphere, and the roughly hewn white pine was a good choice. The 12,000-square-foot lodge could seat 250 for lunch and dinner, and the tasty food at the resort has always had a country-cooking flavor. Built around a huge, rustic stone fireplace, the lounge area provided a comfortable place to socialize and warm up by the fire. Entertainment was available in the lounge area, although no alcoholic beverages have ever been sold there. This lodge also included a store and rental shop for ski clothing and equipment. (Both, courtesy of the Appalachian Ski Mountain Collection.)

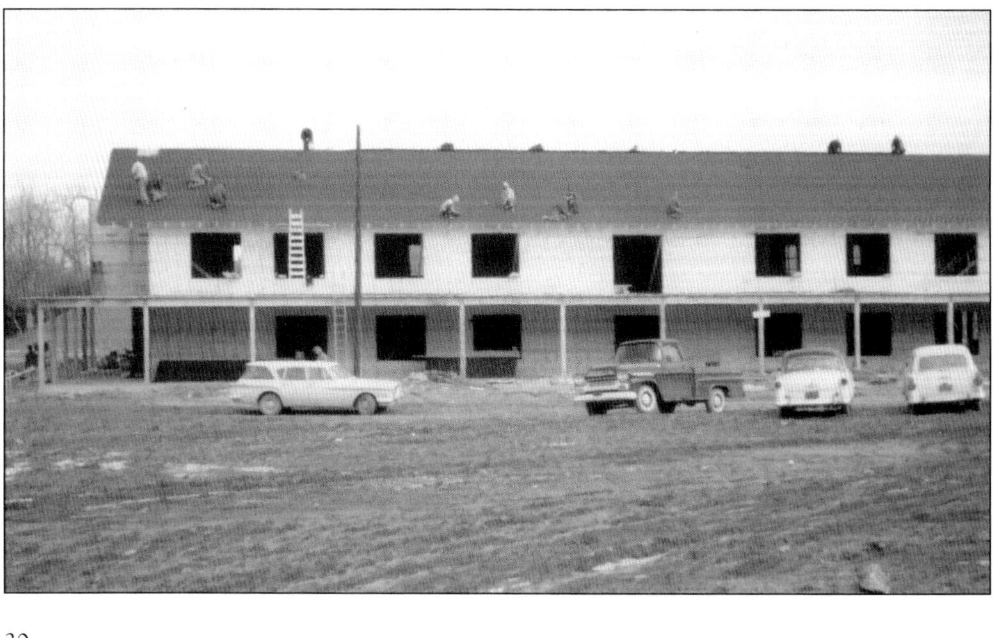

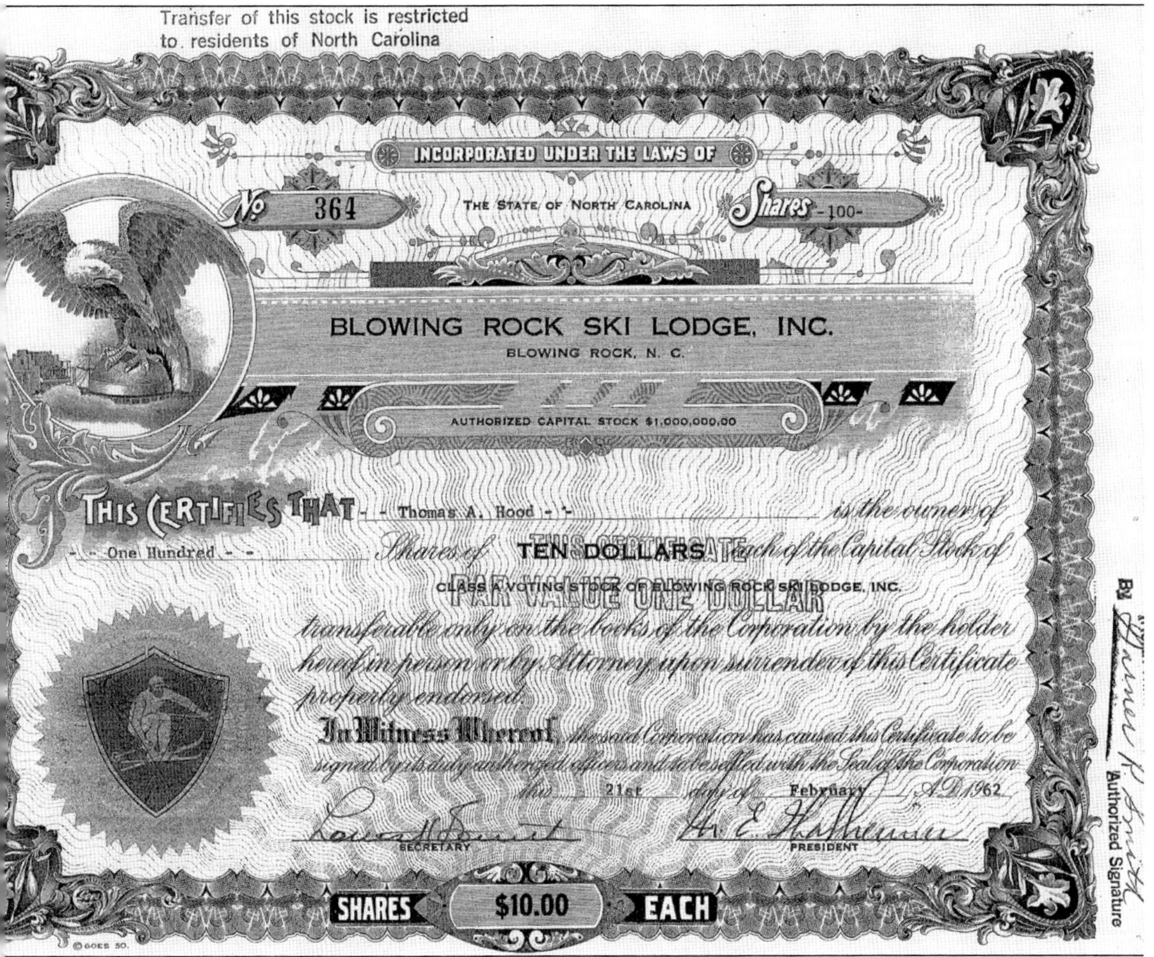

This copy of an original stock certificate for Blowing Rock Ski Lodge, Inc., was issued on February 21, 1962. The State of North Carolina limited the stock price to $1 because it viewed the lodge as a speculative investment. This is certificate number 364, representing 100 shares. It was issued to Thomas A. Hood and was signed by Bill Thalheimer. Stock sales capped out at $305,000. Northwestern Bank held the loan and later recalled it due to the resort's financial troubles. Note that the stock is also restricted to residents of North Carolina. Many investors became active board members, and a group of them ended up purchasing the resort during 1967–1968, after Blowing Rock Ski Lodge went into bankruptcy. (Courtesy of the Appalachian Ski Mountain Collection.)

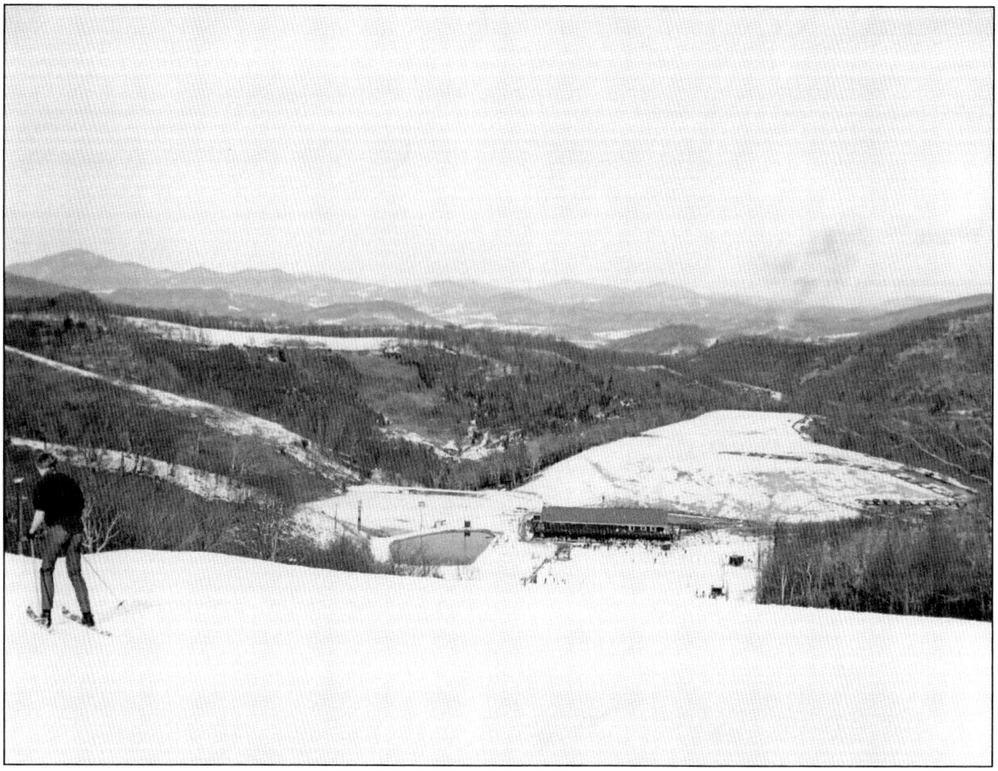

The Blue Ridge Mountains loom in the background of this c. 1965 photograph taken at the top of the slopes. The pond on the left is likely the water source for the simple snowblowing equipment used at this time. The parking area is visible behind the lodge. The resort appears busy, providing skiing on its three slopes on this snowy day. (Courtesy of the French-Swiss Ski College Collection.)

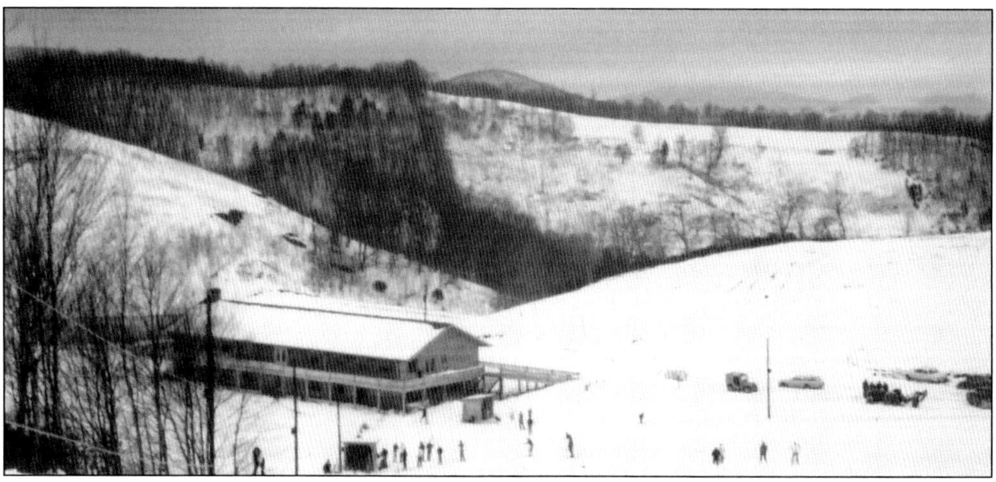

This photograph depicts the lodge from a different angle, showing the large sundeck that wraps around it to provide plenty of viewing space for spectators. Skiers can be seen on the T-bar at the bottom of the photograph, and a group appears to be lined up for a lesson. Natural snow covers the nearby hills, but the snowmaking equipment was always there to supplement the natural snow. (Courtesy of the Appalachian Ski Mountain Collection.)

This c. 1965 ski brochure advertises the rates for skiing at Blowing Rock Ski Lodge, which have increased quite a bit today. Instead of a lift ticket, the resort provided a daily tow ticket, since this preceded the installation of lifts. Marketing has always been integral to the resort's success, and this particular season offered ladies and men's days at special discounts. (Courtesy of the Appalachian Ski Mountain Collection.)

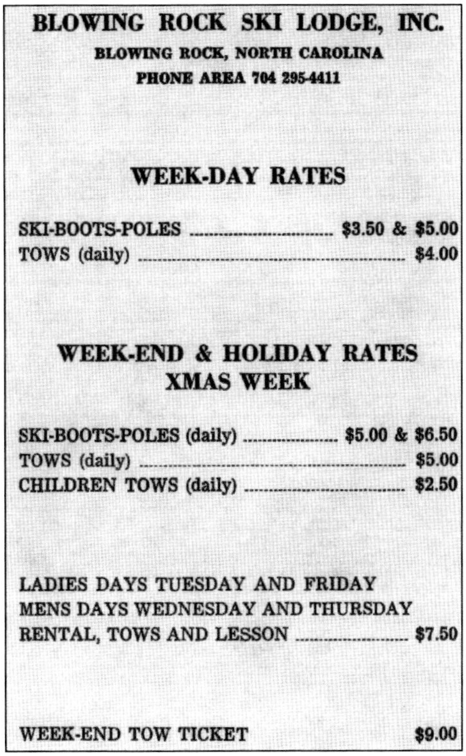

BLOWING ROCK SKI LODGE, INC.
BLOWING ROCK, NORTH CAROLINA
PHONE AREA 704 295-4411

WEEK-DAY RATES

SKI-BOOTS-POLES .... $3.50 & $5.00
TOWS (daily) $4.00

WEEK-END & HOLIDAY RATES
XMAS WEEK

SKI-BOOTS-POLES (daily) .... $5.00 & $6.50
TOWS (daily) $5.00
CHILDREN TOWS (daily) $2.50

LADIES DAYS TUESDAY AND FRIDAY
MENS DAYS WEDNESDAY AND THURSDAY
RENTAL, TOWS AND LESSON $7.50

WEEK-END TOW TICKET $9.00

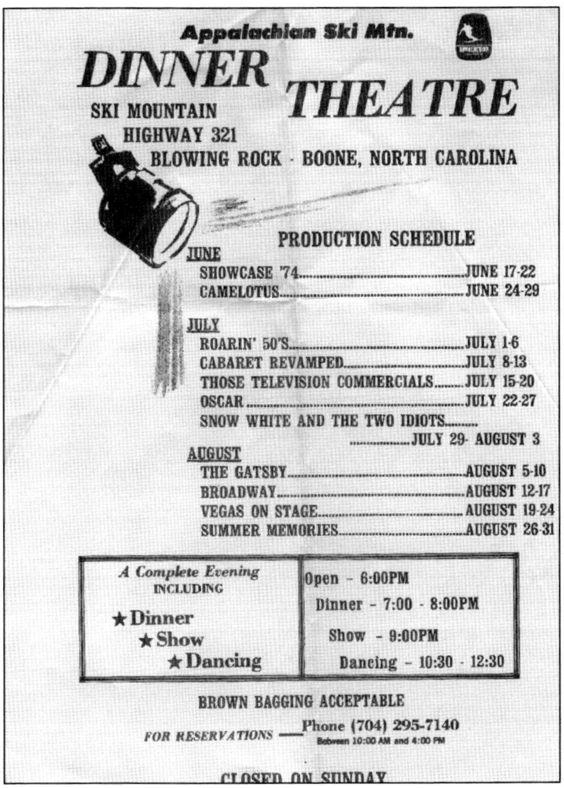

Appalachian Ski Mtn.
DINNER THEATRE
SKI MOUNTAIN
HIGHWAY 321
BLOWING ROCK · BOONE, NORTH CAROLINA

PRODUCTION SCHEDULE

JUNE
SHOWCASE '74 .... JUNE 17-22
CAMELOTUS .... JUNE 24-29

JULY
ROARIN' 50'S .... JULY 1-6
CABARET REVAMPED .... JULY 8-13
THOSE TELEVISION COMMERCIALS .... JULY 15-20
OSCAR .... JULY 22-27
SNOW WHITE AND THE TWO IDIOTS .... JULY 29- AUGUST 3

AUGUST
THE GATSBY .... AUGUST 5-10
BROADWAY .... AUGUST 12-17
VEGAS ON STAGE .... AUGUST 19-24
SUMMER MEMORIES .... AUGUST 26-31

A Complete Evening INCLUDING ★Dinner ★Show ★Dancing	Open - 6:00PM Dinner - 7:00 - 8:00PM Show - 9:00PM Dancing - 10:30 - 12:30

BROWN BAGGING ACCEPTABLE
FOR RESERVATIONS — Phone (704) 295-7140
Between 10:00 AM and 4:00 PM
CLOSED ON SUNDAY

The Dinner Theatre at Appalachian Ski Mountain provided a show, dinner, and dancing in the evenings. Note that alcohol was not sold at this popular attraction (it still is not), though the flyer states, "Brown Bagging Acceptable." (Courtesy of Appalachian Ski Mountain Collection.)

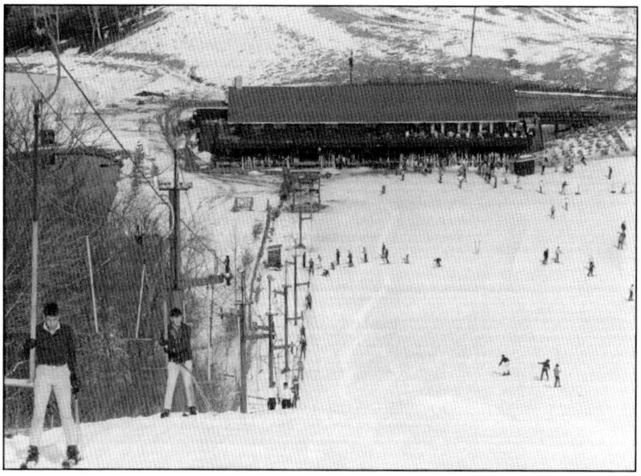

This c. 1965 photograph from the top of the slopes shows young skiers on the towrope and a lodge sundeck that is crowded with visitors. Note that the boys appear to be wearing regular pants, as ski bibs and insulated ski pants were not common or available in the Southeast. Scant natural snow is visible around the resort, so the snow guns had surely been blowing hard over the previous few days. (Courtesy of the Appalachian Ski Mountain Collection.)

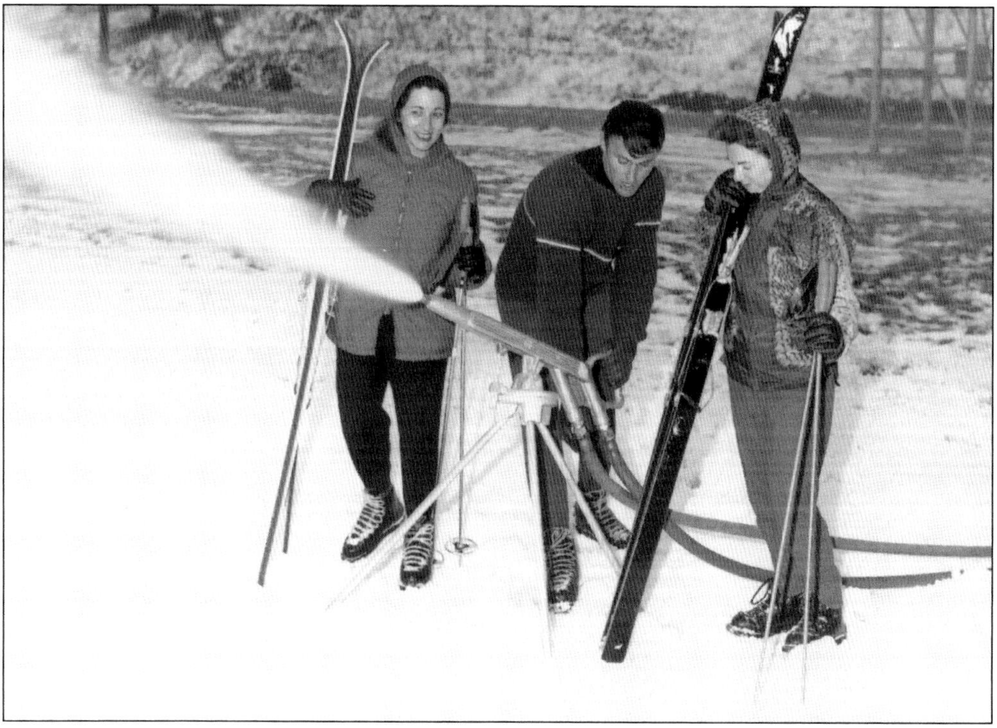

Here, an Appalachian staff member adjusts an early snowblower around 1965, while two ladies observe. Note the lace-up boots and binding cords that were used at the time. Thalheimer invested in state-of-the-art snowblowers, but their capacity was much less than that of the blowers available today. Frank Coffey, chief train engineer at Tweetsie Railroad—a nearby amusement park centered on a steam train—installed the first snowmaking equipment at this resort and others. In *Southern Snow: The Winter Guide to Dixie*, Randy Johnson notes that Hardin Greene—who worked at Blowing Rock and the other ski resorts—would, when he was planning to make large amounts of snow, comment, "I'm going to tilt the mountain tonight." Snowmaking was the key to the success of the southern resorts because it offered better quality and more controlled amounts of snow, allowed the resorts to open earlier, and extended the season for the sport. In fact, the southern ski areas were the world's first resorts to depend solely on snowmaking. (Courtesy of the Appalachian Ski Mountain Collection.)

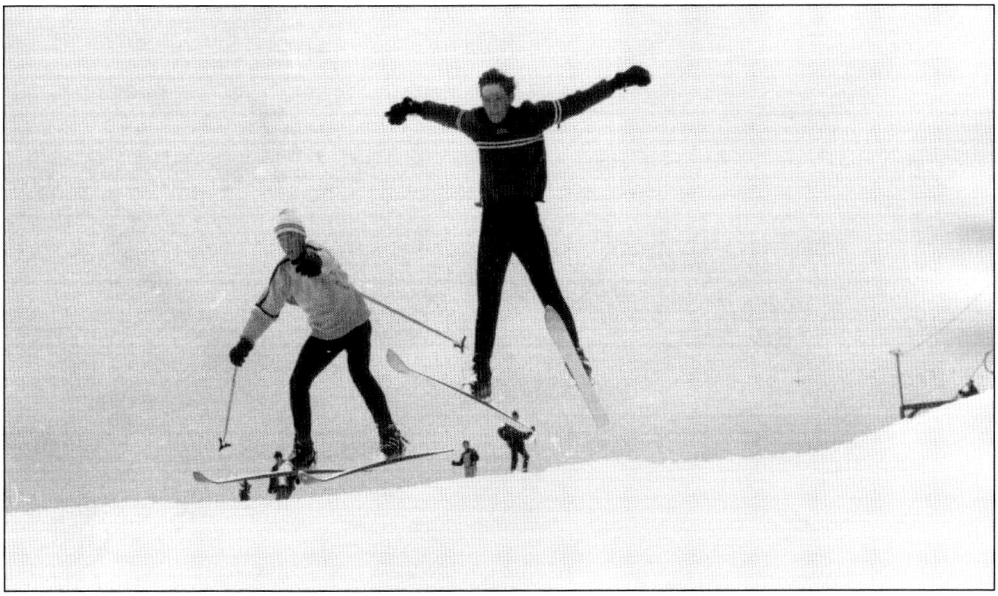

Two skiers are hotdogging on the slopes in this c. 1965 photograph. The man on the right appears to be a ski instructor, as he is wearing the official sweater visible in other photographs. This resort was, and still is, known for the quality of its ski instruction—particularly for novice skiers. (Courtesy of the Appalachian Ski Mountain Collection.)

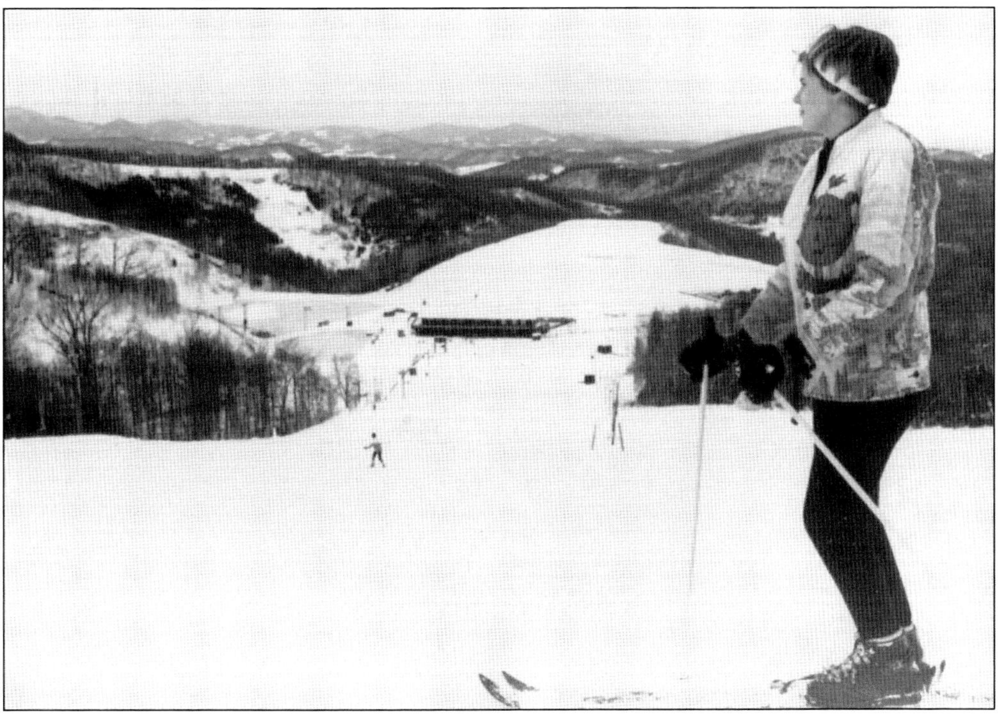

Gazing over the far mountains, this female skier seems to be trying to decide if she should ski down or just enjoy the view. Note the lace-up boots and straps used for bindings that were in use in 1965, when this photograph was taken. Deep natural snow covers most of the area, so the snow guns probably were not running. (Courtesy of the Appalachian Ski Mountain Collection.)

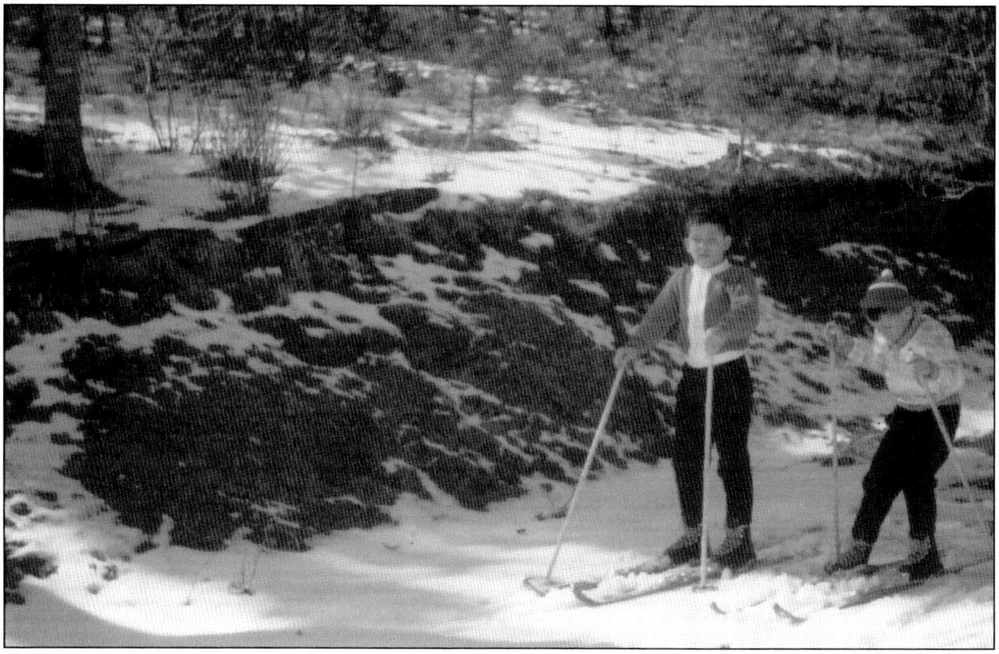

These two young boys are enjoying a day at Blowing Rock Ski Lodge, even if the snow appears slightly slushy. Their light outerwear indicates temperate weather on this late winter's day. Skiers were still using lace-up boots, which were later replaced with much safer buckles. (Courtesy of the Appalachian Ski Mountain Collection.)

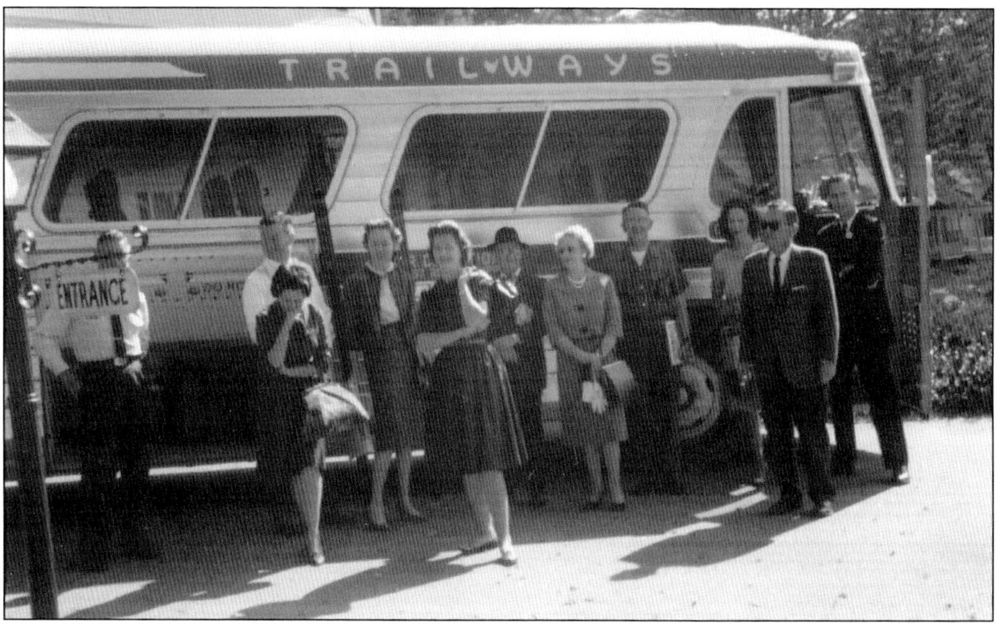

Showing sharp marketing skills, the resort began to partner with bus companies that arranged bus tours and brought tourists up the mountain. This was done not only in warm weather, as shown in this c. 1965 image, but in colder weather as well. Partnerships with local motels provided special rates for skiers, and rooms were often packaged with ski passes. (Courtesy of the Appalachian Ski Mountain Collection.)

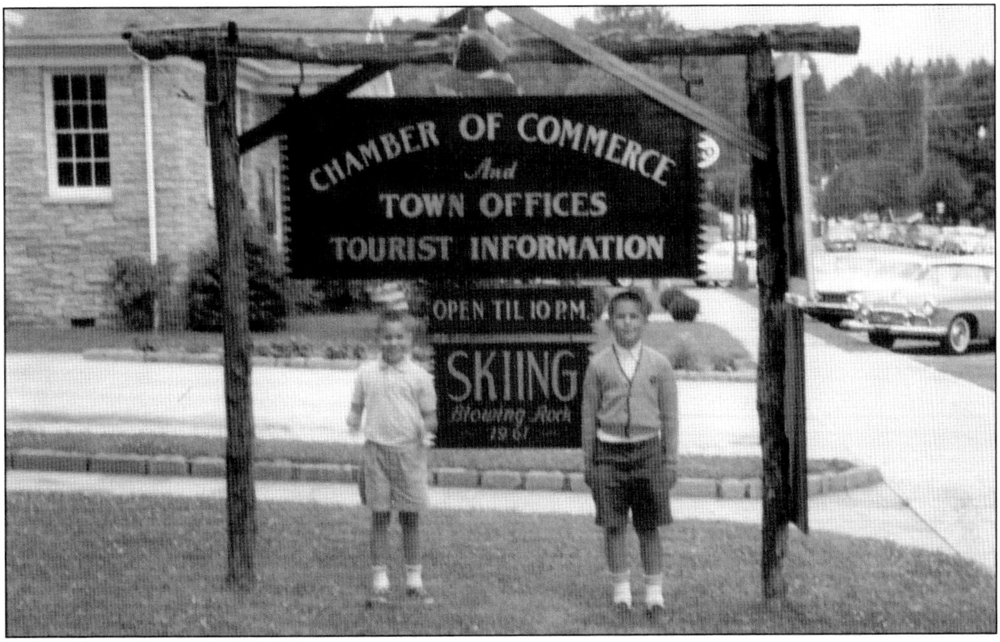

These two young boys are a perfect welcoming party to the town of Blowing Rock. Even though it is summer in this photograph, the chamber of commerce is advertising the resort's ski offering. Local governments wanted year-round recreation to add to the economies of these rural areas, and they have always been very supportive to the resorts. (Courtesy of the Appalachian Ski Mountain Collection.)

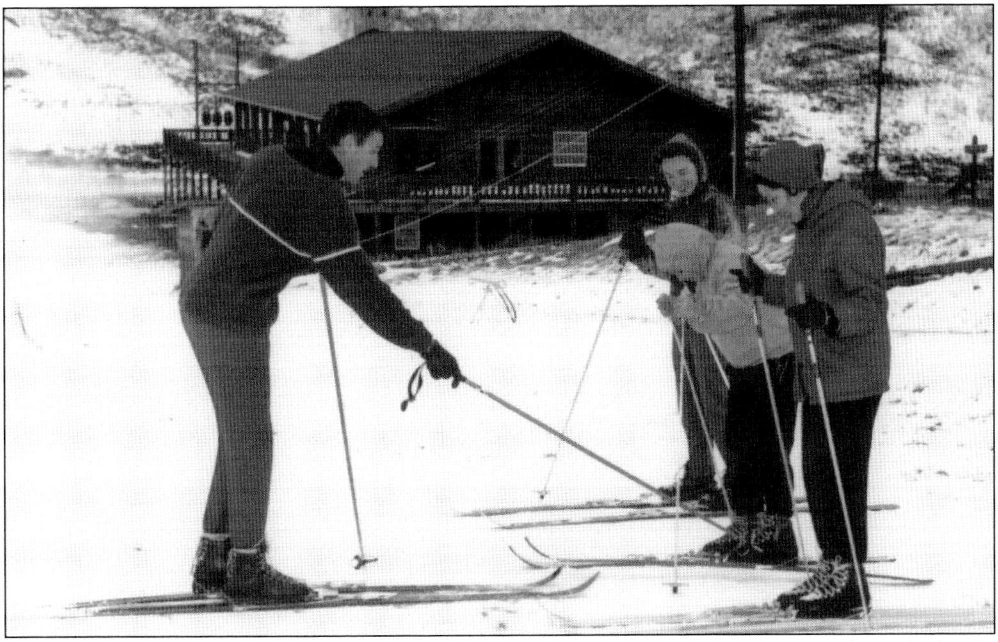

A ski instructor (left) is providing a lesson to three skiers in this c. 1967 photograph, with the ski lodge visible in the background. The snow surrounding the lodge appears sparse, so perhaps this photograph was taken late in the season. The ski boots are still the old-fashioned type fastened with lace-up ties. (Courtesy of the Appalachian Ski Mountain Collection.)

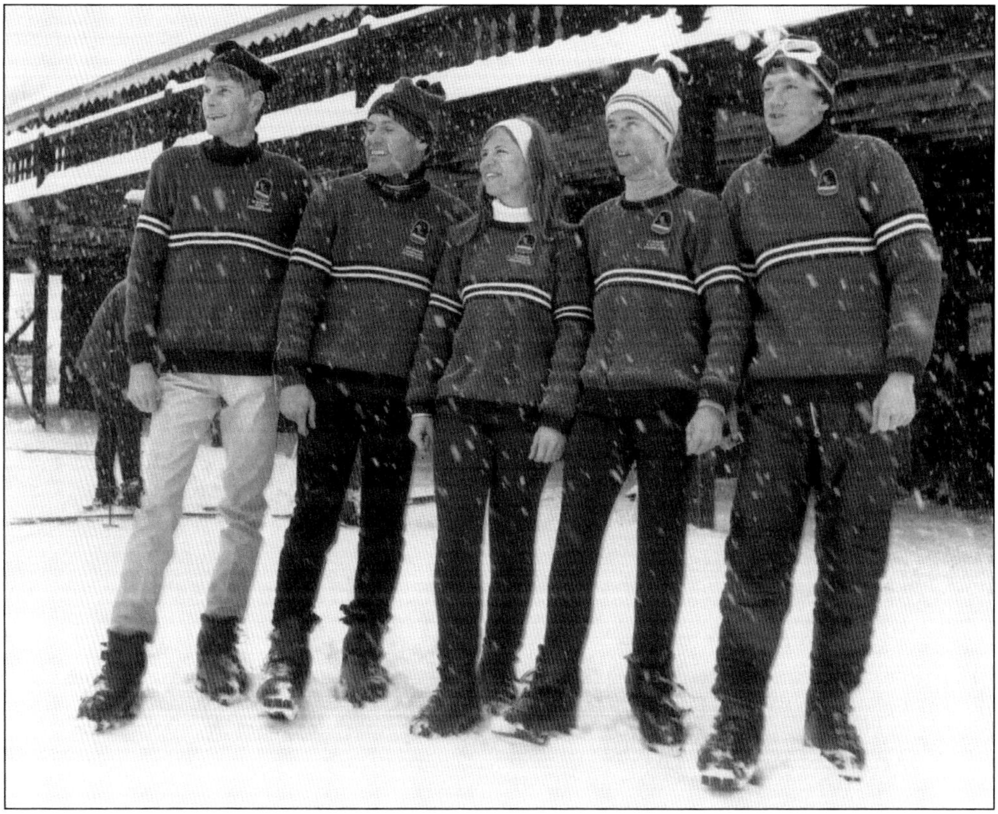

Above, these five ski instructors pose in front of the Blowing Rock Ski lodge around 1965, proudly wearing their ski sweaters on this snowy day. Below, the same group shows that they know how to have fun as well, by building a human pyramid. One of the instructors has goggles on his cap, which would have been unusual at the time. Rigorous testing ensured that ski instructors were of the highest caliber and that they emphasized safety for skiers. (Courtesy of the Appalachian Ski Mountain Collection.)

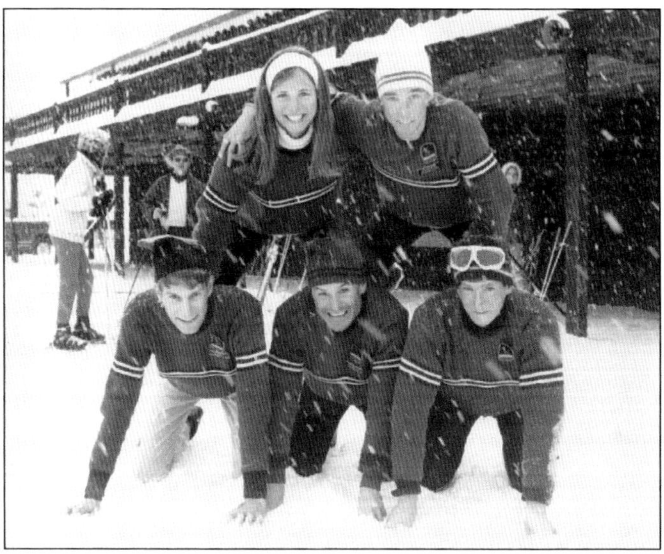

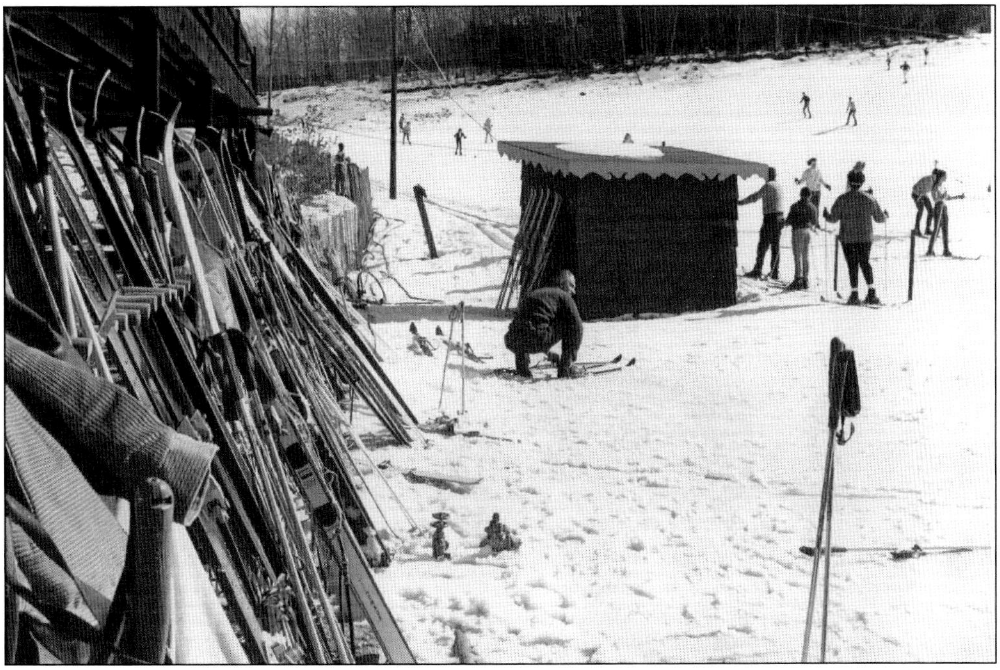

In this c. 1965 photograph, skis are lined up outside of the lodge, awaiting riders. The beginner slope is visible, along with the outbuilding for the rope tow. Note the wavy trim on the building, which mimics that on the ski lodge and adds to the alpine atmosphere. While these skis are still attached to boots by cable bindings, they do feature early-release toes. (Courtesy of the Appalachian Ski Mountain Collection.)

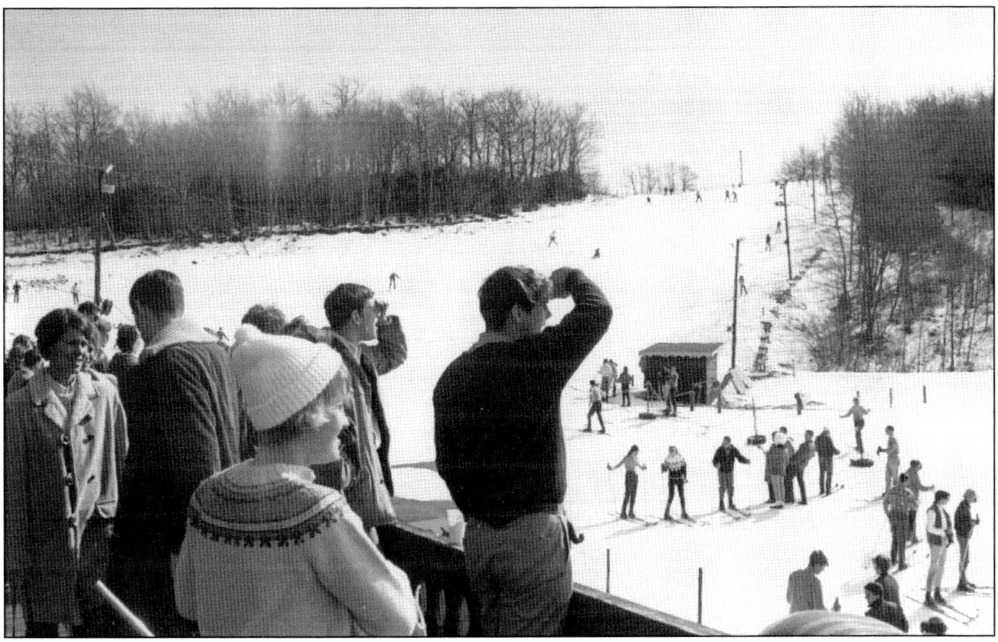

Visitors scan the slopes for their friends and family members on this sunny day at Appalachian. A lesson is taking place in the right foreground of this c. 1965 photograph. The beginner slope can be seen in the background. (Courtesy of the Appalachian Ski Mountain Collection.)

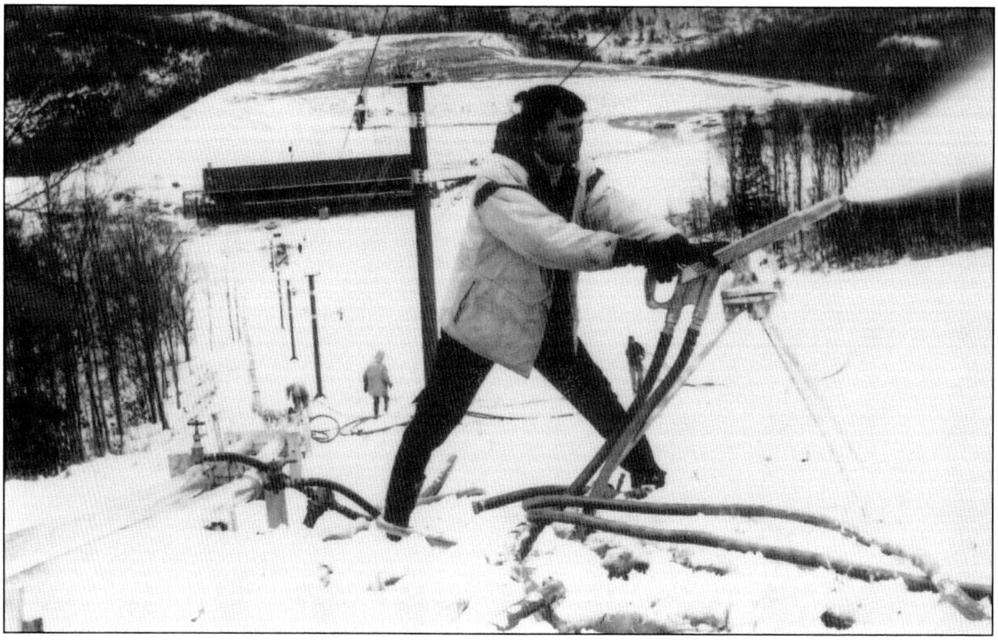

A snow gun operator adjusts the equipment on the slopes to provide the best snow coverage. These hoses and guns worked, but today's snowblowing techniques dwarf these simple guns. Without these, the Southeast would not have been able to develop and maintain its ski resorts. (Courtesy of the Appalachian Ski Mountain Collection.)

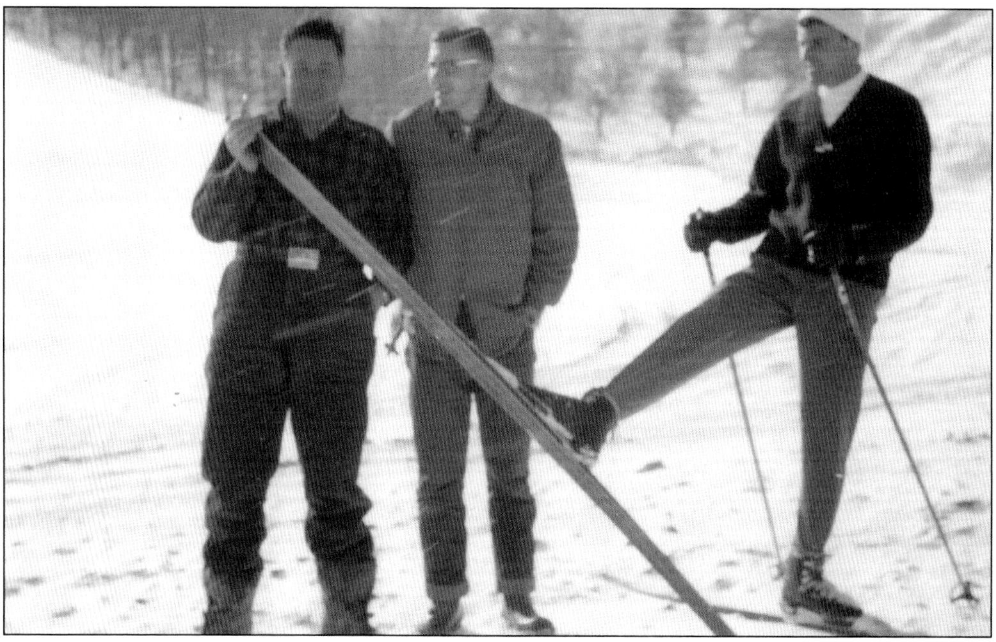

The man at left seems to be checking the tips of another man's skis in this scene from about 1967. Snow appears to be falling, and the two men on the left seem content to observe the skiing. (Courtesy of the Appalachian Ski Mountain Collection.)

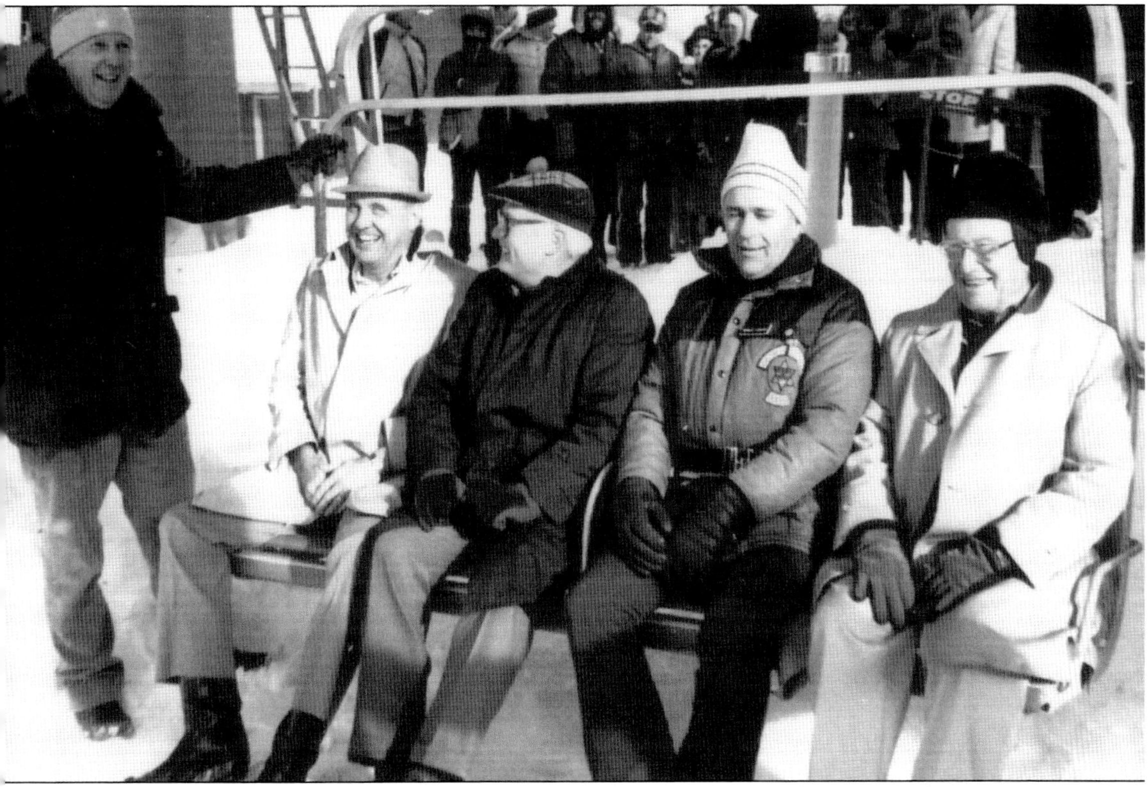

Dignitaries visited the slopes to show their support for the resort's contributions. In this c. 1975 photograph, an unidentified staff person assists the guests from the chairlift, including, from left to right, Appalachian State University chancellor Herbert Walter Wey (1969–1979), unidentified, North Carolina governor James Holshouser Jr. (1973–1977), and unidentified. Local and state support were key to the slope's endurance and continued success. (Courtesy of the Appalachian Ski Mountain Collection.)

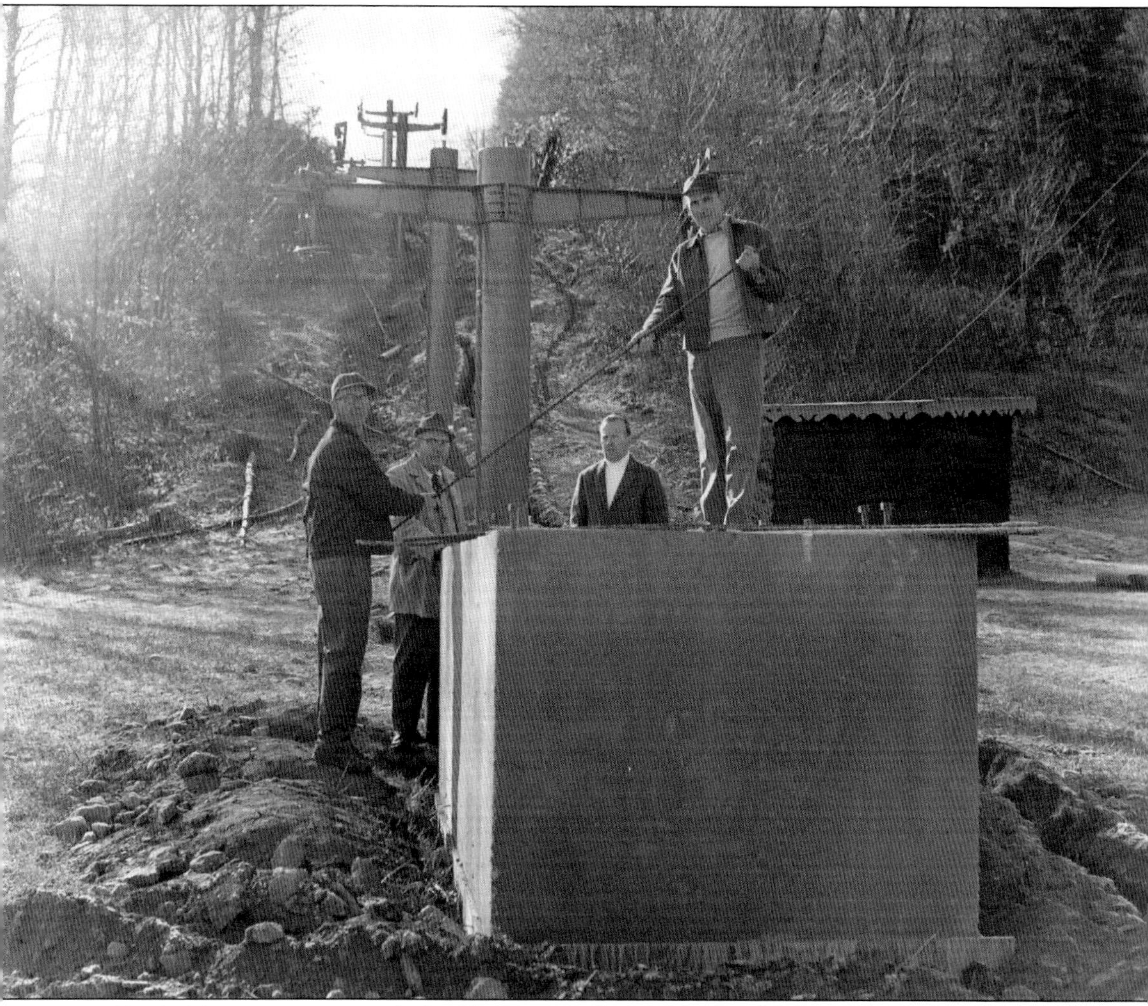

Grady Moretz, contractor for building materials; Herb Reynolds, grading contractor; and Earl Searcy were among the original board members who had an investment in the resort when it went bankrupt. They added Lloyd Caudle and W. Harold Mitchell to their group of investors and paid the loan off with Northwestern Bank. These same owners, with the exception of Searcy, who died, and Herb Reynolds, who was replaced by his son Jon, have held the company until the present day. The new owners reopened the resort during 1968–1969, renamed it the Appalachian Ski Mountain, and made many improvements over the next few years. The first chairlift at the resort is being installed in this c. 1969 photograph, which features, from left to right, an unidentified resort employee, Sam Goforth, Grady Moretz, and a second unidentified employee. Lifts enabled the resort to transport more people up the slope at a greater rate, lessened the waiting time, and were safer than rope tows. (Courtesy of the Appalachian Ski Mountain Collection.)

Photographed in 1969, Grady Moretz points to the newly installed lift system, while Sam Goforth examines it in more detail. This system was constructed at a significant cost to the newly named resort, but it increased the speed and numbers of skiers that could move up the hill. This double chairlift went to the top of the Strudel and Appaljack slopes and is still running today. (Courtesy of the Appalachian Ski Mountain Collection.)

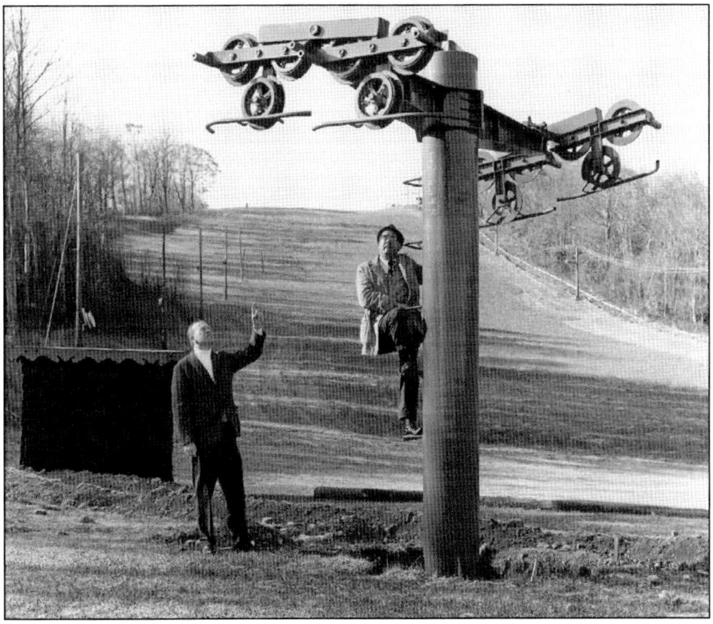

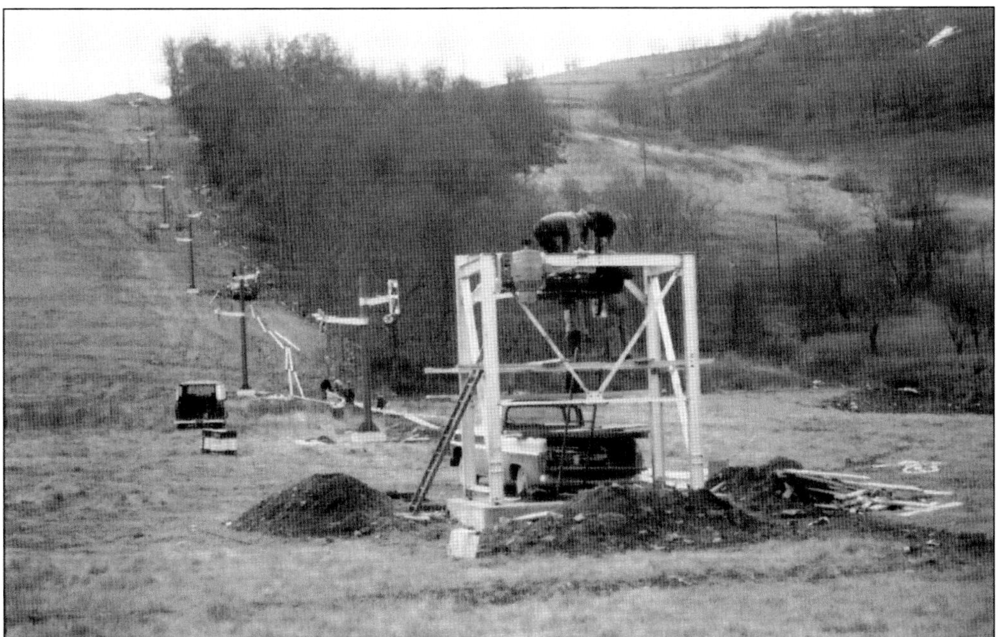

The snowmaking system is being installed along the rope tow in this c. 1969 photograph. Note the pipes lying on the ground. Grady and Reba Moretz and their partners—as new owners—made many improvements to the resort, including upgrading the snowmaking system. (Courtesy of the Appalachian Ski Mountain Collection.)

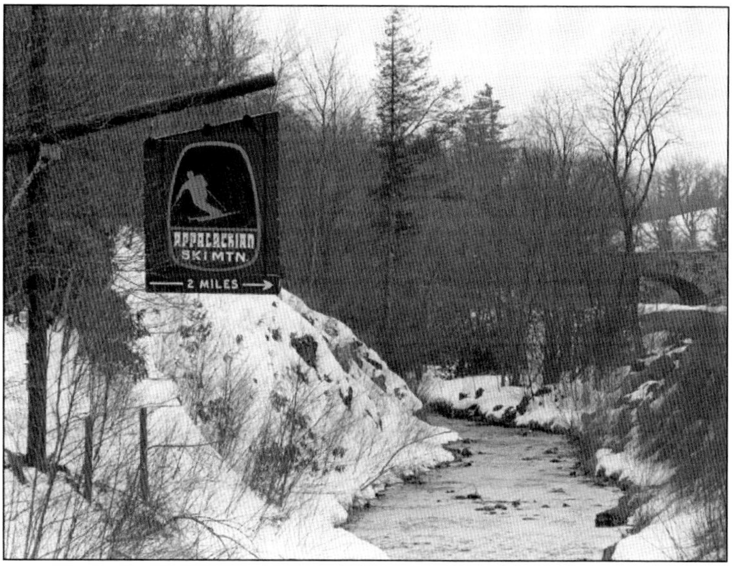

This modest wooden sign stood alongside the creek for many years, where visitors would turn from US Highway 321 up to the resort. A nearby native stone bridge stands where the Blue Ridge Parkway crosses Highway 321. This sign was later replaced by a billboard, which still stands in the same location. (Courtesy of the Appalachian Ski Mountain Collection.)

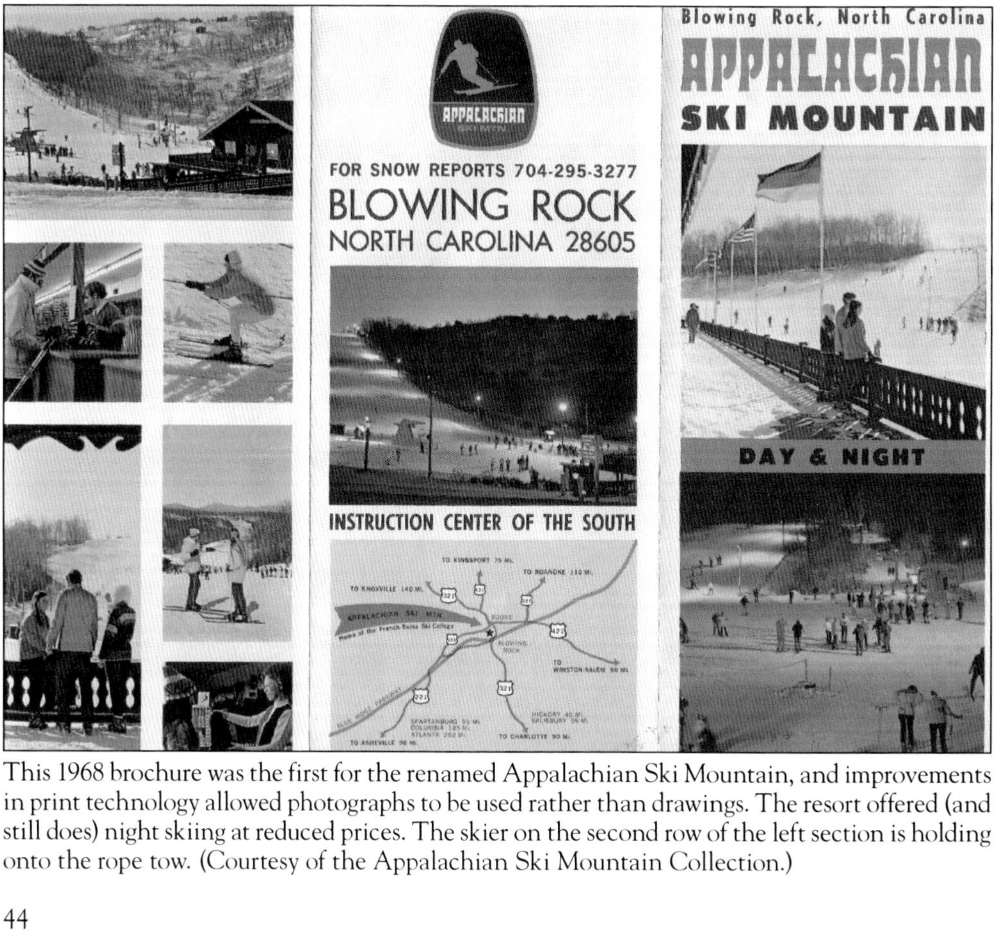

This 1968 brochure was the first for the renamed Appalachian Ski Mountain, and improvements in print technology allowed photographs to be used rather than drawings. The resort offered (and still does) night skiing at reduced prices. The skier on the second row of the left section is holding onto the rope tow. (Courtesy of the Appalachian Ski Mountain Collection.)

This c. 1970 photograph shows the base of the newly installed double chairlift on the left, and the rope tow along the right, as they move skiers to the top of the slopes. A first aid sled is visible at the bottom left of the photograph, as the ski patrol works at keeping the slopes safe. (Courtesy of the Appalachian Ski Mountain Collection.)

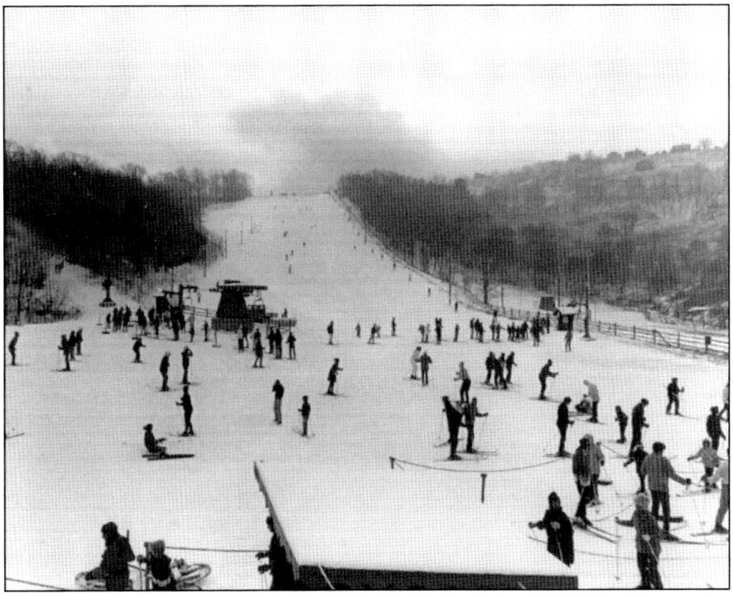

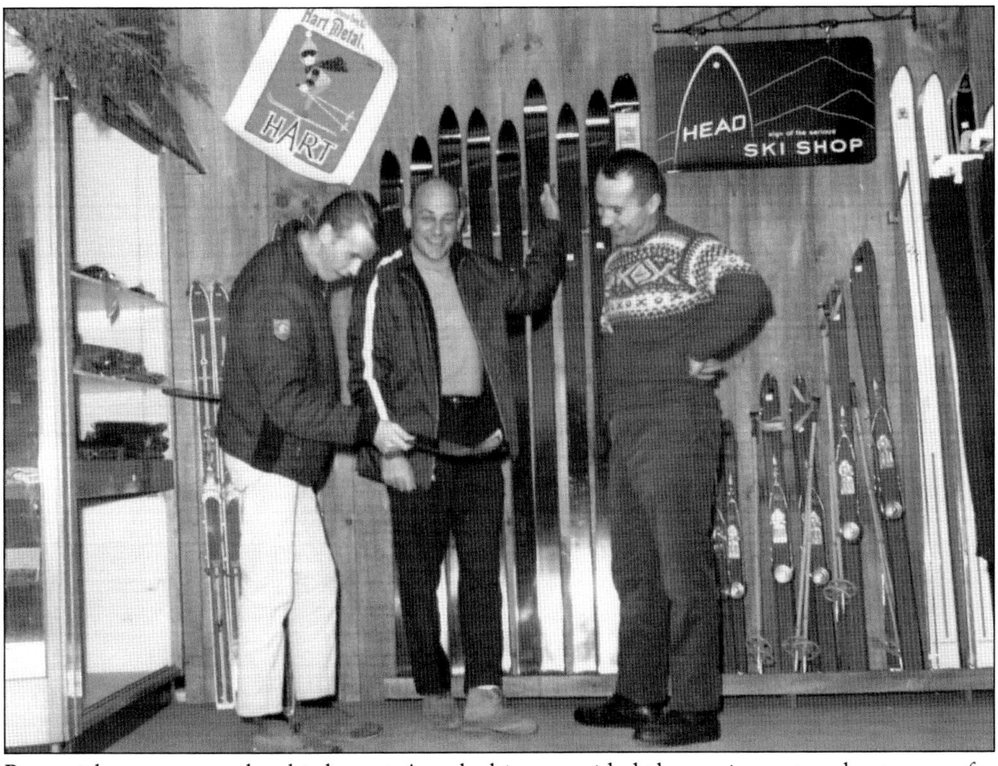

Busy with customers, the ski shop at Appalachian provided the equipment and outerwear for skiers. Head skis, the leading brand in the United States at that time, were being advertised in the store. Howard Head developed the first laminated metal skis in 1947, and the brand became an industry leader. The varying lengths of skis on display may be for skiers of different heights, or they may be part of the Graduated Length Method of skiing education. (Courtesy of William L. Eury Collection, Appalachian State University.)

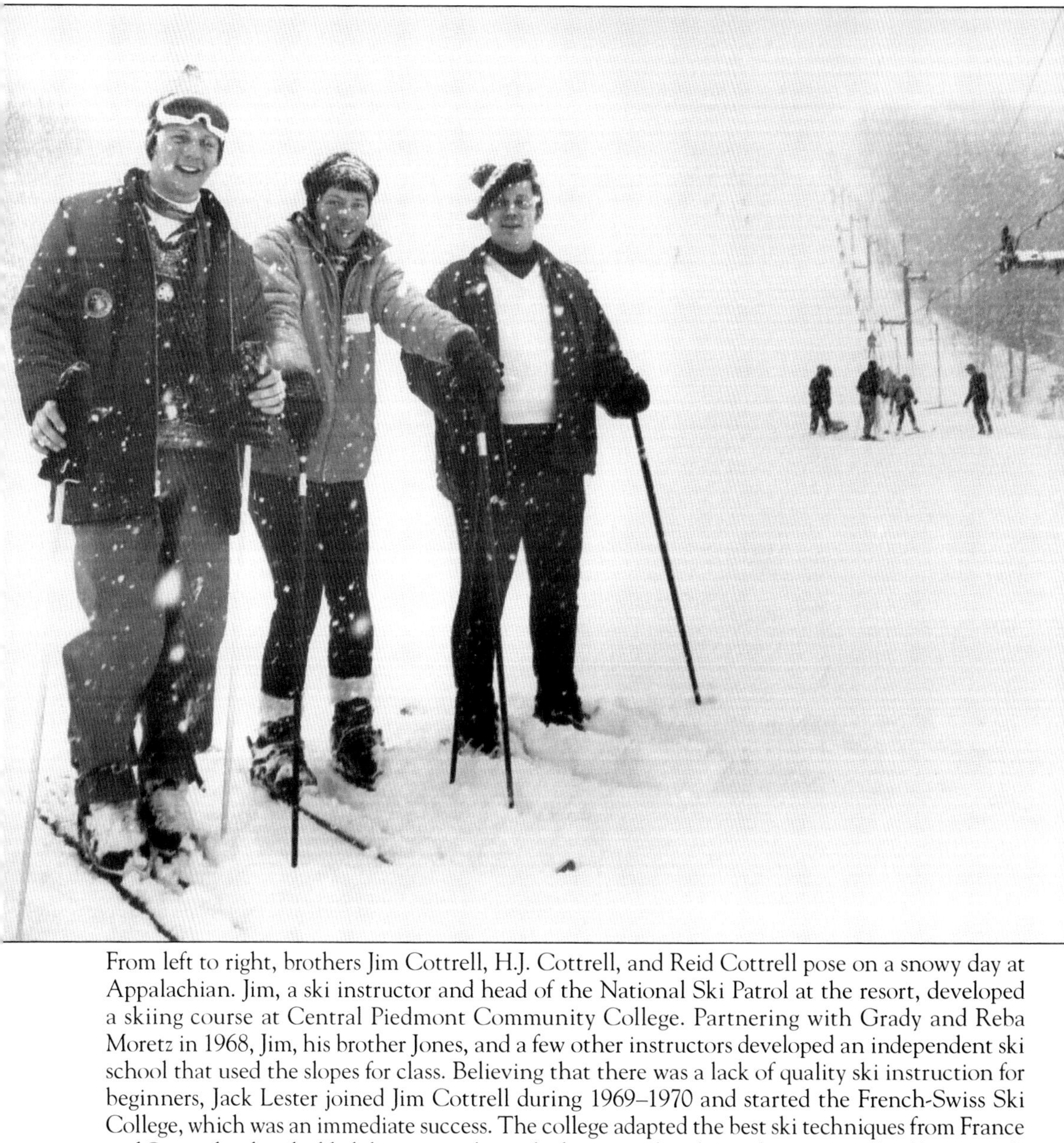

From left to right, brothers Jim Cottrell, H.J. Cottrell, and Reid Cottrell pose on a snowy day at Appalachian. Jim, a ski instructor and head of the National Ski Patrol at the resort, developed a skiing course at Central Piedmont Community College. Partnering with Grady and Reba Moretz in 1968, Jim, his brother Jones, and a few other instructors developed an independent ski school that used the slopes for class. Believing that there was a lack of quality ski instruction for beginners, Jack Lester joined Jim Cottrell during 1969–1970 and started the French-Swiss Ski College, which was an immediate success. The college adapted the best ski techniques from France and Switzerland and added skiing as a physical education class for credit at regional colleges. With Jack Lester's brilliant promotion, the school took off and, by 1975, had a full-time staff of 50 and a part-time staff of 105. In 1976, Cottrell hosted the first North Carolina Winter Special Olympics, and the school has hosted the Southeastern Winter Special Olympics ever since. In 1982, Eunice Kennedy Shriver, founder of the Special Olympics, visited the slopes and was impressed with the program. (Courtesy of the Appalachian Ski Mountain Collection.)

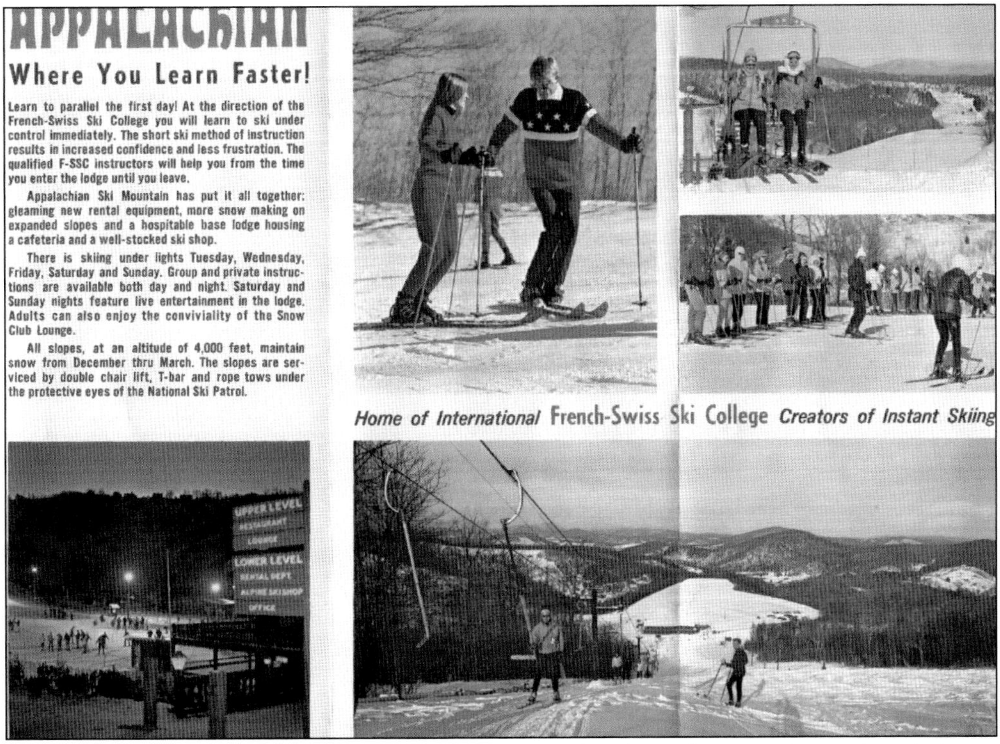

According to this c. 1970 brochure, Appalachian was the place where one learned to ski faster. Jim Cottrell's innovative French-Swiss Ski College started new skiers on short skies that helped establish control and confidence. This made it possible to get students on the slopes quickly. By 2005, the college had given more than a million lessons. (Courtesy of Wilson King Collection.)

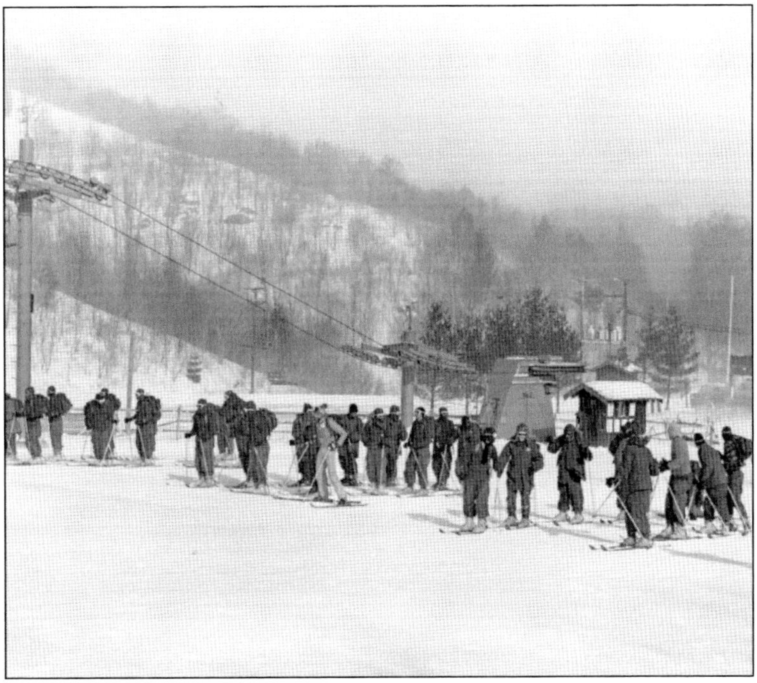

Beginning in 1972, hundreds of Special Forces Green Beret troops began training at French-Swiss, which was a first for a southern ski school. It is impressive that the Army decided for the first time to do ski training in North Carolina, driving home the idea that North Carolina was a good place to learn to ski. (Courtesy of French-Swiss Ski College Collection.)

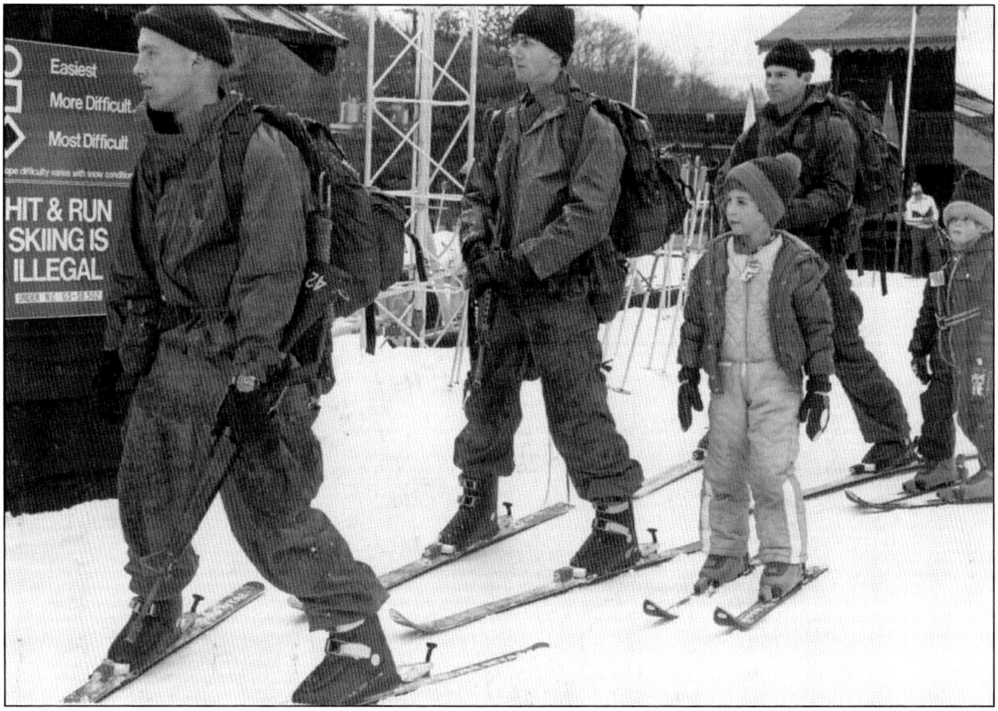

Imagine the surprise of these children to be riding a lift with gun-toting soldiers (the guns were unloaded, of course). Jim Cottrell's French-Swiss Ski College is proud of having trained thousands of groups of soldiers from US Army Special Forces, Navy Seals, and other divisions. The units set up tents, camped at the resort, and also received wilderness survival training. At the end of their training, the soldiers held races to see who had become the fastest skiers—as shown below. Jim Cottrell remains at Appalachian as the director of this prestigious ski school and has published a book, *Skiing Everyone*, that explains his methodology and training. (Courtesy of French-Swiss Ski College Collection.)

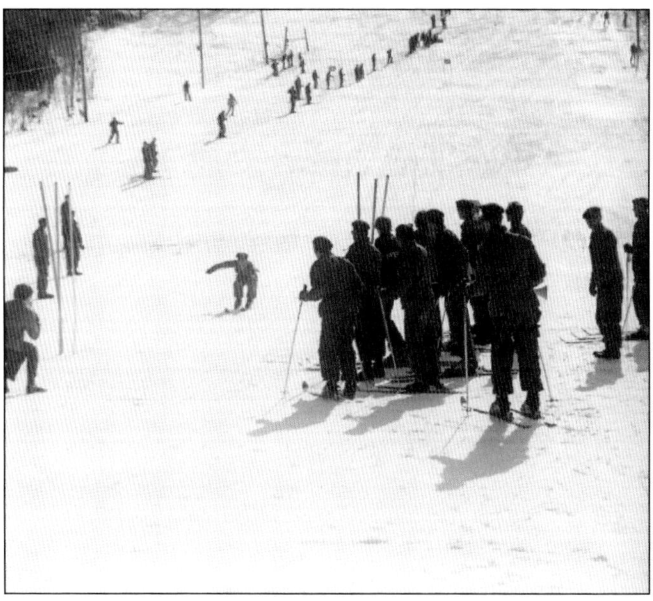

This soldier is loaded down to simulate combat conditions as he skis on Appalachian's slopes. His boots feature a more modern style of bindings, rather than the previously noted laces. Thousands of armed forces members learned or honed their ski skills through classes at the French-Swiss Ski School. (Courtesy of French-Swiss Ski College Collection.)

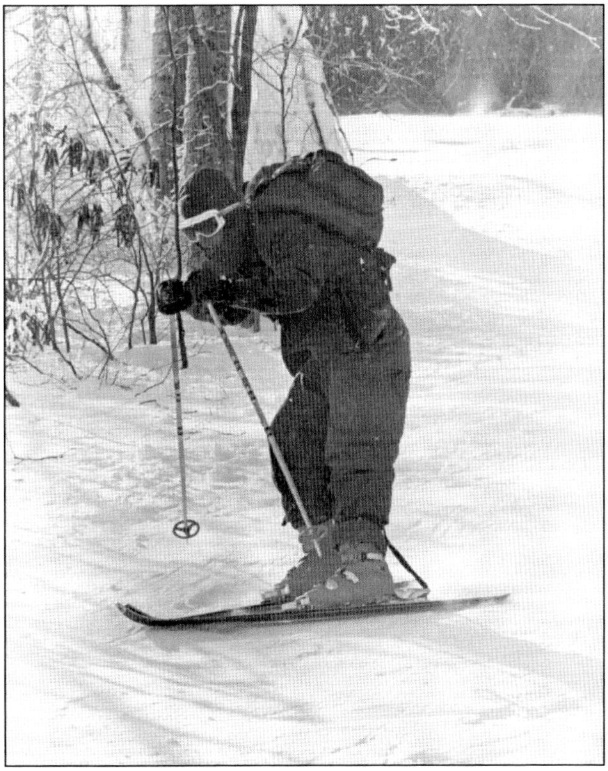

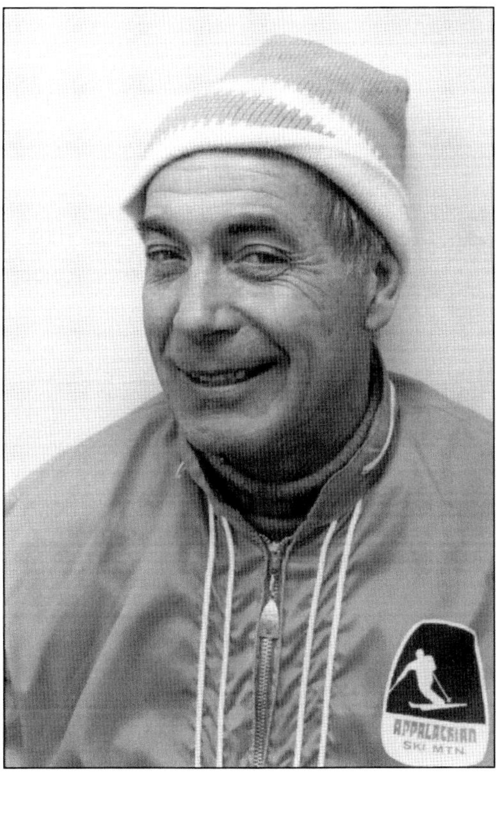

Eric DeGroat, an early ski instructor and ski patrol member, was instrumental to the success of Appalachian. He is credited with starting a physical education class in skiing at the nearby Appalachian State University and worked at the resort for many years. It is believed that he suggested the new name for the resort during 1968–1969. (Courtesy of the Appalachian Ski Mountain Collection.)

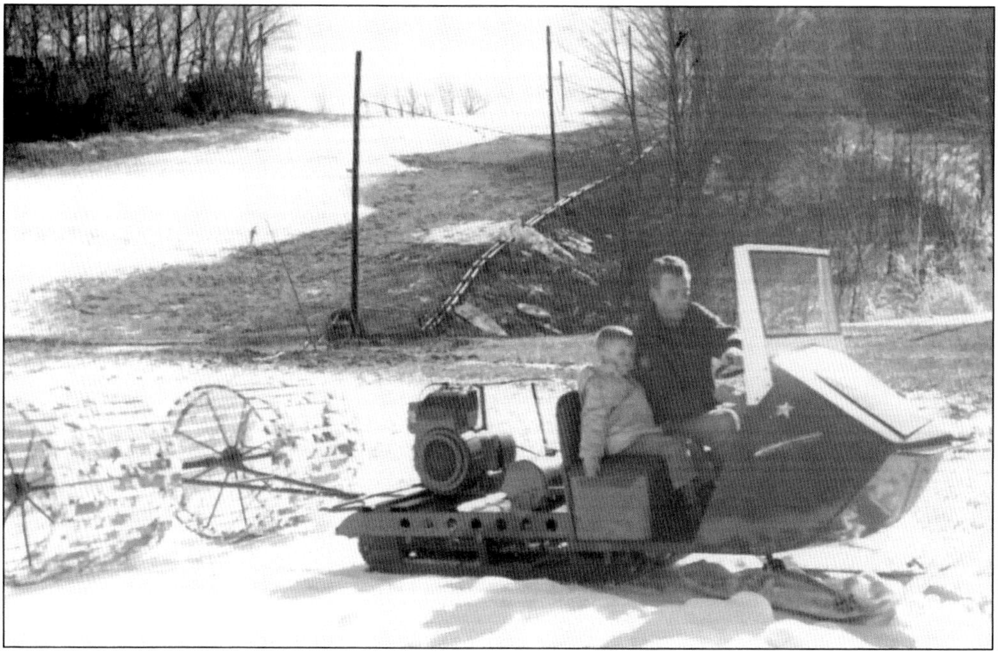

An employee appears to be giving a young child a ride on an early snow-grooming machine in this c. 1970 photograph. These early groomers were closely related to tractors and used similar equipment to shape the snow—a far cry from modern high-tech groomers. Pipes for snowmaking are visible on the nearby hill. (Courtesy of the Appalachian Ski Mountain Collection.)

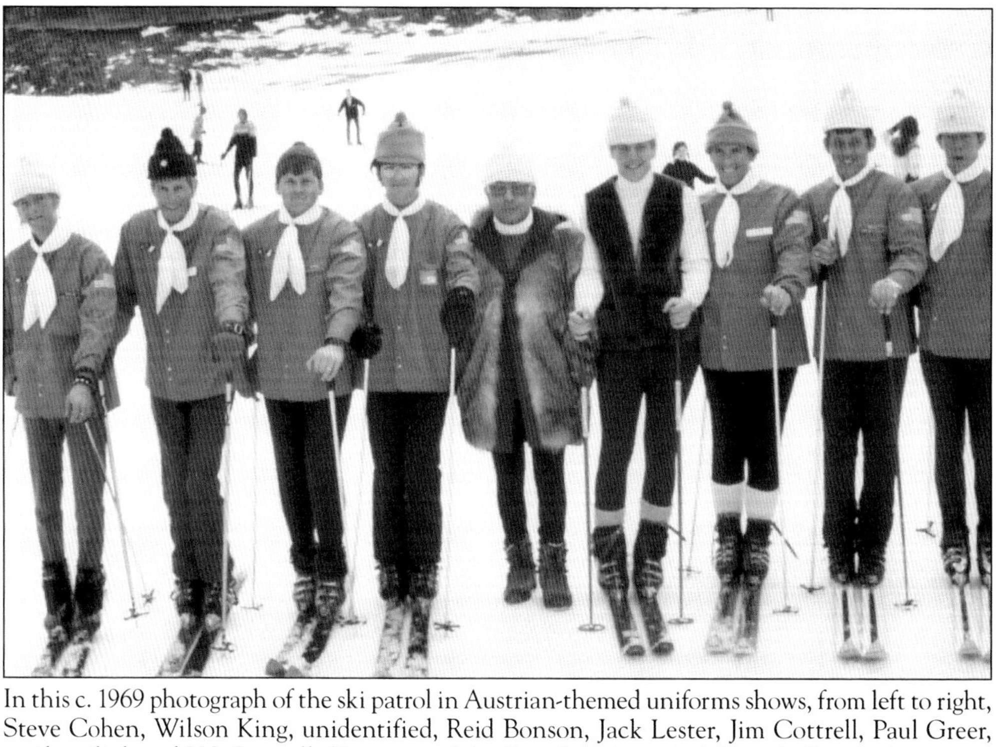

In this c. 1969 photograph of the ski patrol in Austrian-themed uniforms shows, from left to right, Steve Cohen, Wilson King, unidentified, Reid Bonson, Jack Lester, Jim Cottrell, Paul Greer, unidentified, and H.J. Cottrell. (Courtesy of the French-Swiss Ski College Collection.)

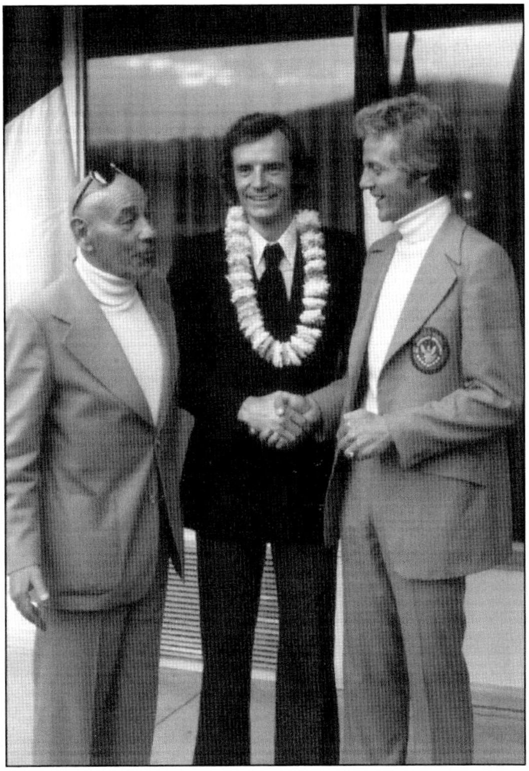

In 1972, the French-Swiss school brought French skier Jean-Claude Killy to the resort. Killy, regarded as the world's greatest skier, was the winner of three Olympic gold medals. Pictured at right during his three-day visit, Killy (center) posed with Jack Lester (left) and Jim Cottrell (right). In the photograph below, Killy rides the double chairlift with a lucky resort employee. Many believe that this marketing feat helped build up the southern ski industry and the French-Swiss Ski College. Jack Lester, a former manager for Marilyn Monroe and The Ink Spots, initiated an aggressive, colorful marketing plan for the resort during his tenure. Although his immodesty irritated some, Lester accomplished his goals and put North Carolina's ski resorts in the news. (Both, courtesy of the Appalachian Ski Mountain Collection.)

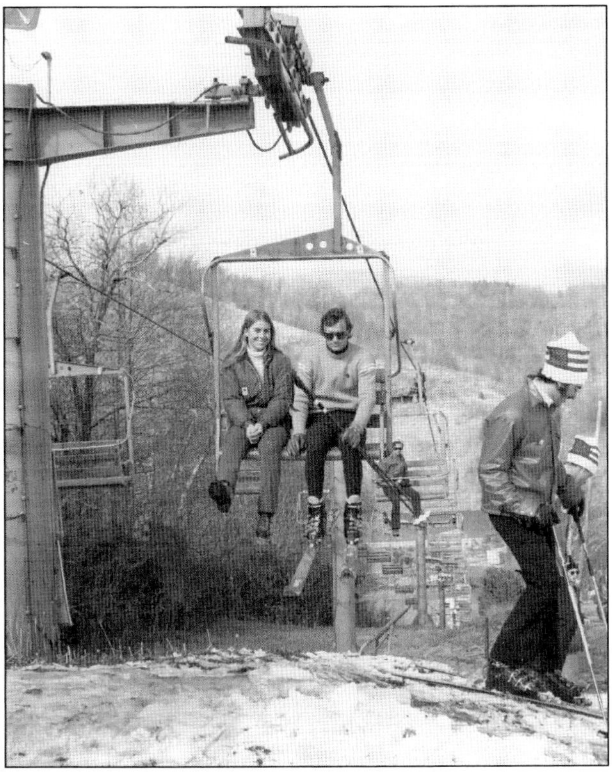

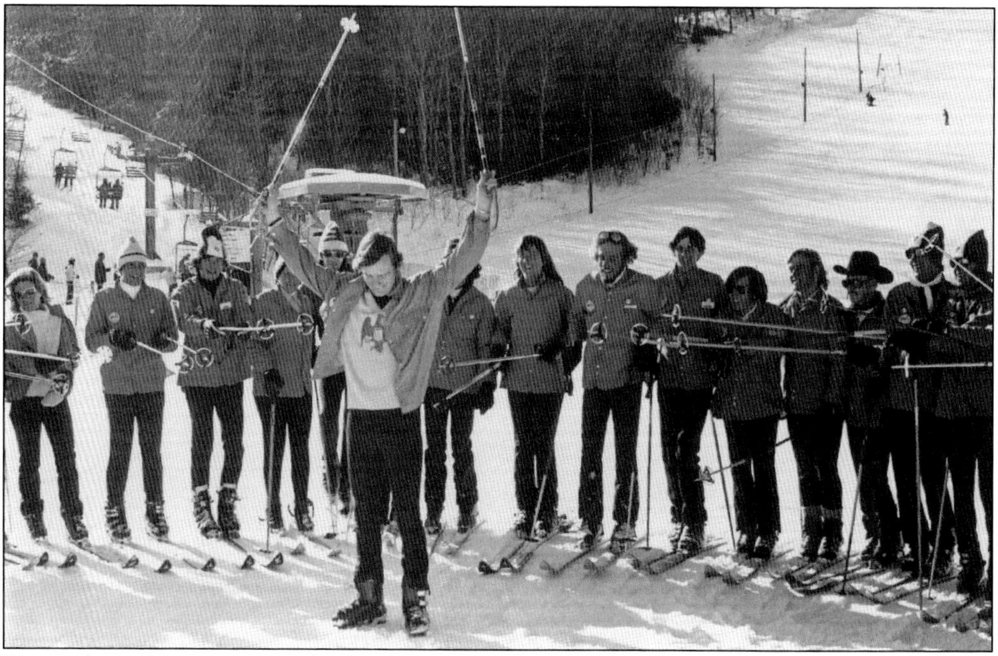

During his 1972 visit, Jean-Claude Killy's first film, *Snow Job*, premiered in nearby Boone. His visit was an enormous media event, bringing national press to Appalachian Ski Mountain. In this photograph, Killy is providing instruction to the resort's ski instructors. The "American Eagle" sweaters were designed for the occasion of Killy's visit. (Courtesy of the Appalachian Ski Mountain Collection.)

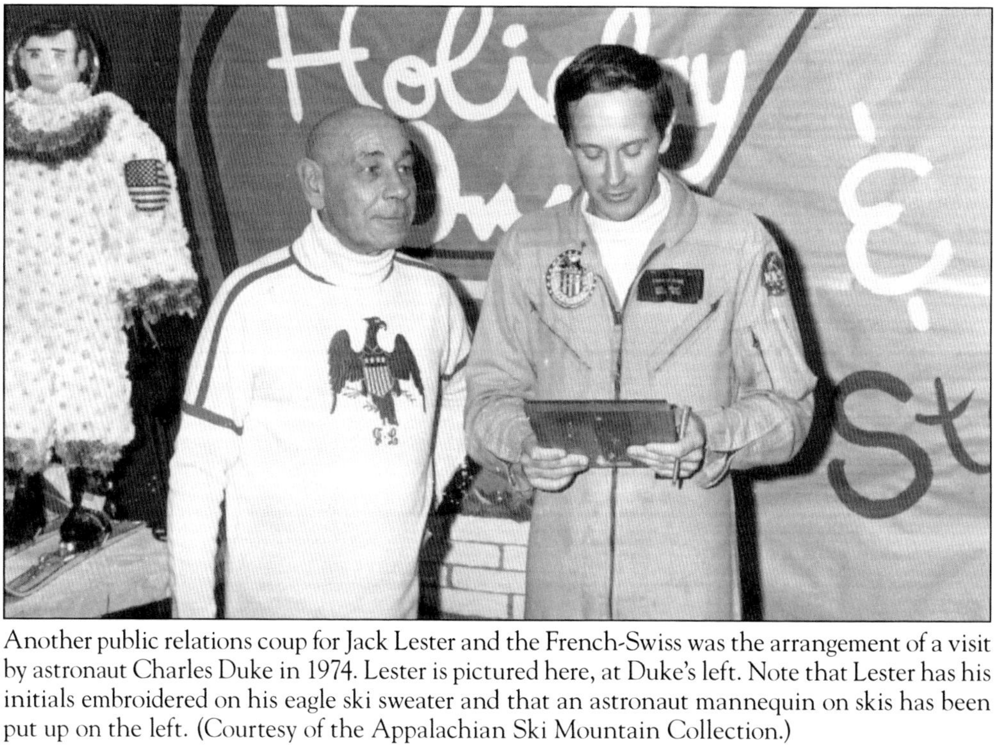

Another public relations coup for Jack Lester and the French-Swiss was the arrangement of a visit by astronaut Charles Duke in 1974. Lester is pictured here, at Duke's left. Note that Lester has his initials embroidered on his eagle ski sweater and that an astronaut mannequin on skis has been put up on the left. (Courtesy of the Appalachian Ski Mountain Collection.)

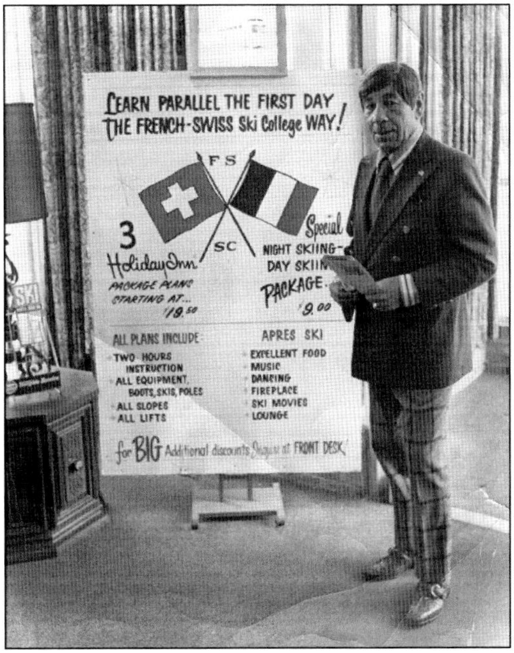

Another successful marketing campaign involved organizing ski and lodging packages with Continental Trailways and Holiday Inn. Jack Lester, pictured, would take the details of these packages to trade shows, where he would answer questions and book customers on a trip to the resort. (Courtesy of the French-Swiss Ski College Collection.)

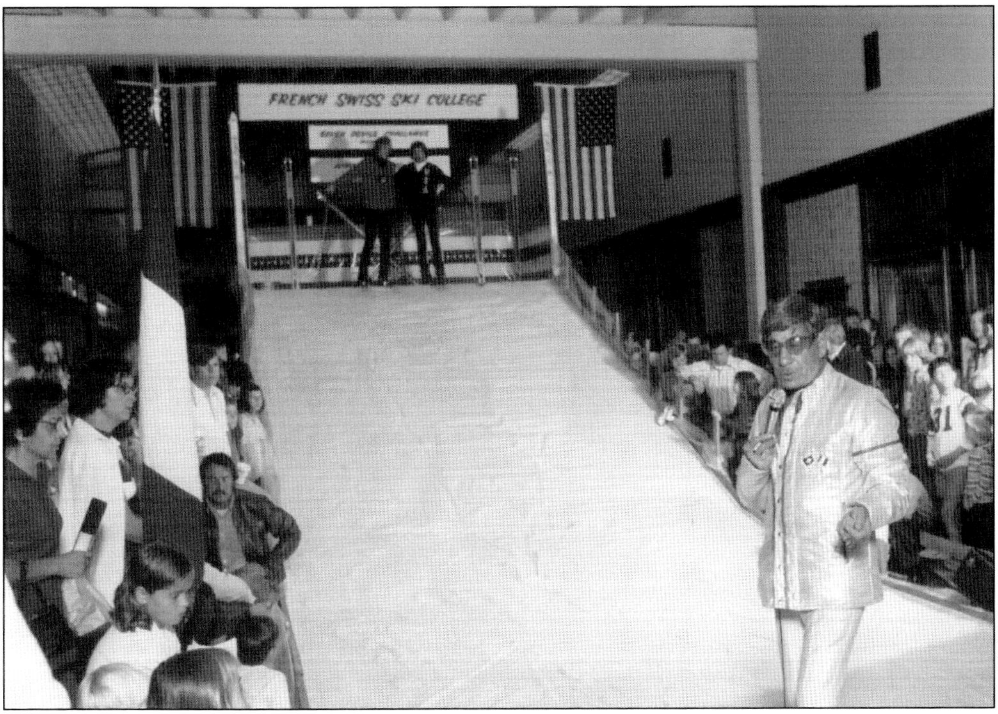

Resplendent in a fancy ski outfit, Jack Lester announces the French-Swiss Ski Revue around 1974. Realizing that Southerners needed to be wooed to ski, Lester and Jim Cottrell developed a mobile ski ramp made of poly snow and traveled around the Southeast to market their ski instruction and resort. Lester died after just a few years at the resort, but his aggressive marketing techniques—and the subsequent group marketing approach of Jim Cottrell—built French-Swiss into a leader in ski instruction. (Courtesy of the French-Swiss Ski College Collection.)

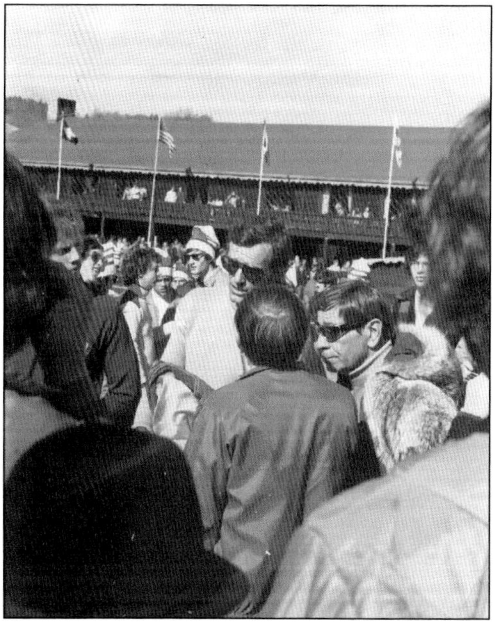

Wearing sunglasses and a light sweater, Jean-Claude Killy stands at the center, with Jack Lester to the right of him, in this 1972 photograph taken during his visit to Appalachian and the premiere of his first feature film, *Snow Job*. Killy's visit to the ski slope brought welcome national publicity to the slopes and to North Carolina's ski industry. (Courtesy of Appalachian Ski Mountain Collection)

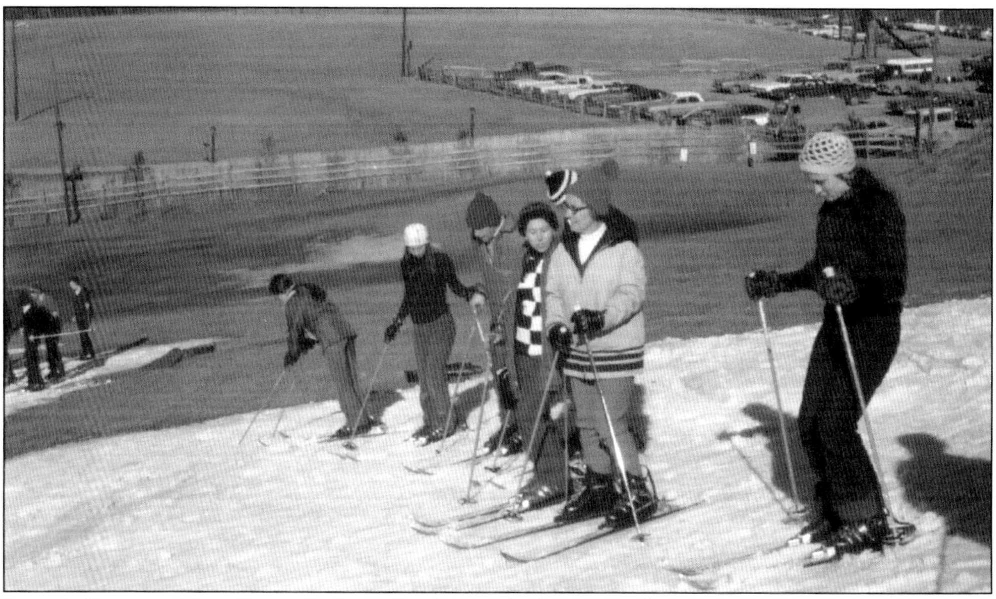

French-Swiss and Jim Cottrell also offered "patch skiing," a ski program that enabled students to learn to ski on little or no snow; it became the basis for the "dryland skiing" used by the International Special Olympics and ski clubs. This safe and unintimidating method of ski instruction convinced many cautious would-be skiers to hit the slopes, and, according to author Randy Johnson, the French-Swiss Ski College has been one of the main factors in the success of the southern ski market. The Moretz family, current owners of Appalachian, gives Cottrell credit for much of the growth of their resort and the High Country's ski industry, as well as praising his significant contribution to national ski instruction. Due to demand, Cottrell penned a book, *Skiing Everyone*, which outlined his innovative method. Today, Jim Cottrell remains a modest, yet inspiring, figure in the ski industry and can be found on the slopes every morning of the season. (Courtesy of the French-Swiss Ski College Collection.)

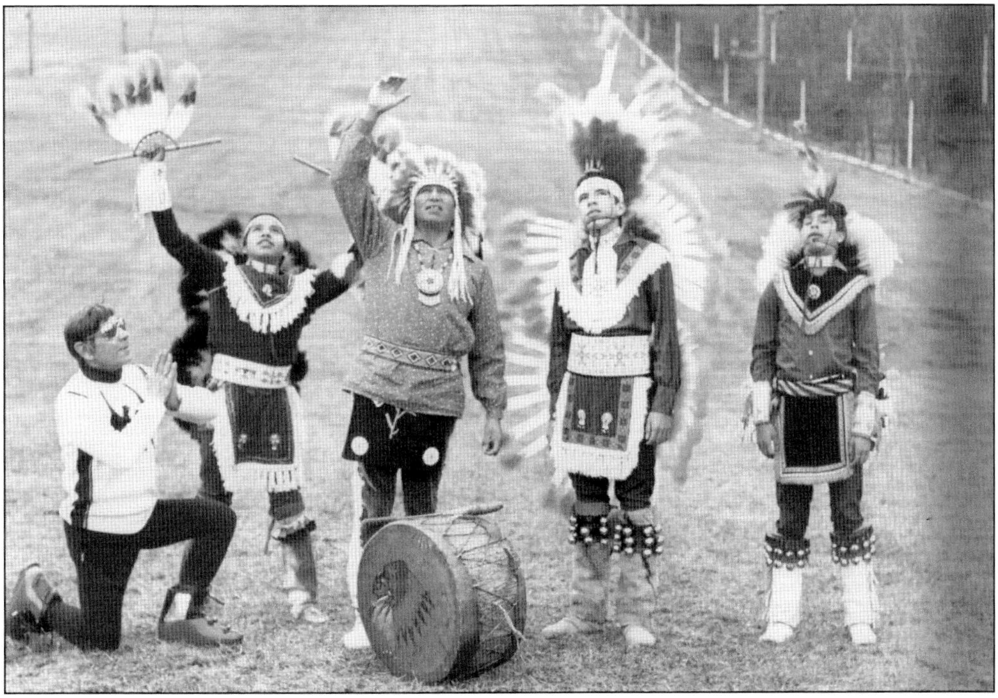

Jack Lester arranged for Cherokee tribe members to stage a "snow dance" and bring snow to the resort during a dry winter in 1971. Once again, Lester's genius provided the press with a story that featured French-Swiss and Appalachian and conveyed their message to Southern skiers. (Courtesy of the French-Swiss Ski College Collection.)

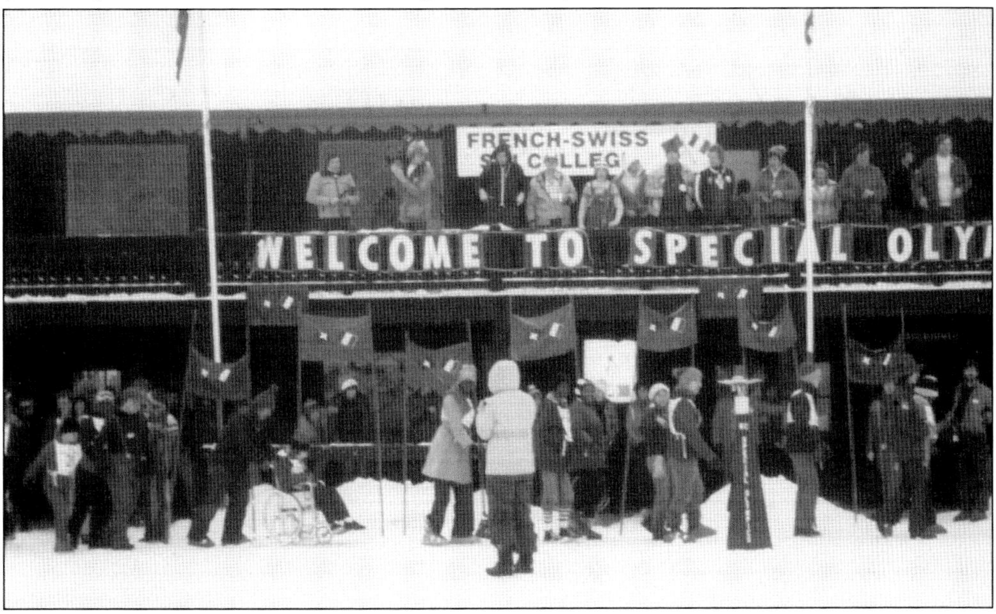

This c. 1976 photograph shows the resort hosting the Winter Special Olympics, which has since become a regular event. In 1982, Eunice Kennedy Shriver, founder of the Special Olympics, visited the slopes to congratulate French-Swiss for adding the event. (Courtesy of the French-Swiss Ski College Collection.)

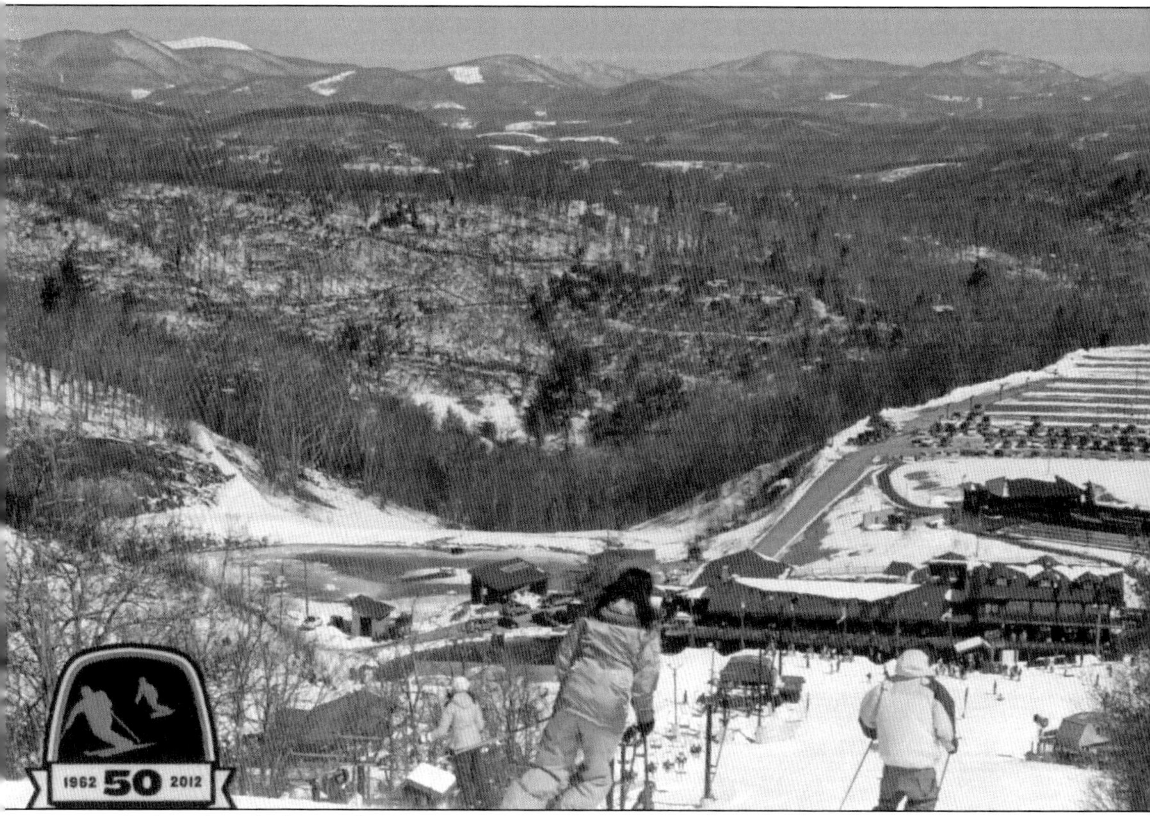

Today, Appalachian Ski Mountain is one of best family resorts in the state, offering easier access and more of a family atmosphere than some of the other resorts. Grady and Reba Moretz have mainly handed off management to their children, Brenda and Brad, but Jim Cottrell is still running the highly acclaimed French-Swiss Ski College. A mainstay of the local economy, the resort continues to bring in visitors for winter recreation and it has expanded significantly. With 27 skiable acres and a vertical drop of only 365 feet, Appalachian features 11 slopes and trails and six lifts capable of moving 7.884 visitors per hour. (Courtesy of the Appalachian Ski Mountain Collection.)

Three

Beech Mountain Resort

Beech Mountain Resort was the result of the vision of Tom "Doc" Brigham, Serena "Chessie" and George MacRae, and the Robbins brothers. In March 1960, Brigham and MacRae formed a corporation with Ted Randolph, John Grenier, and Joe Simpson, purchasing the land at the top of Beech Mountain for the development of a ski resort. Financing challenges caused Brigham to bring in Grover and Harold Robbins—successful developers then working on the Hound Ears golf community—and eventually sell Beech to them in 1968. The Robbins brothers then formed the Carolina Caribbean Corporation, a residential development partnership, which matched up buyers wanting to live in the mountains during the summer and St. Croix in the winter.

Initial land sales were brisk, and, until the early 1970s, Beech Mountain was a leading development. Opened in the winter of 1967–1968, the ski resort featured a replica of an alpine pedestrian village (designed by Claus Moberg), an Austrian ski school, the Beechtree Inn, and a golf course. The golf course was once noted as the second highest golf course in the United States. Additionally, Willi Falger brought in ski instructors from Austria, which brought in increased numbers of visitors. Beech's charm was also showcased with the Land of Oz attraction. Opened by the Robbins brothers in 1970, Oz was a delightful park—inspired by the novels of L. Frank Baum. Sadly, a fire burned the Emerald City in 1976, and the park closed in 1980. For the past 20 years and continuing today, a group hosted Autumn in Oz events—weekends when the park open for tours designed to raise funds for reconstruction.

Carolina Caribbean was hit hard by the recession of the 1970s, and the winters of 1972–1974 were warm and light of snow. The company's bankruptcy—which began in 1975—was the state's largest and continued until the 1980s. The Tri-South Mortgage Company purchased the resort and brought in a retired colonel, Norman Smith, to improve the resort. With no owners to operate the ski resort, the Beech Property Owners Associates, including Robert Yelton, George Handley, Alan Holcombe, and Fench Moore, leased the ski area from the bank in the winter of 1975–1976. Beech was improved again in 1982, when Sepp Gmuender and Paul Bousquet used their resort management experience to refurbish the facilities, add a new lift, expand the resort's snowmaking equipment, and establish the annual Winterfest event. In 1986, Ray Costin and Wayne Holman purchased the resort, and in 2001, Ray and his family began to manage the resort. Today, Ray's sons, Ryan and Jack Costin, continue to expand the ski resort's offerings and increase its popularity.

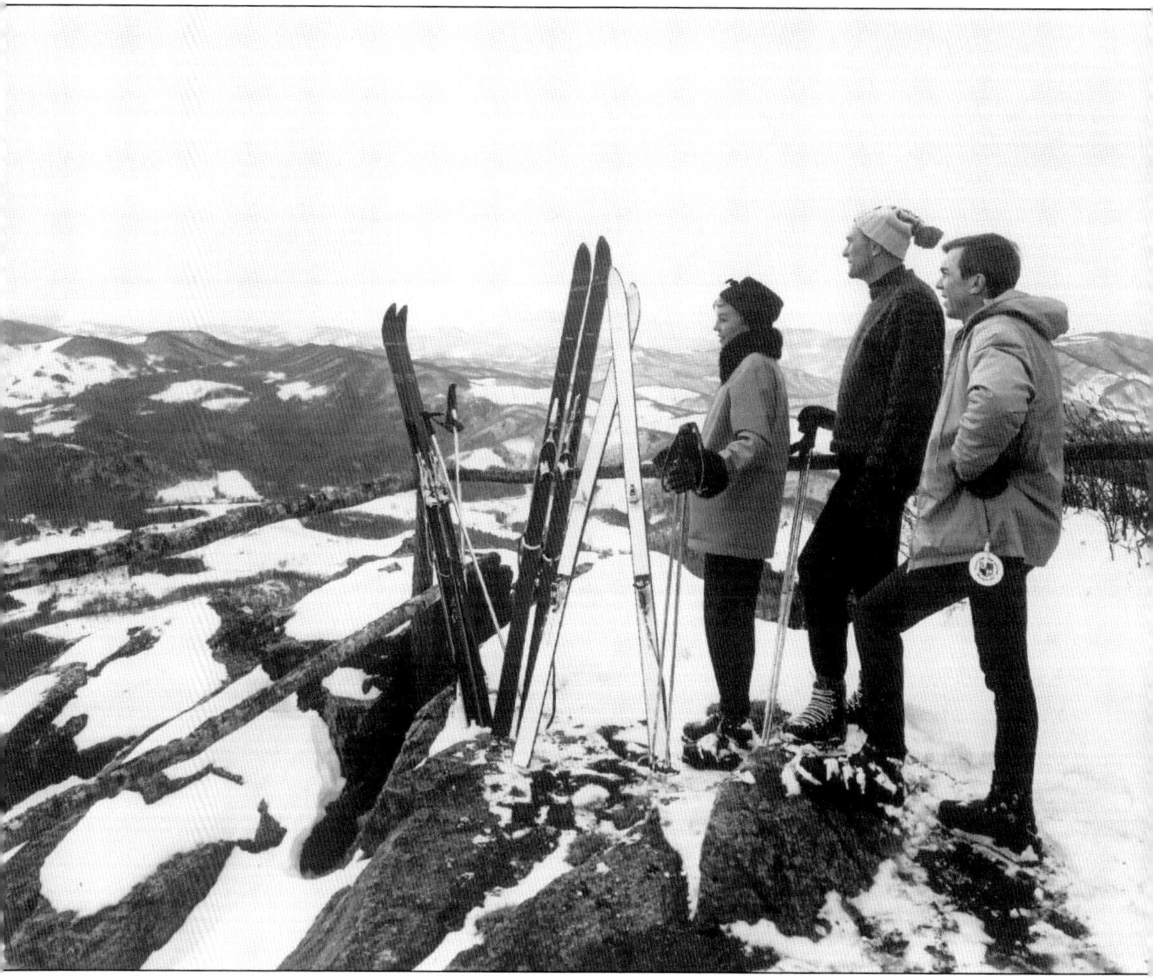

The creators of Beech Mountain Resort are pictured here in 1970, peering over the mountainous view from the pinnacle. They are, from left to right, Barbara J. Robbins, Tom Brigham, and Grover C. Robbins. Grover and his brother Harold built several theme parks and residential developments, mainly in the northwest North Carolina mountains, including the Tweetsie Railroad theme park in the late 1950s, the Hound Ears Club in 1962, and Linville Land Harbor. After selling Beech Mountain to the Robbins brothers in 1968, Brigham and the MacRaes joined other developers and purchased land on Sugar Mountain—developing a residential and recreational area that also included a ski resort. The Robbins brothers formed the Carolina Caribbean Corporation to offer buyers an interest in St. Croix and Beech Mountain, and Beech was a major development in the early 1970s. Despite the company's eventual bankruptcy, the residential and recreational development persevered and continues to offer skiing and other amenities. Many Carolina Caribbean employees remained, such as Jim Brooks, and have been key to the resort's success today. (Courtesy of Jim Brooks Collection.)

Developed by Grover and Harry Robbins and the Carolina Caribbean Corporation, the Beech Mountain development was designed on a grand scale and included winter and summer recreational activities. The resort was not developed as shown, but this map reflects the careful, widespread planning that the development involved. (Courtesy of Jim Brooks Collection.)

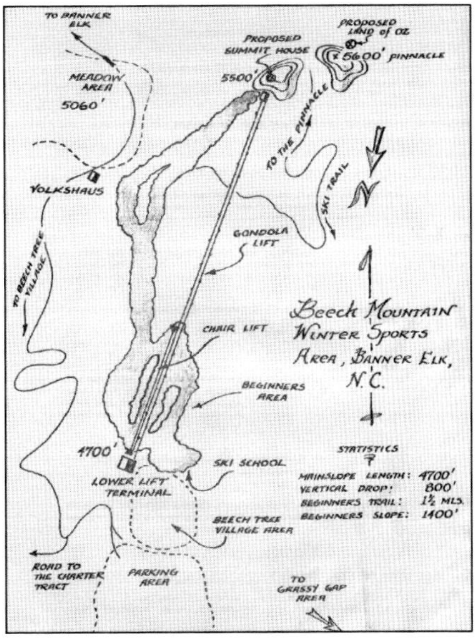

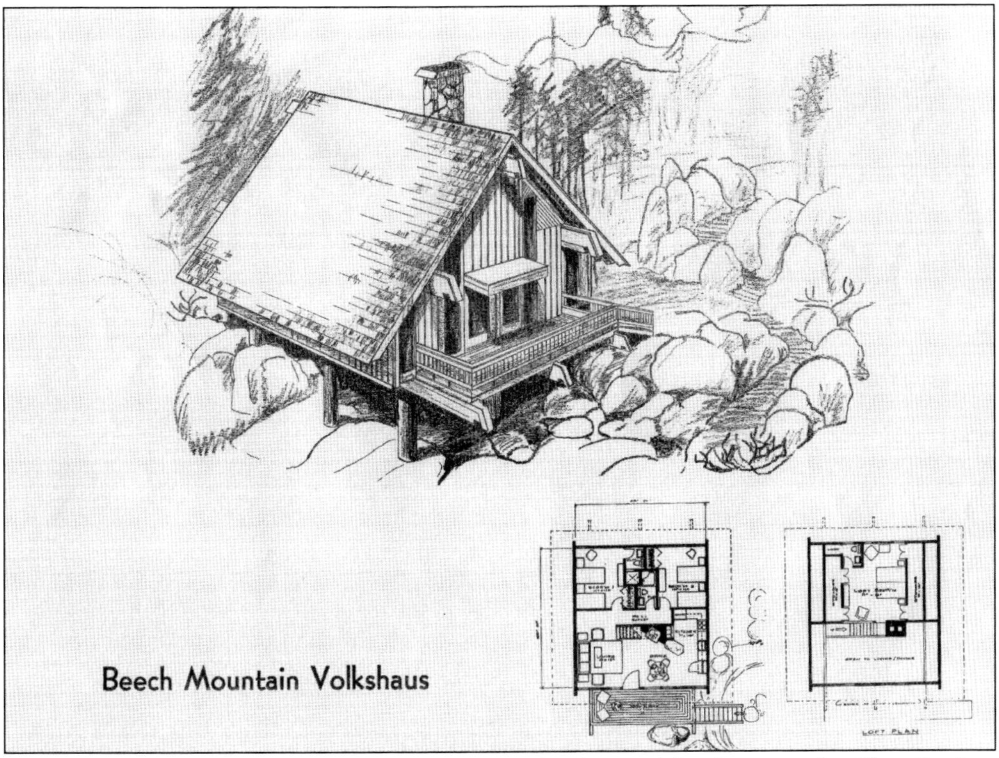

The Volkhaus was one of five charming house styles designed for the resort by Claus Reuben Moberg, a Yale-educated, nationally renowned architect. Moberg designed many unique buildings in the area, including Beech's Alpine Village, the Blowing Rock Country Clubhouse, the Hound Ears clubhouse, and many local residences. Carolina Caribbean exercised architectural control, approved Moberg's five residential designs—the Volkhaus, Alpenhaus, Kleinhaus, Skihaus, and Berghaus—and also allowed the round house to be built in the resort. (Courtesy of Jim Brooks Collection.)

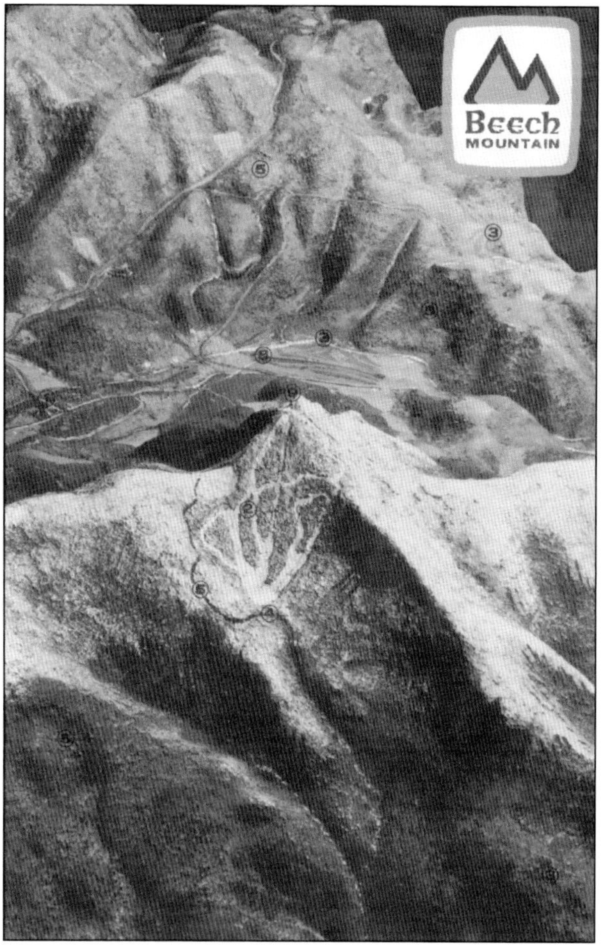

This early marketing brochure for the Beech Mountain development shows the ski resort area and advertises that it provides the highest skiing in the East. Golf courses, the Beech Tree Village, homesites, and the Land of Oz are also marked on the map. Additional golf courses and ski slopes were planned for the adjacent valley, and a 3,600-foot-long airstrip was constructed. Today, those areas are part of the Elk River Club. (Courtesy of Jim Brooks Collection.)

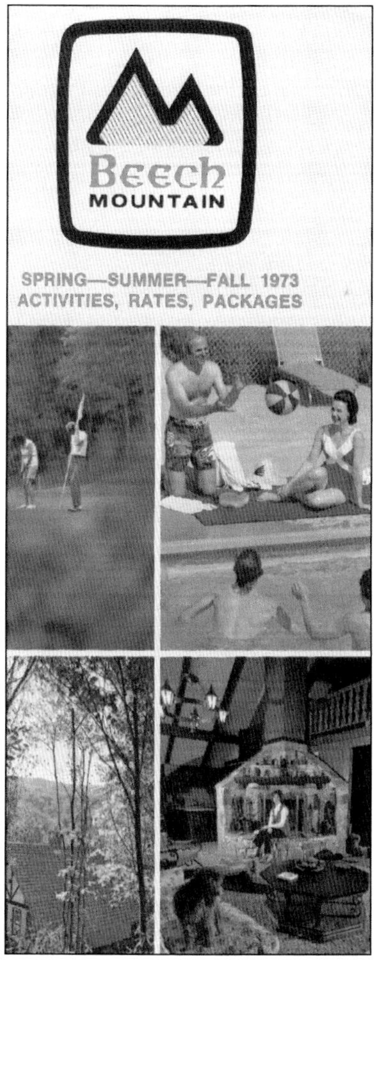

As seen in this early marketing brochure, the resort offered activities for every season. Beech Mountain included activities such as fishing, hiking, camping, horseback riding, golf, restaurants, and the Land of Oz attraction. Additionally, Beech Tree Village was a pedestrian center for entertainment, dining, and shopping, and the golf course could claim to be the built at the highest elevation on the East Coast—until the Elk River Club constructed one nearby that is a bit higher. (Courtesy of Jim Brooks Collection.)

Here, two skiers pause at the top of Beech Mountain to take in a view of the neighboring mountains. From the top of Beech Mountain, it is possible for visitors to see all of the way to the mountains of Tennessee and Virginia. (Courtesy of Wilson King Collection.)

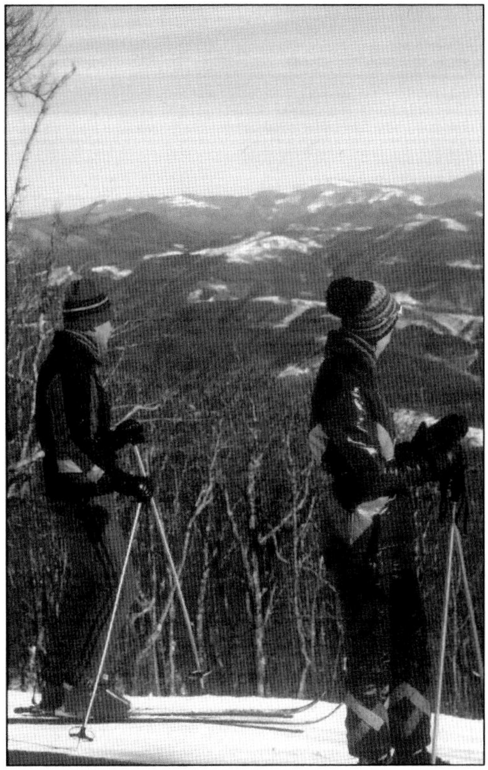

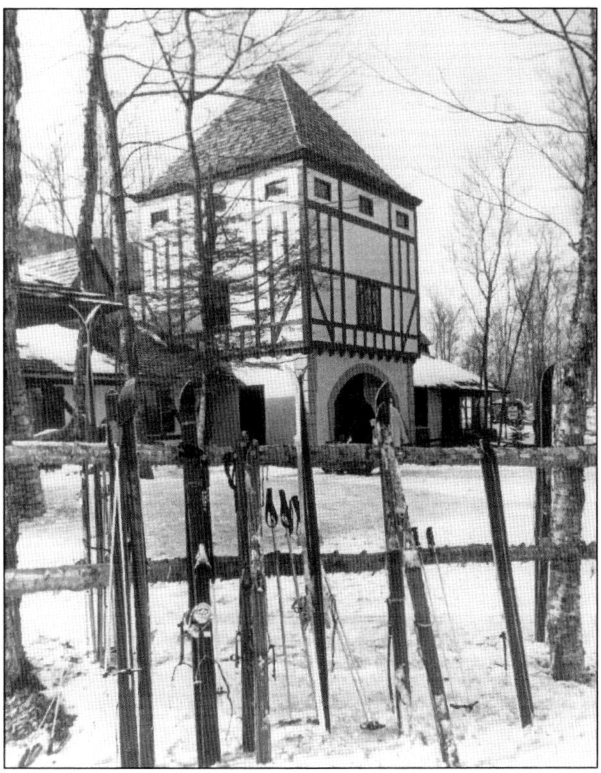

The Beech Mountain Resort Gallery is featured in this c. 1969 photograph, with skis propped along the fence. The building is a part of Beech Tree Village, which was designed by nationally renowned architect Claus Moberg, and it still sets the tone for the entrance to the ski area. On the season's opening day in 1976, the trees were covered in rime ice and it was only two degrees, but the resort still ran out of food and rental boots. (Courtesy of Jim Brooks Collection.)

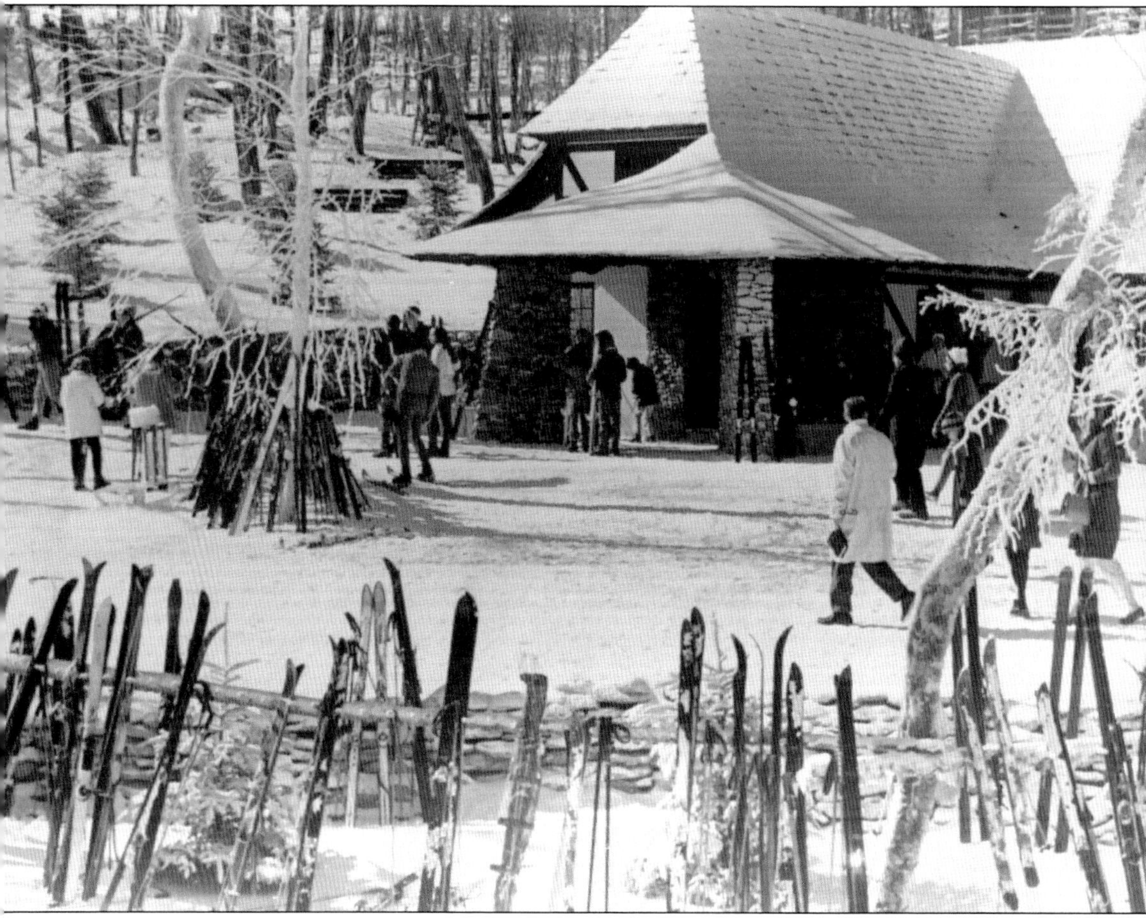

This building was at one end of the Beech Tree Village and originally contained the ski office—selling lift tickets and renting ski equipment. Each building was painstakingly crafted to resemble alpine architecture and provide a rustic and welcoming flavor to the ski resort. The village was advertised as "a picturesque Alpine Village providing services and facilities for the entire resort. Included in the village will be restaurants, ski lodge and cafeteria, ski rental and repair shop and sports and specialty shops." The buildings remain today, and, while some have closed and fallen into disrepair, the resort is working to open new businesses there. In fact, a brewery recently opened in one of the buildings. (Courtesy of Jim Brooks Collection.)

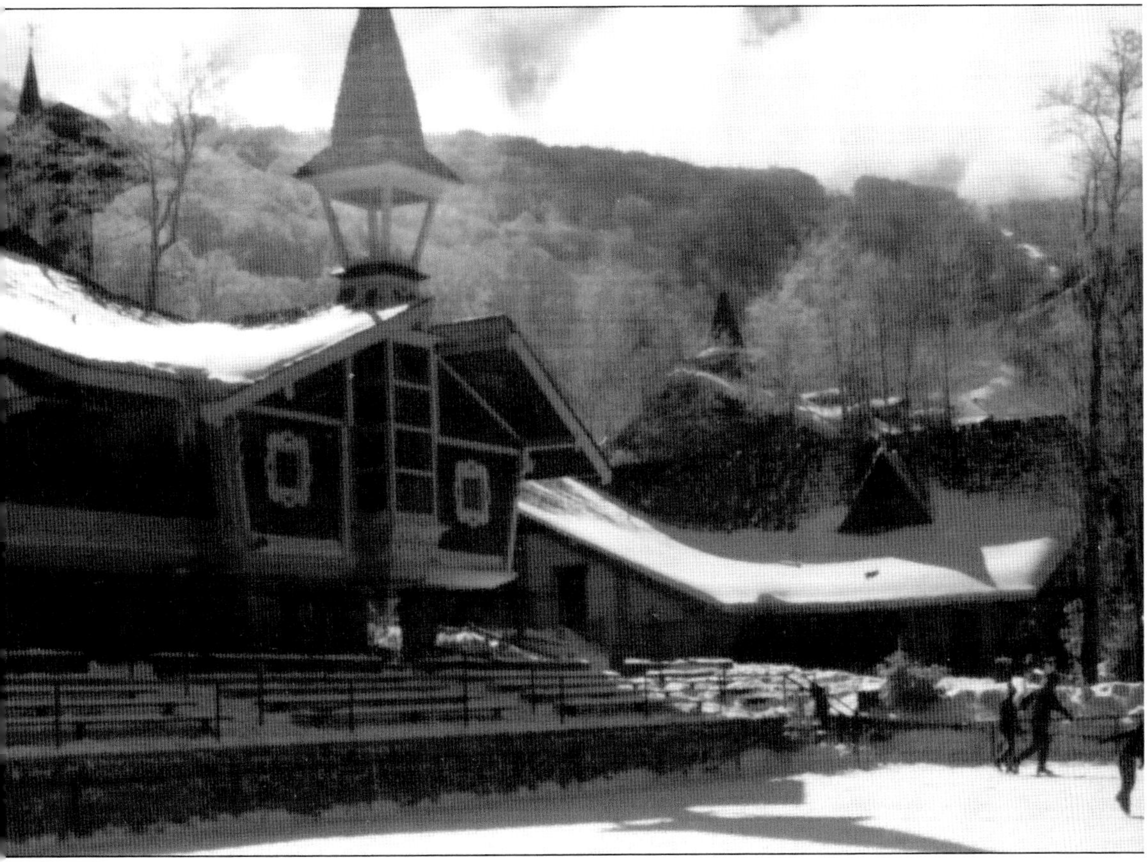

Beech Tree Village also provided an ice-skating rink for those interested in another winter sport. The rink was very popular and hosted several well-known skaters at competitions. Today, the rink is 7,000 square feet and open during the ski season. (Courtesy of Beech Mountain Resort.)

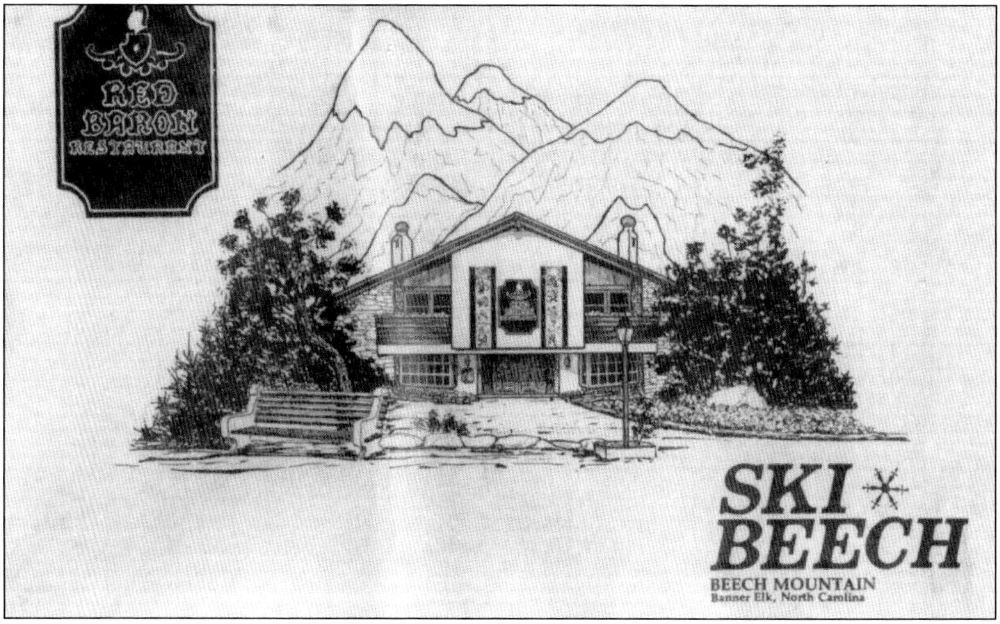

The Red Baron Club was established in the basement of the Beech Tree Inn in 1970, where it operated for many years. With its authentic French bar from 1917 and $100 annual membership fee, the club was a favorite social spot for skiers, locals, and paying members. Compared to saloons in the Wild West by some alumni, the club allowed brown bagging and sold alcoholic drinks while providing a unique ambience that included a partial airplane and other World War I aerial decor. Within, the honorable Red Baron award was bestowed upon successful Carolina Caribbean salespersons. While Beech Mountain became "wet" in the 1980s, a Watauga County raid for illegal alcohol in the 1970s gathered $10,000 worth of beverages from the club. As seen below, the owners had a creative sense of humor and named drinks for different air squadrons to honor their reputations. Unfortunately, the club is no longer in operation, although the inn does have a popular lounge area with live entertainment. (Both, courtesy of Beech Mountain Resort.)

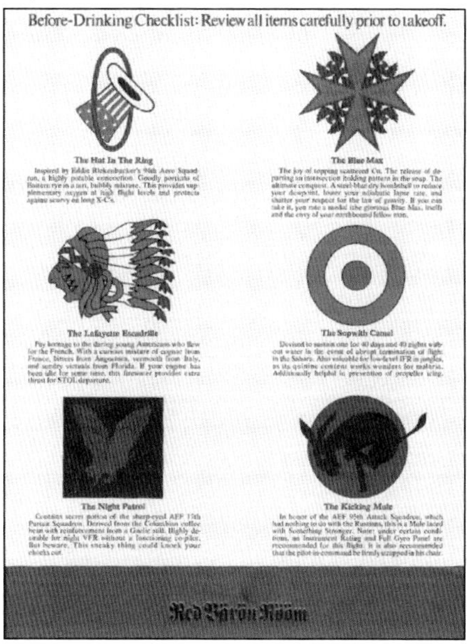

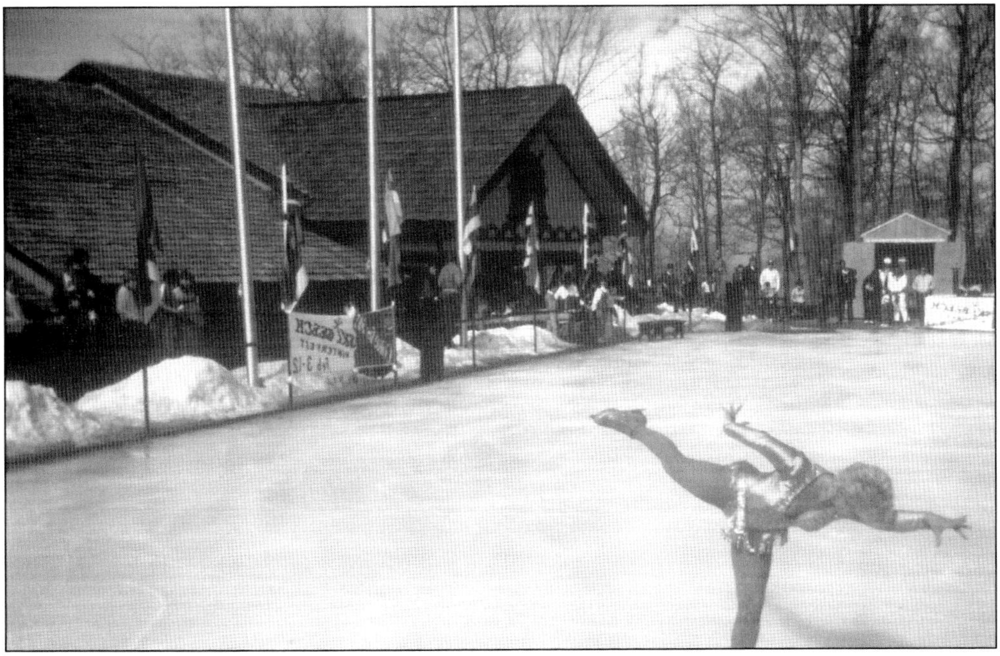

The talented skater in the above photograph provides a show at the Beech Tree Village ice-skating rink on a sunny day in 1970. Below, parents skate alongside their children in this fun family activity that was either an alternative, or addition, to skiing the slopes. The rink has hosted several competitions and shows—featuring well-known skaters—throughout its history and continues to operate today. The Beech Mountain Resort ice rink has a reputation as an excellent place to learn the art of ice-skating. (Both, courtesy of Beech Mountain Resort.)

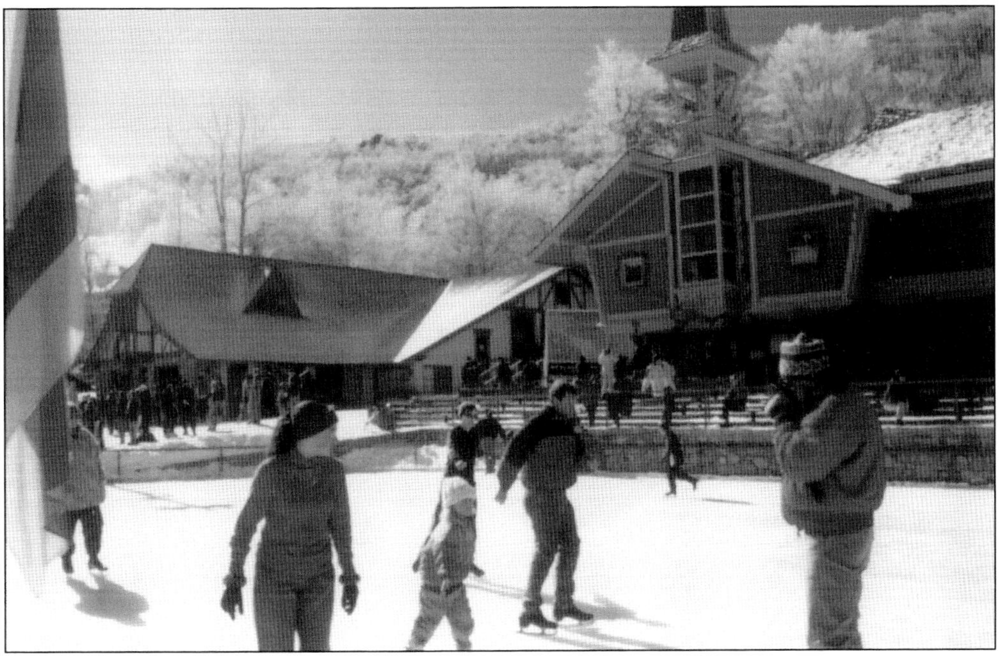

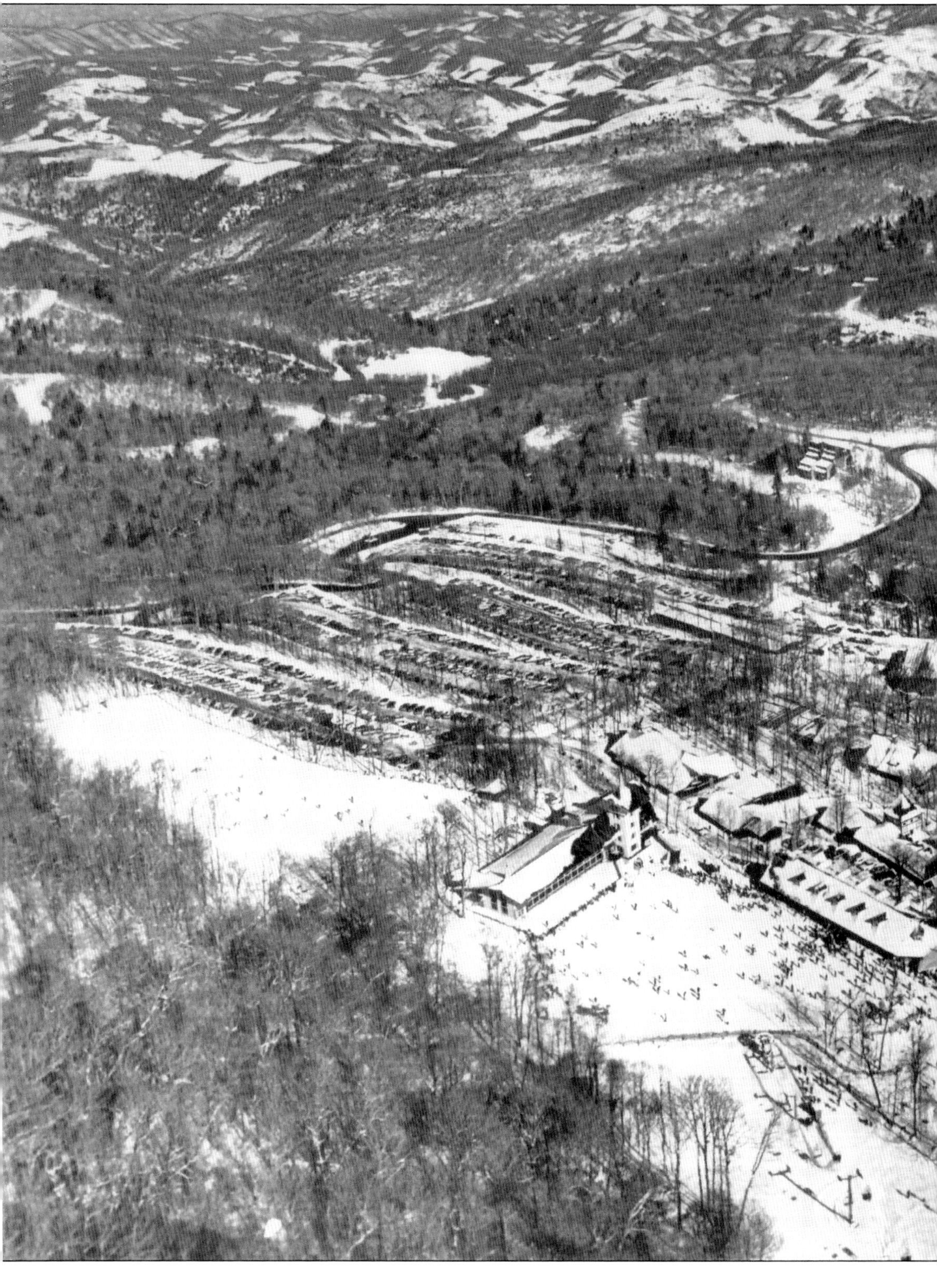

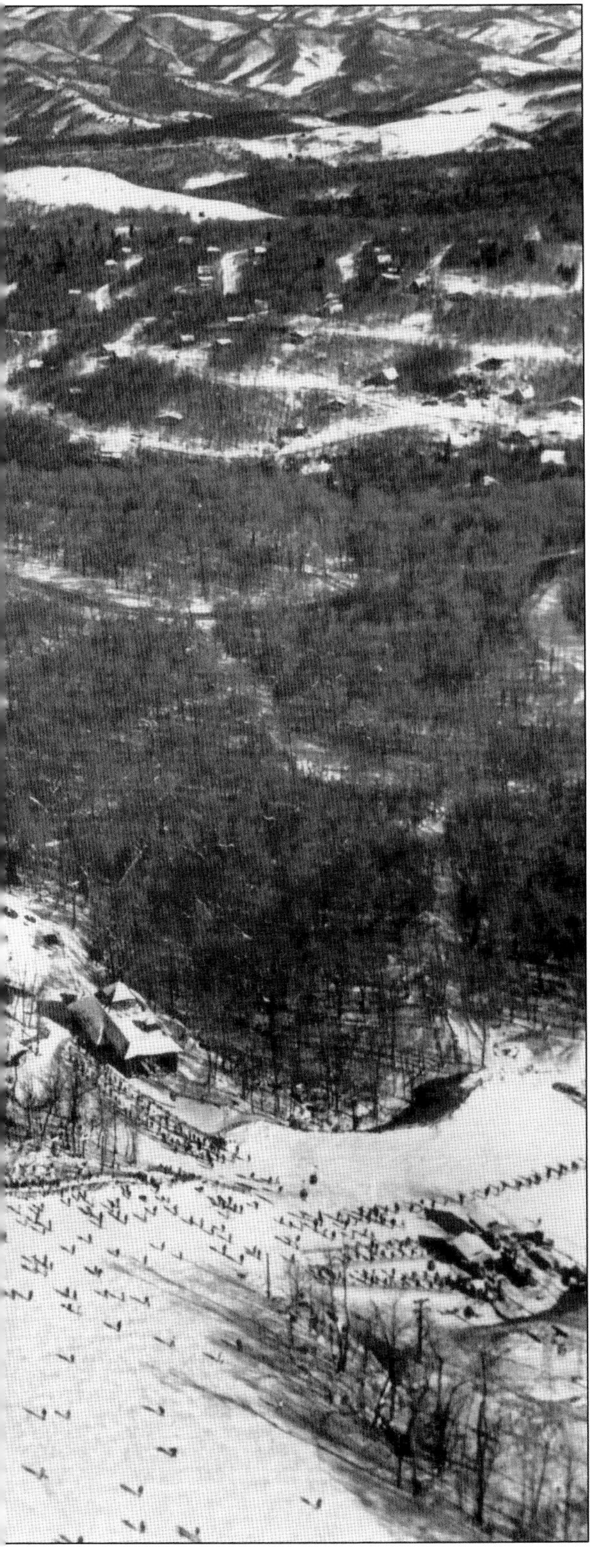

This incredible aerial view of the Beech Mountain Resort in 1970 gives one a better perspective on the scale and plan of the entire mountain development. The parking area for the ski slopes is visible in the middle left portion of the image, while Beech Tree Village and the ski buildings are in the middle of the photograph. Skiers can be seen as tiny black shapes scattered along the slopes, and small residential developments are scattered throughout the woods. Today, there are additional neighborhoods, but they have remained at a low density and retained much of the green space and wilderness area of the original plan. The mountains at the top of the photograph are actually in Virginia and Tennessee. (Courtesy of Jim Brooks Collection.)

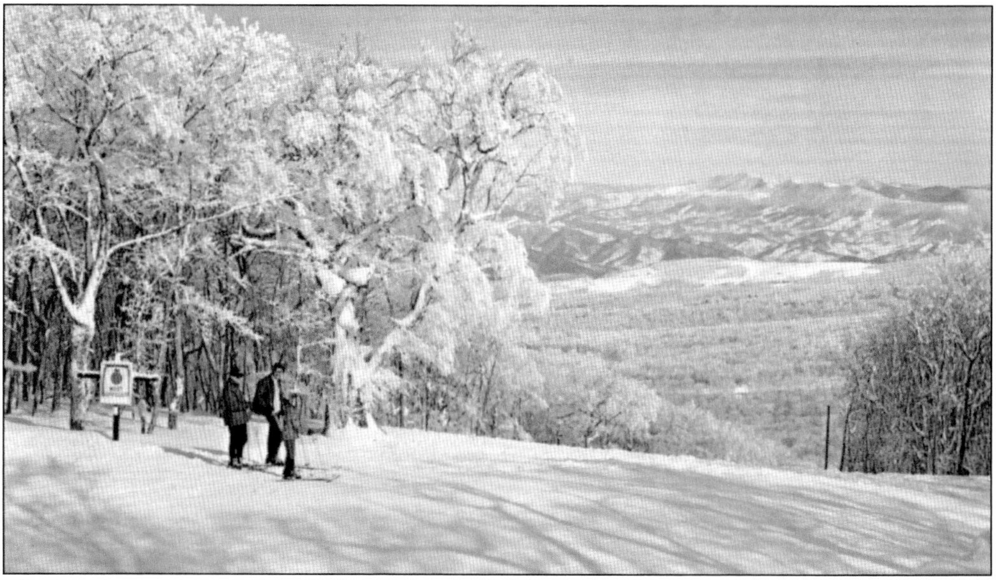

This c. 1970 postcard from Beech Mountain shows the inspiring view from the top. The postcard reads, "Two miles of the highest ski slope in Eastern America, served by gondola, double chair lifts and T-bars with uphill capacity of 3000 skiers per hour." Beech learned that marketing was key to bringing Southerners up their mountain to ski. (Photograph by Hugh Morton; courtesy of Cindy Keller.)

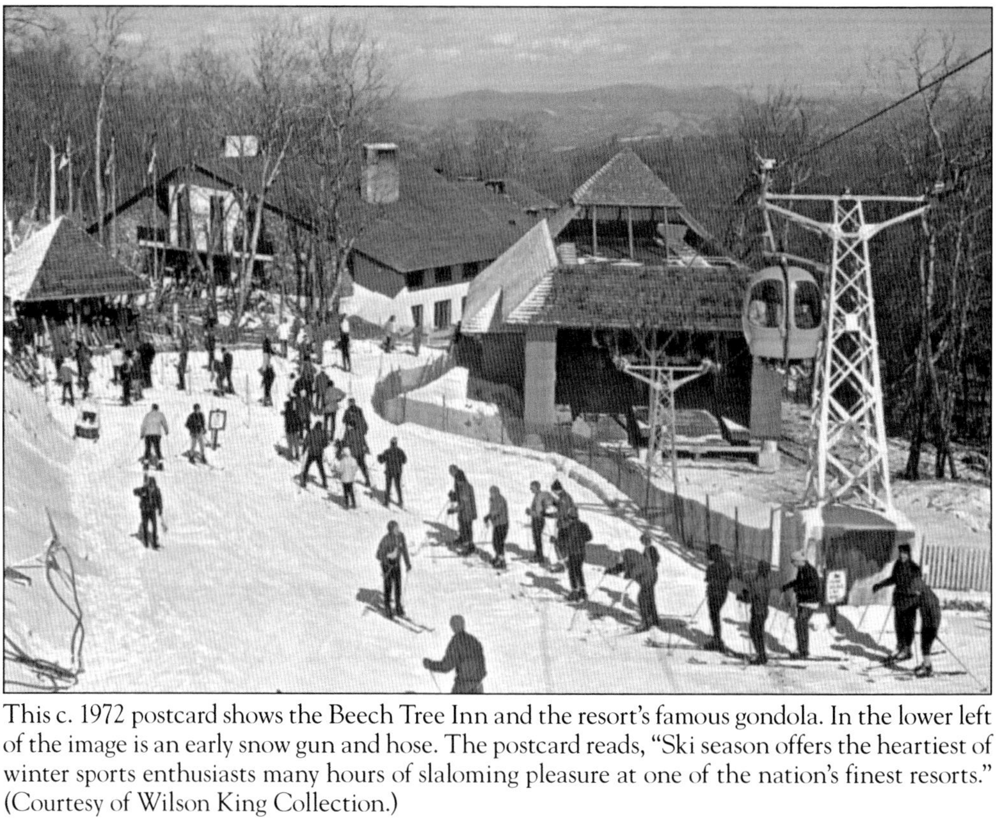

This c. 1972 postcard shows the Beech Tree Inn and the resort's famous gondola. In the lower left of the image is an early snow gun and hose. The postcard reads, "Ski season offers the heartiest of winter sports enthusiasts many hours of slaloming pleasure at one of the nation's finest resorts." (Courtesy of Wilson King Collection.)

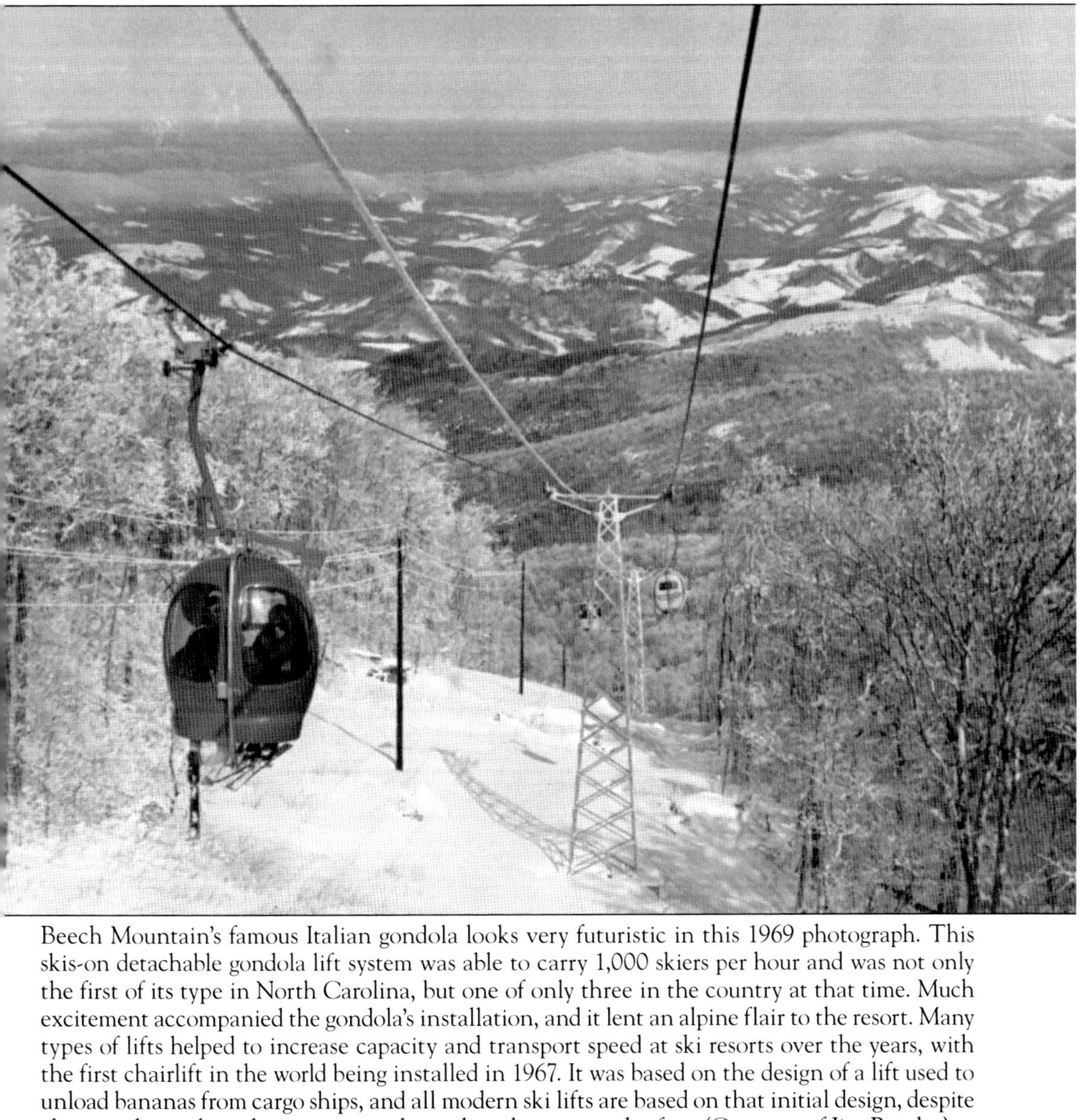

Beech Mountain's famous Italian gondola looks very futuristic in this 1969 photograph. This skis-on detachable gondola lift system was able to carry 1,000 skiers per hour and was not only the first of its type in North Carolina, but one of only three in the country at that time. Much excitement accompanied the gondola's installation, and it lent an alpine flair to the resort. Many types of lifts helped to increase capacity and transport speed at ski resorts over the years, with the first chairlift in the world being installed in 1967. It was based on the design of a lift used to unload bananas from cargo ships, and all modern ski lifts are based on that initial design, despite changes that enlarged cars, increased speed, and augmented safety. (Courtesy of Jim Brooks.)

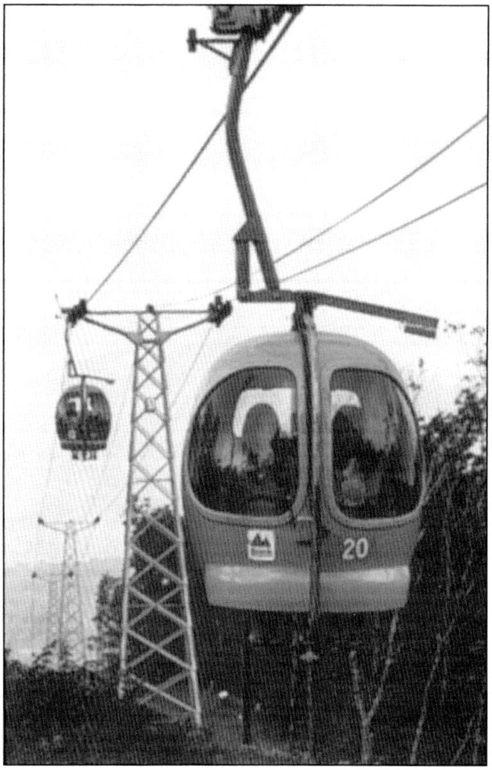

Beech's famous Italian gondola was made by Carlevaro & Savio of Turin, Italy. This was the first enclosed car at Beech, offering weather protection for skiers and allowing their skis to hang from the open bottom. It was one of several improvements made by general manager Sepp Gmuender, who also had the slopes regraded and upgraded the snowmaking equipment. (Courtesy of Jim Brooks.)

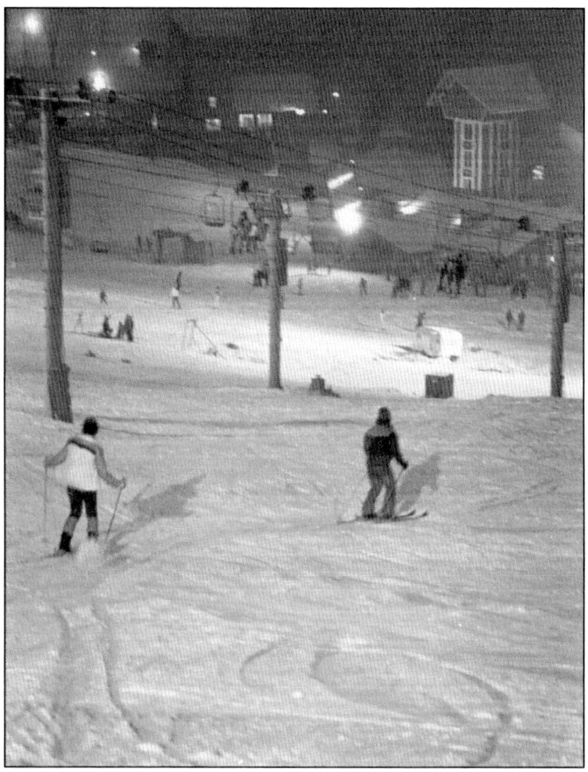

This c. 1970 photograph shows the magic of nighttime skiing at Beech. Special deals on lift tickets were usually offered to help reduce the congestion of the slopes, while lights provided plenty of illumination for skiers to slalom down the slopes. (Courtesy of Jim Brooks.)

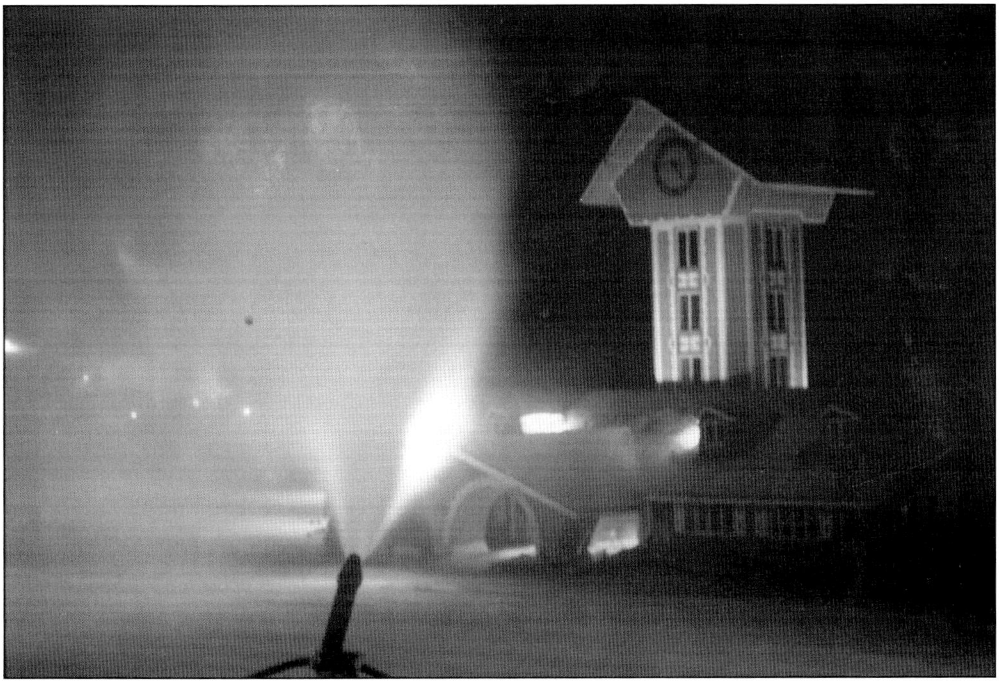

The snow blasting from this early, simple snow gun shines in the darkness and partially obscures the View Haus and its clock tower. The ski slope adopts an ethereal atmosphere in the darkness, as more snow is blown and deposited for next day's skiing crowd. (Courtesy of Jim Brooks Collection.)

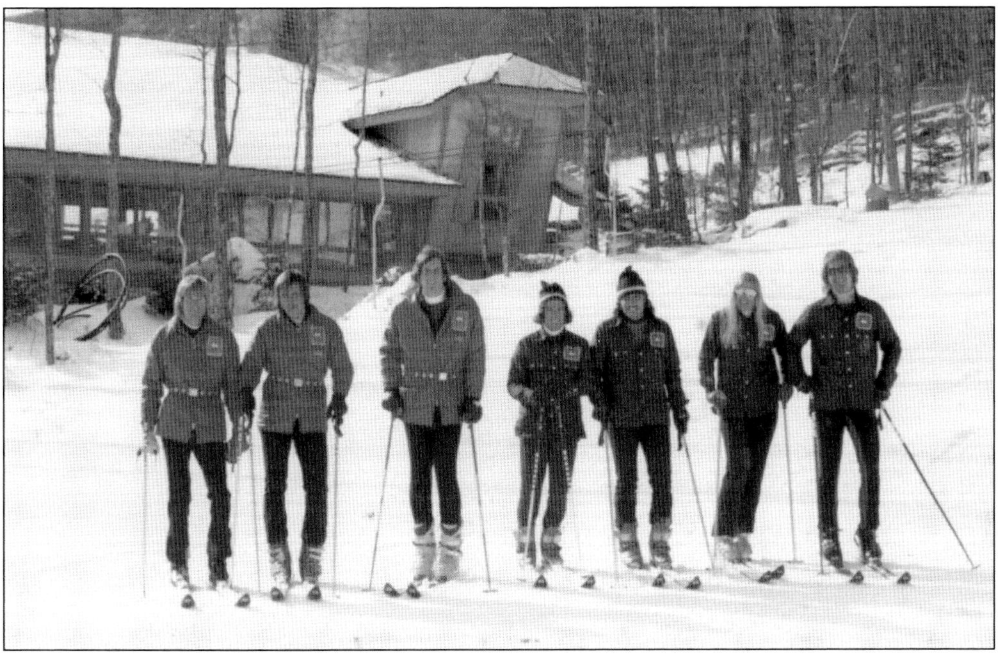

Committed, high-caliber ski instructors (many of them students from the nearby Appalachian State University) contributed to Beech's excellent reputation. These instructors paused for a photograph during the 1973–1974 season. From left to right, they are Wilson King, Bruce Mehl, Lindsey ?, Joe Merlini, Jack Mehl, unidentified, and Rusty ?. (Courtesy of Wilson King Collection.)

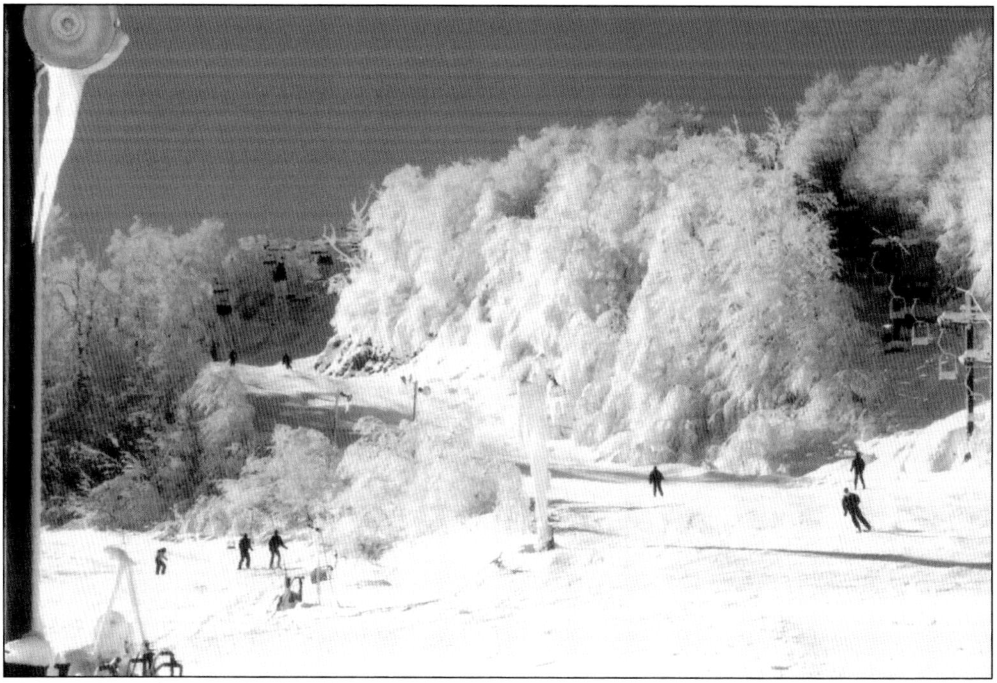

The tree branches are weighed down with snow in this photograph from 1970. An icicle is even suspended from the lift pole on the right of the image. Staying warm may have been a challenge on this day. (Courtesy of Wilson King Collection.)

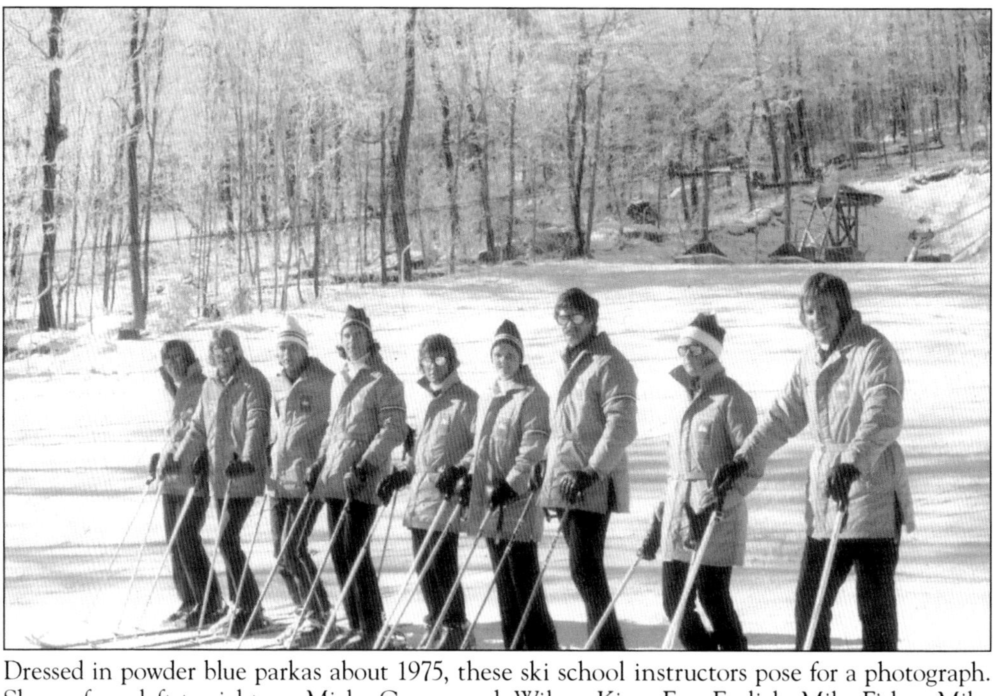

Dressed in powder blue parkas about 1975, these ski school instructors pose for a photograph. Shown from left to right are Micky Greenwood, Wilson King, Ewe Earlich, Mike Fisher, Mike Barrett, Jeannie Schlichting, Sam Robinson, Anita Alred, and Bruce Mehl. (Courtesy of Wilson King Collection.)

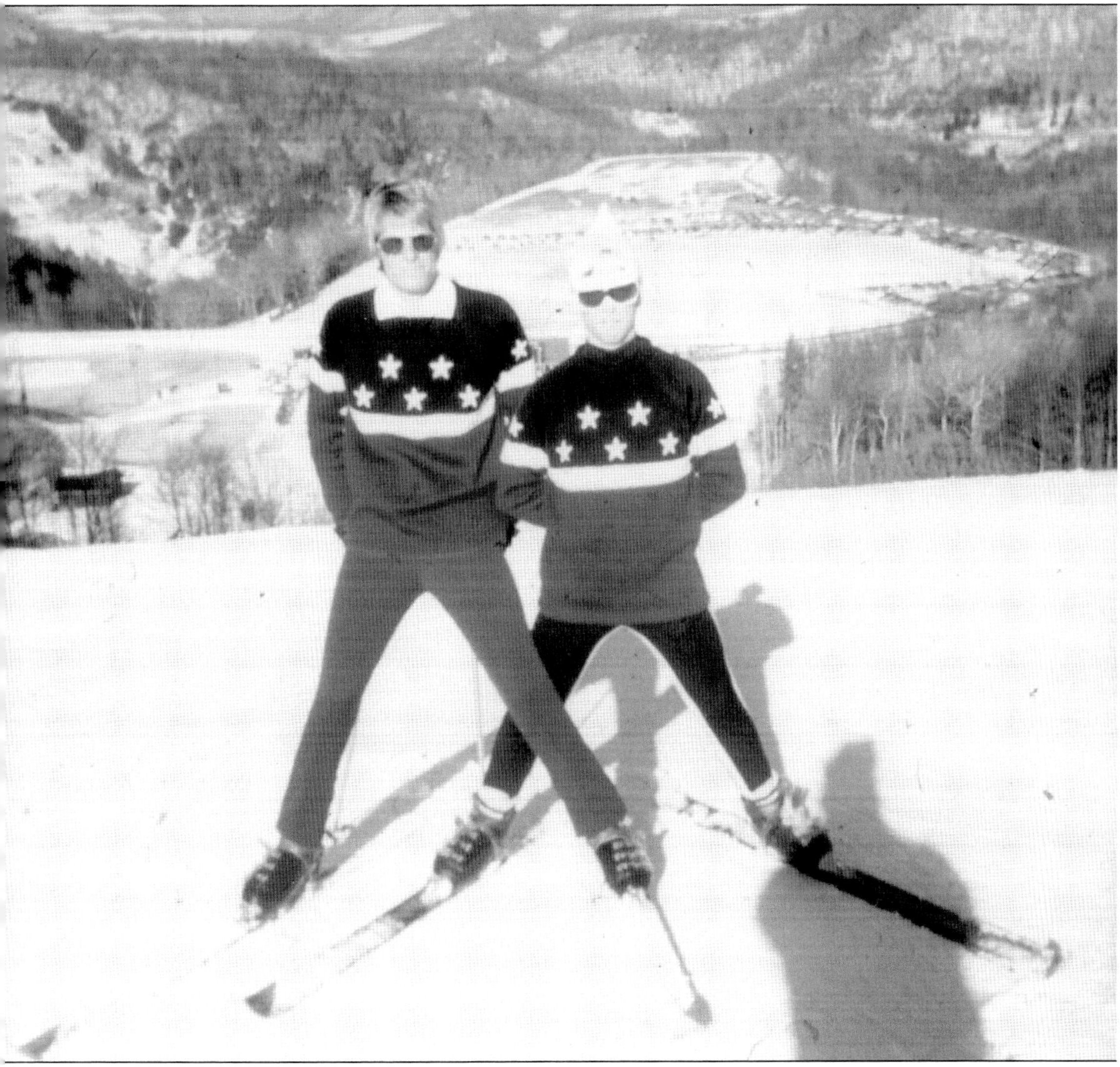

This c. 1975 photograph shows two men who were instrumental in building up Beech's reputation: Wilson King (left) and Mike Barrett (right), the director of the ski school. Wilson King worked at Beech for many years before opening the nearby Beech Meadows Ski Shop and Beech Mountain Realty, both of which he still operates today. (Courtesy of Wilson King Collection.)

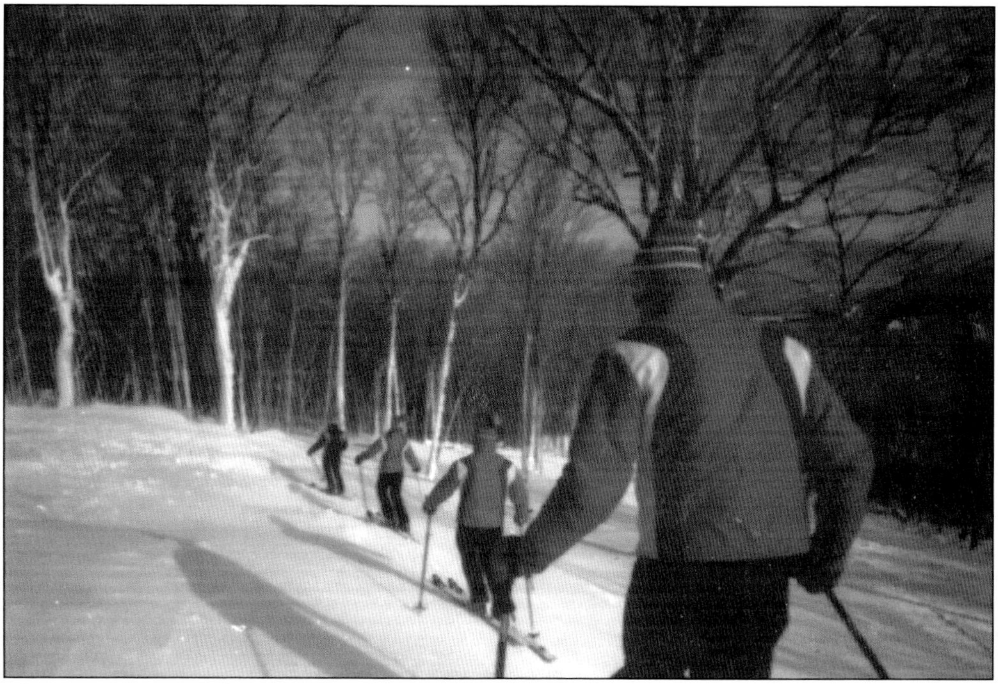

These cross-country skiers are traveling through the woods—enjoying a sport that is still offered at the resort. Over the years, the Town of Beech Mountain has created a system of cross-country trails and rents out skis to visitors. (Courtesy of Beech Mountain Resort.)

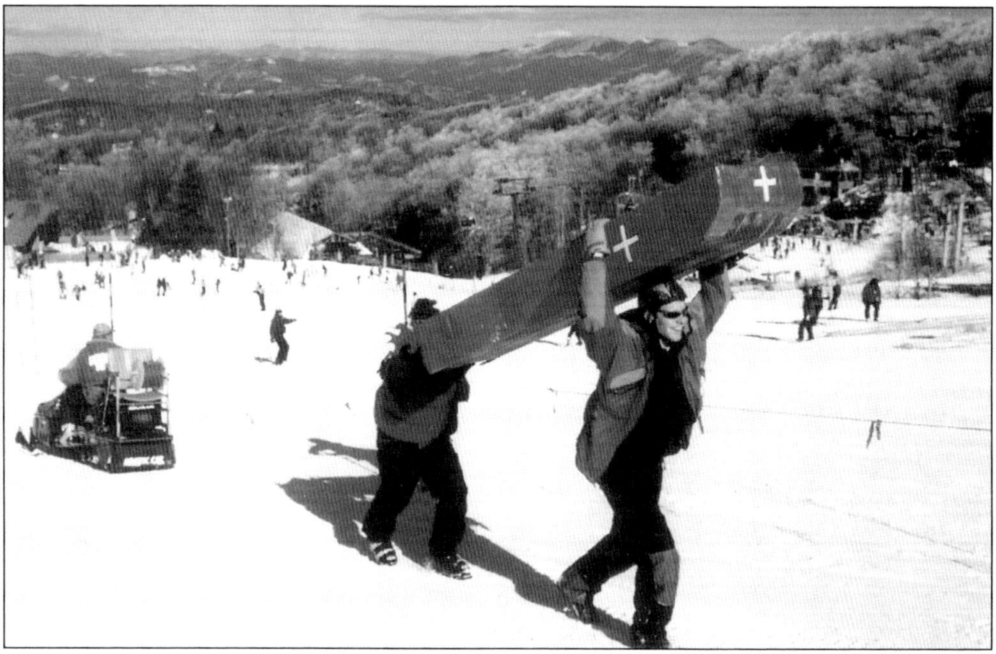

Ski patrol members train with a heavy first aid sled in this photograph from 1970. Another patroller is running an Arctic Cat with some type of cable on the back—something that was, perhaps, used for rescues. Beech's patrollers eventually joined the National Ski Patrol, the first national ski organization to come to the South. (Courtesy of Beech Mountain Resort.)

Created by the Robbins brothers and designed by Jack Pentes, the 28-acre Land of Oz attraction opened in 1970 and provided entertainment at Beech Mountain until it was damaged by fire in 1980. Over 40,000 yellow bricks were installed for the yellow brick road. The postcard on the right for the Land of Oz reads, "Wicked Witch of the West brews her evil stew in front of her castle in the Land of Oz, watched by the Cowardly Lion, Dorothy, the Scarecrow, and The Tin Woodsman as Dorothy disappears." This stage show captivated audiences of all ages, and thousands of visitors enjoyed their visits to the park. Many fans mourn the loss of the park even today. Fortunately, a group, led by Cindy Keller, takes care of the remaining buildings and grounds, rents the site for reunions and weddings, and plans to restore it to its former appearance. For the past 20 years, in an effort to raise funds to restore the park, the remaining buildings have been opened for tours one weekend every fall. (Both, courtesy of Cindy Keller.)

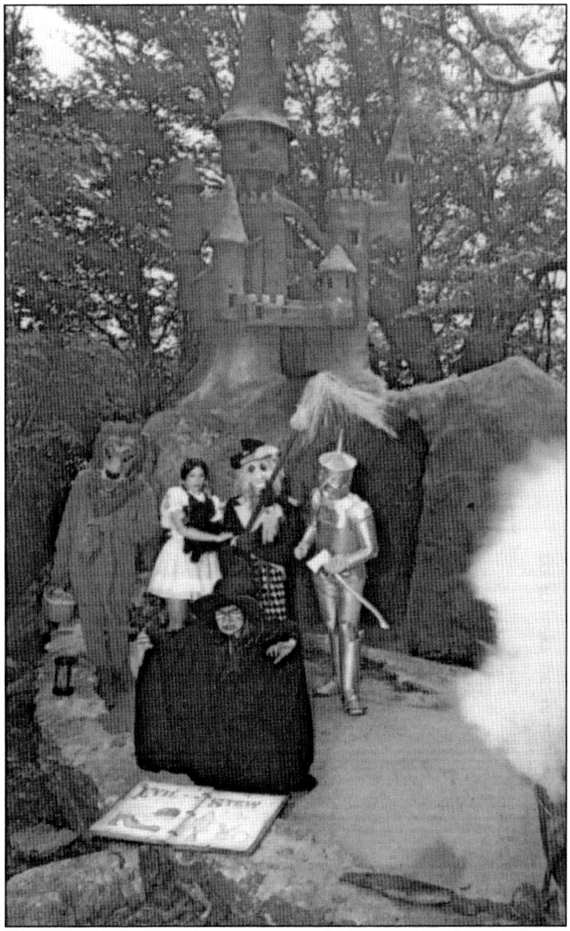

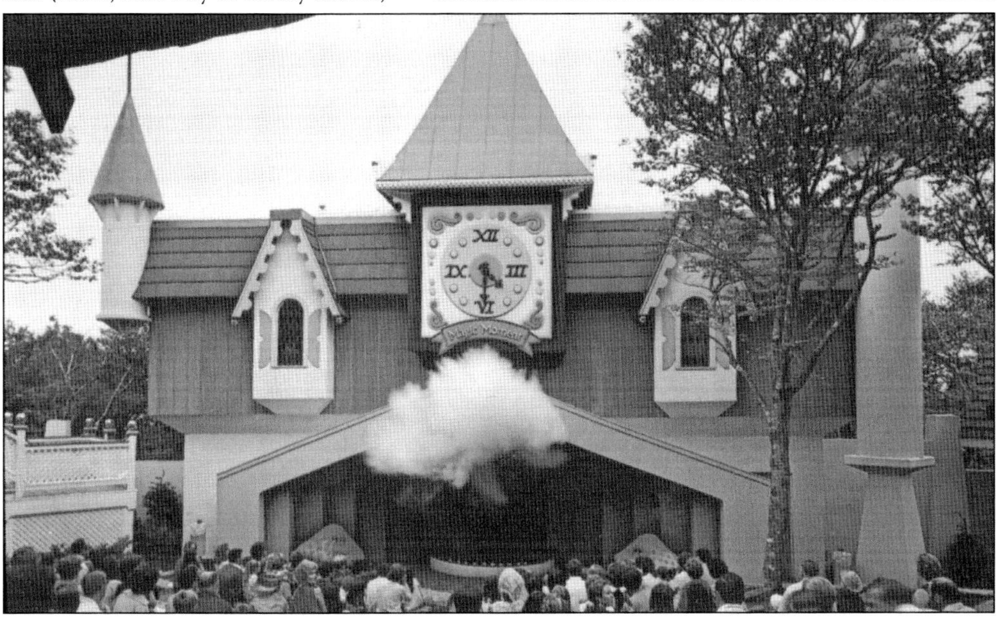

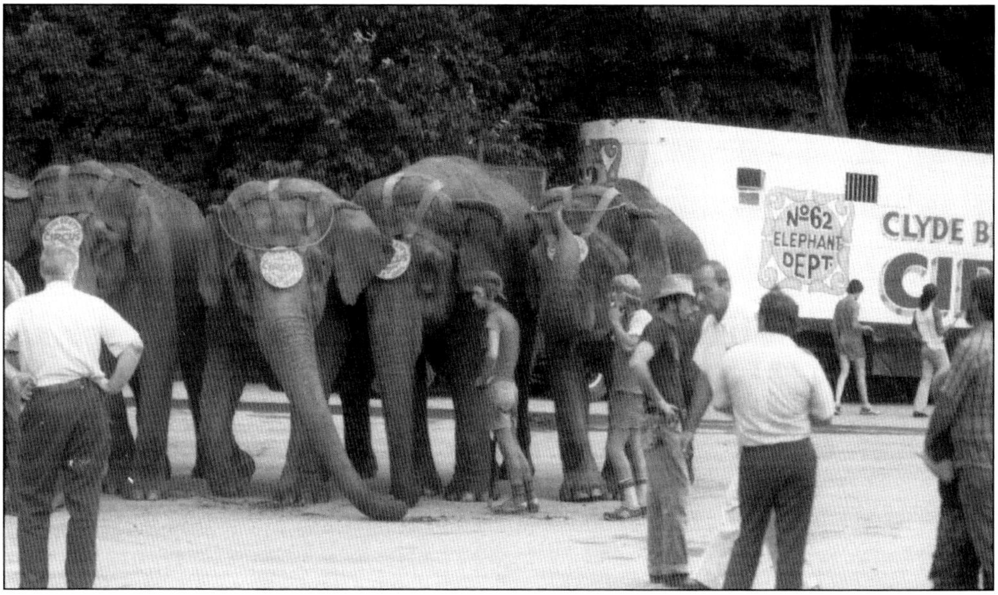

In this photograph from the early 1980s, the Clyde Beatty circus visits the top of Beech Mountain. Unfortunately, the circus's elephants were too heavy for the trucks, and the poor beasts had to walk several miles up the steep grade. This created quite a spectacle, which many residents remember. Others recall seeing large, mysterious patties dotting the Beech Mountain Parkway and wondering about them. (Courtesy of Jim Brooks Collection.)

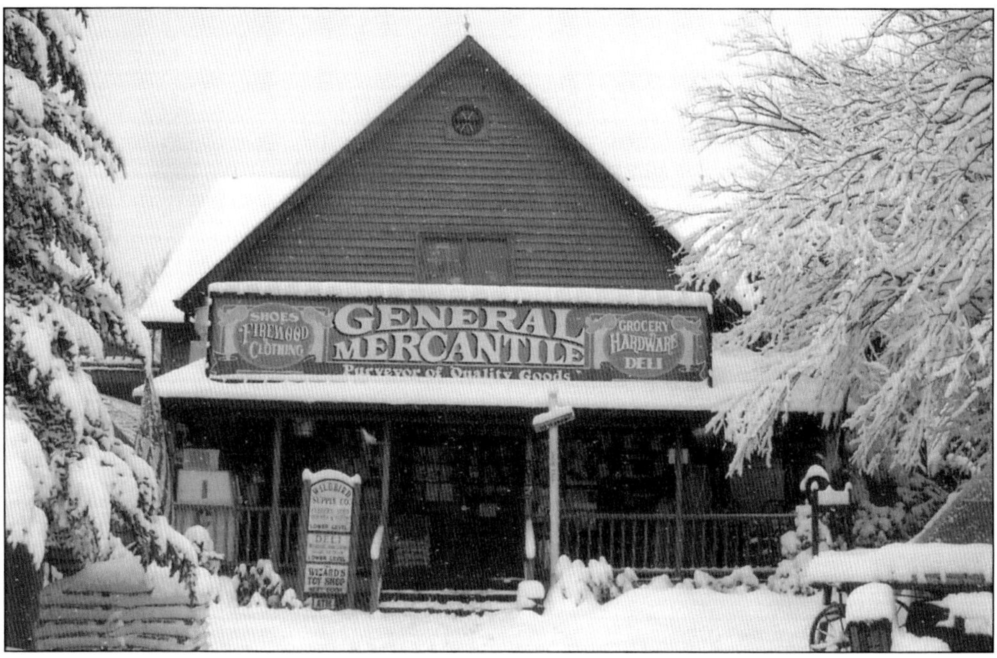

Fred's General Mercantile has been a mainstay of the Beech Mountain community since 1979. Fred Pfohl, who worked at the ski resort for several years, purchased a small, useless tract of land and developed it into a thriving business that offered a little bit of everything, excellent customer service, a restaurant, and a ski shop and rentals. This has made the store an essential stop for thousands of visiting skiers. (Courtesy of Fred Pfohl.)

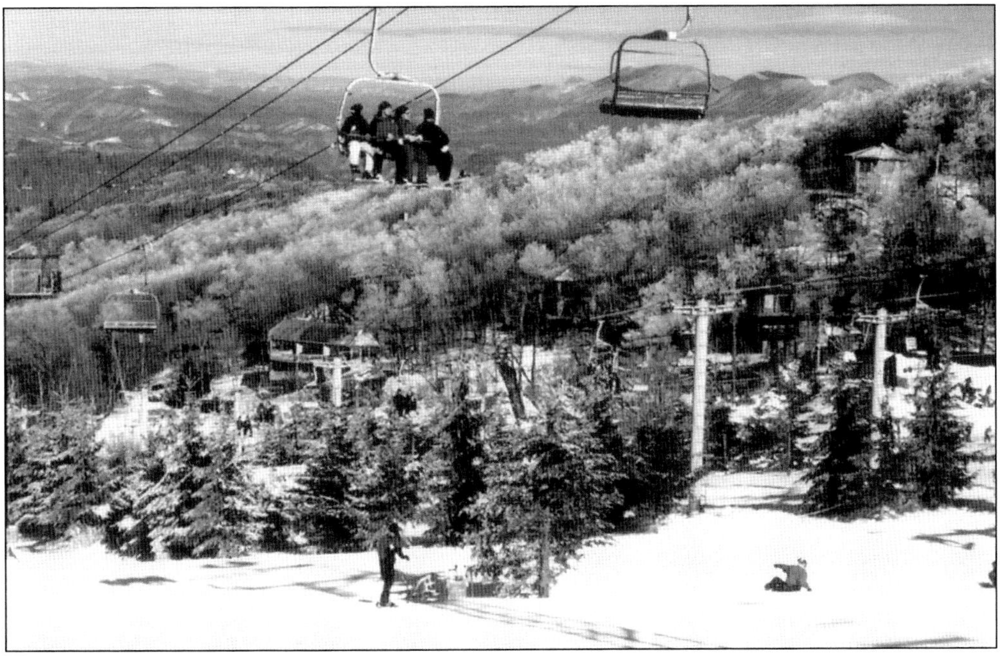

The quad lift transports skiers up the slope in this c. 1980 photograph, taken on a snowy day on the mountain. Several houses are visible along the slopes, including one of the "mushroom" houses, which proliferated in the area during the 1970s. (Courtesy of Beech Mountain Collection.)

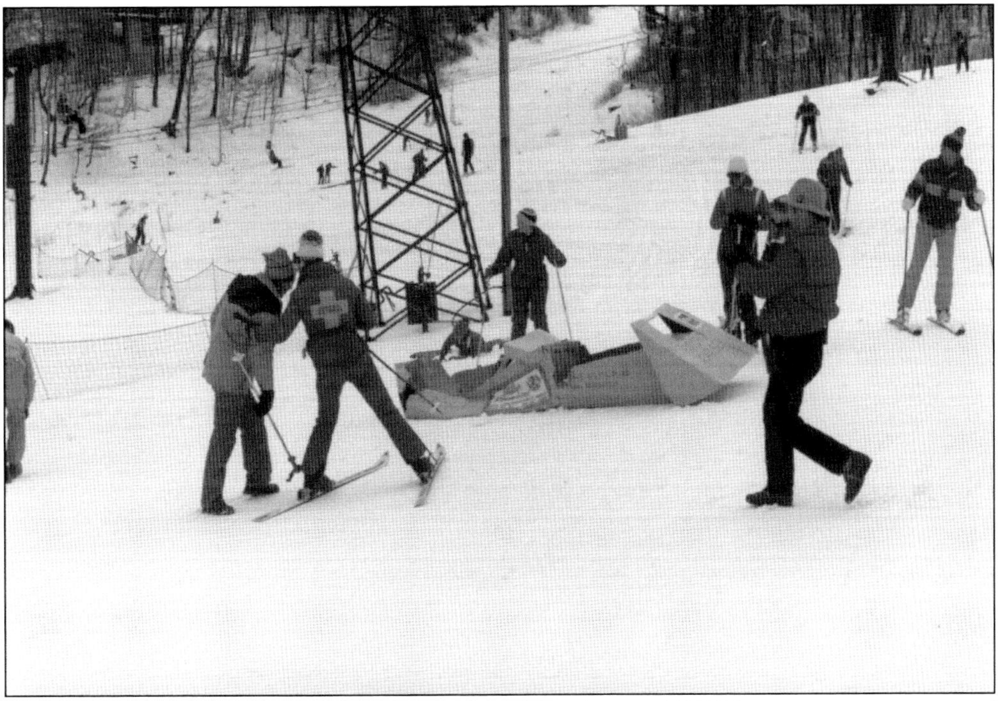

The always popular cardboard box derby races are shown here in 1975. These races were sponsored by Budweiser, and prizes were awarded for speed, originality, and creativity. (Courtesy of Jim Brooks Collection.)

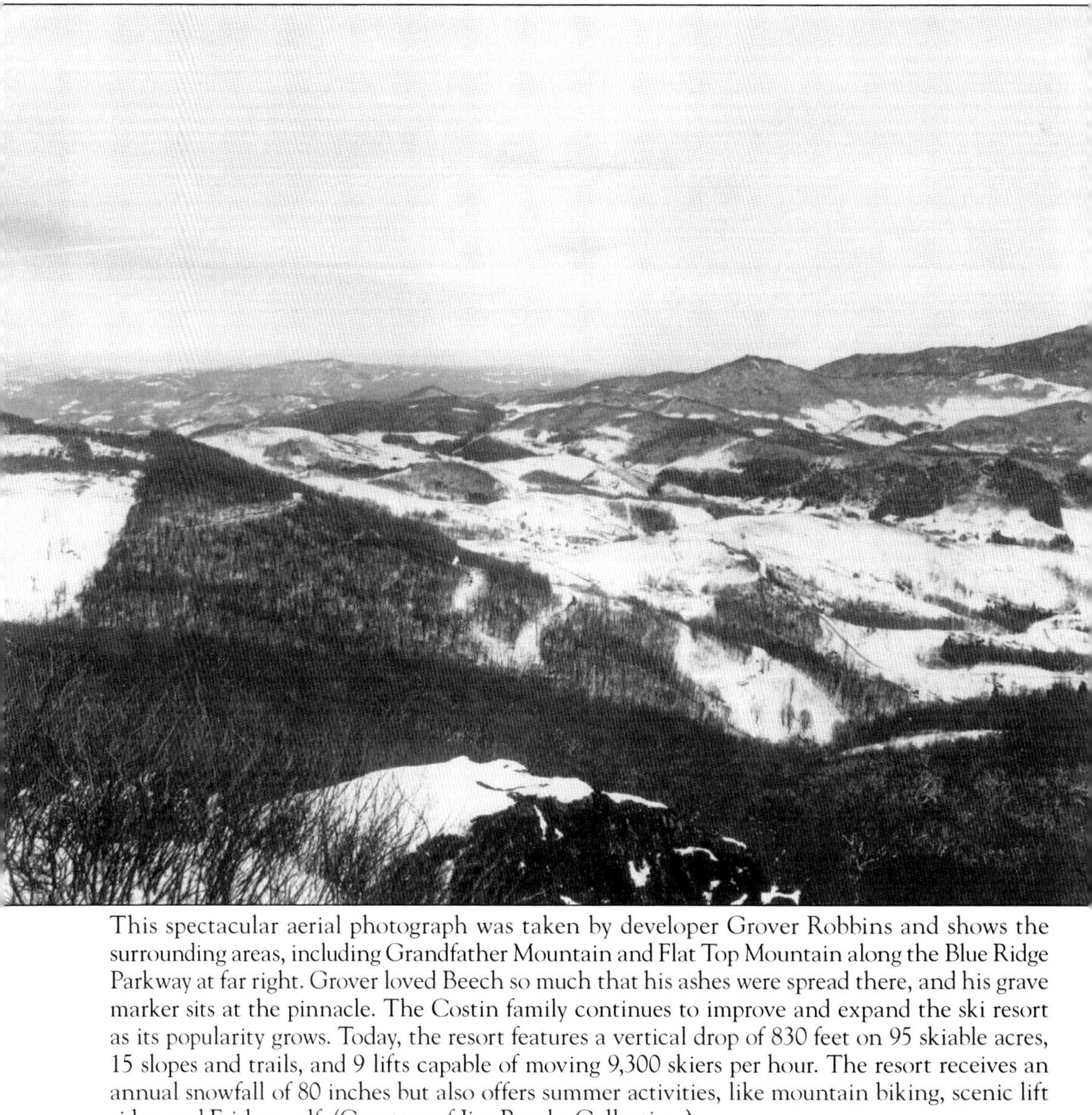

This spectacular aerial photograph was taken by developer Grover Robbins and shows the surrounding areas, including Grandfather Mountain and Flat Top Mountain along the Blue Ridge Parkway at far right. Grover loved Beech so much that his ashes were spread there, and his grave marker sits at the pinnacle. The Costin family continues to improve and expand the ski resort as its popularity grows. Today, the resort features a vertical drop of 830 feet on 95 skiable acres, 15 slopes and trails, and 9 lifts capable of moving 9,300 skiers per hour. The resort receives an annual snowfall of 80 inches but also offers summer activities, like mountain biking, scenic lift rides, and Frisbee golf. (Courtesy of Jim Brooks Collection.)

Four

Sugar Mountain Resort

After Tom Brigham and the MacRaes sold Beech Mountain Resort in 1968, they assembled a new group of partners—including Alex Andrews and Al Johnson— and began to plan a similar development on nearby Sugar Mountain. By not relying on an Austrian theme, the group developed 3,000 acres at only $7.5 million, featuring six ski slopes, a golf course, residential areas, stables, and streams and lakes. Real estate professionals, such as Al Traver, were hired to sell lots, and the resort became a major success. The slopes opened for the skiing in December 1969, with Bob Ash serving as manager and—according to Randy Johnson—Danny Seme as the South's first professional ski patroller. On opening day, the ski center welcomed guests with a beautiful lodge, shops, rental stores, lounges, cafeteria, and 32 condominiums along the slopes. Eric Bindlechner also started teaching his new Headway Method variant of GLM at the resort. In 1969, the resort began hosting the Snow Carnival of the South, which featured ski pros and celebrities such as Mickey Mantle and Bobby Richardson. In 1973, gas shortages and the recession ended the Snow Carnival, and the residential development began to lose money. While the skiing operation remained profitable, it was not enough to keep the entire resort going. Even though several high-level Beech Mountain employees were hired to keep building up the skiing, the resort declared bankruptcy in 1976.

That same year, the resort was leased to experienced ski resort owners Ray Costin and Dale Stancil, and in 1978, they bought the resort for $2.6 million. With Gunther Jochl serving as general manager, the resort became profitable, the lodge was expanded, snowmaking improved, and real estate development increased. Unfortunately, Sugar Mountain is now famous for Sugar Top, a large, 10-story condominium complex built between 1981 and 1985. The gigantic structure angered many, as it obstructed the view of the ridgeline, and in 1984, its construction caused North Carolina to pass a law that restricts the height of buildings on mountain tops. Improvements continued to the slopes, and hiking and biking trails opened in 1993. National mountain biking competitions were held there in 1994, and the resort began to hold its popular Oktoberfest event. Today, the ski area is owned and managed by Gunther and Kim Jochl, and it offers a terrain park, snow tubing, snowshoeing, and ice-skating.

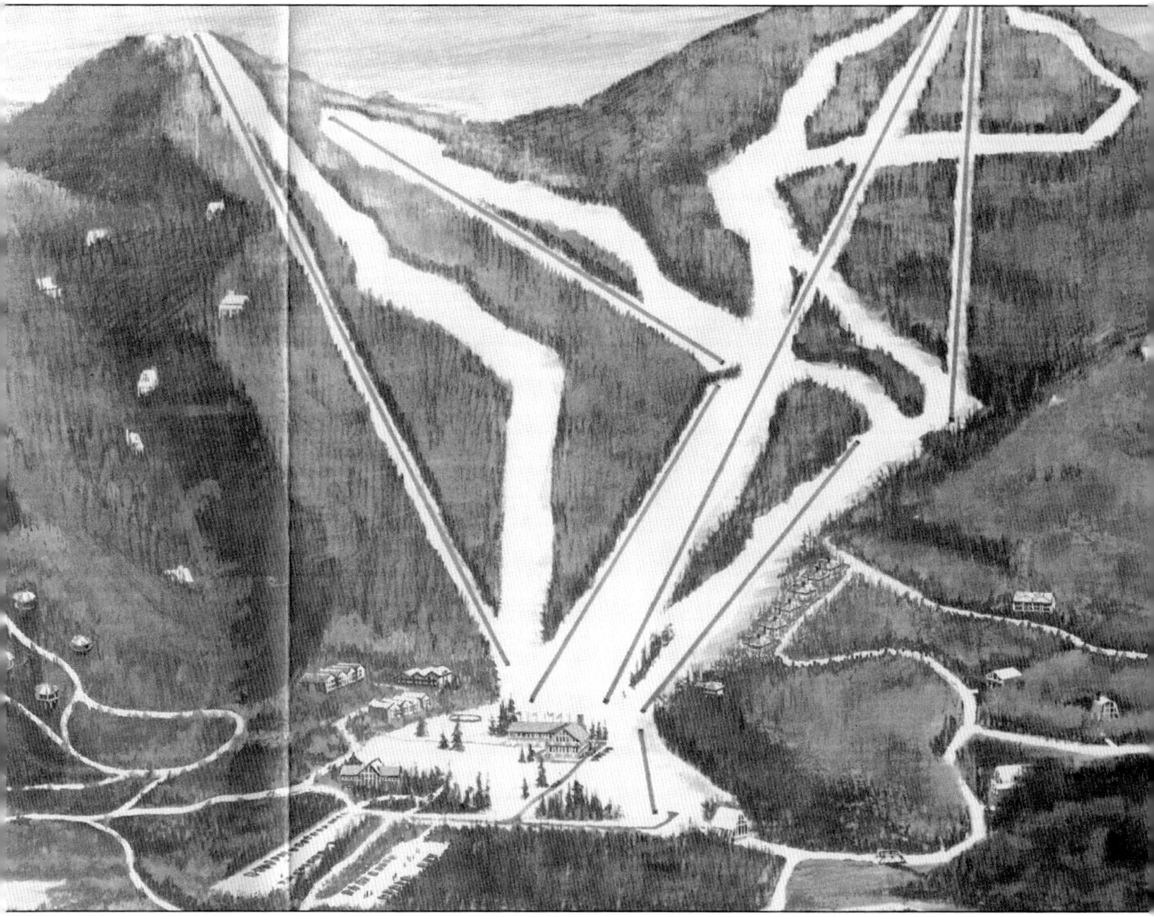

This promotional brochure, published in 1970, shows part of the overall plan for Sugar Mountain. The resort development did follow this slope plan for the most part, as there are houses along the slopes, round houses in several areas (bottom left of image), and houses scattered at low densities throughout the wooded areas. The ski slope on the left was not developed, however. George MacRae planned Sugar's initial houses and developments, which fit into the landscape extremely well. A one-bedroom Hemlock Knob house was initially priced at $18,000, and timeshares were added in later. As if the luxurious lodge, large tennis bubble, dining facilities, golf course, pool facilities, horseback riding, hiking, and dancing were not enough to keep one busy, the resort planned high-end entertainments that included a live performance by the Kingston Trio. A gourmet restaurant was also built on Flat Top Mountain, behind Sugar (now Linville Ridge). Southerners flocked to the resort to try skiing, until the recession of the 1970s. Today, more neighborhoods have been developed, and it remains a popular resort and ski area. (Courtesy of Al Traver Collection.)

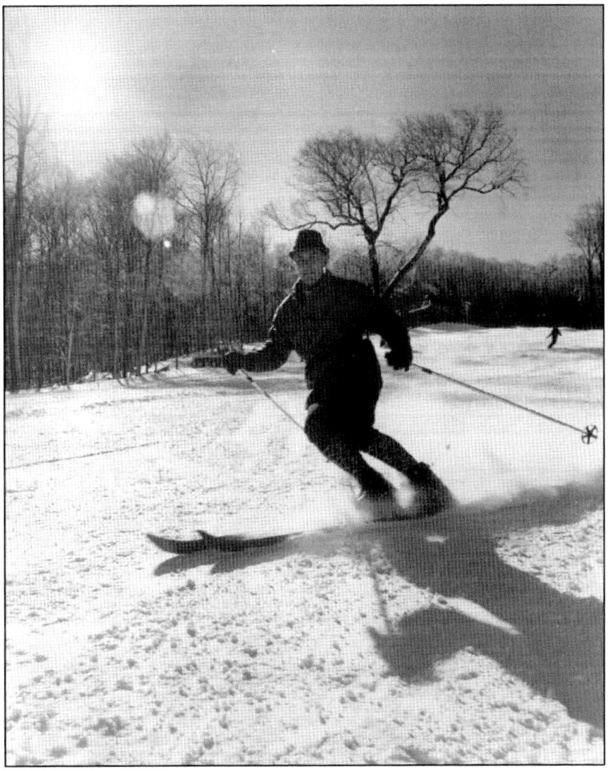

Here, Thomas "Doc" Brigham, the Alabama dentist who believed that snowmaking could permit southern skiing, is shown slicing down a slope. After reading about snowmaking, Brigham dreamed of skiing in Dixie and researched southern weather and the highest mountains. He advised many ski resort developers, helped accumulate land for Beech Mountain, and codeveloped both Sugar Mountain and Snowshoe, in West Virginia. (Photograph by Bob Webb; courtesy of Al Traver Collection.)

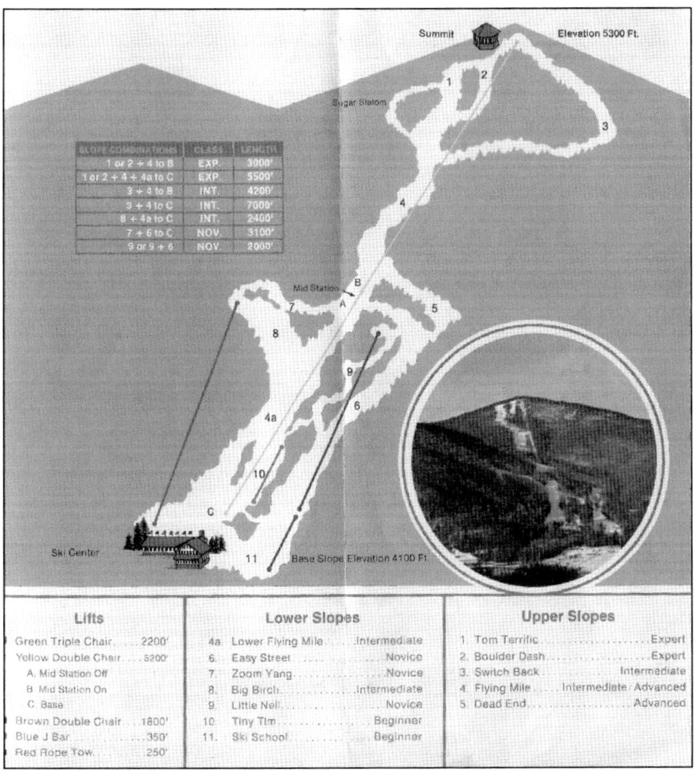

This 1973 Sugar Mountain Resort brochure illustrates which slopes were actually developed. The ski resort drew in thousands of visitors and helped to support the residential component of the development until its 1970s bankruptcy. Tom Terrific remains one of the most popular slopes, and those who ski it are entitled bragging rights. (Courtesy of Al Traver Collection.)

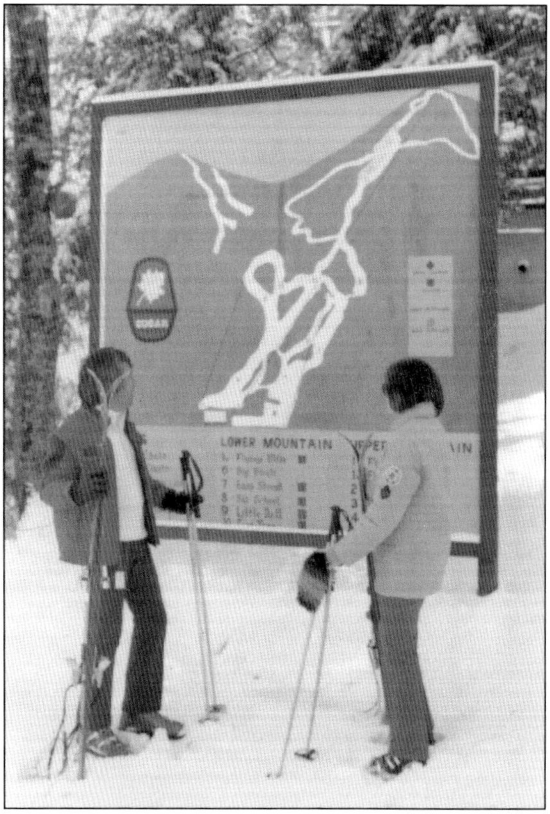

John Starnes (left) and Katie Lyerly examine the ski trail map on a memorable November 15, 1974, when Sugar's slopes had one of their earliest slope openings to this day. Note the slopes shown in the upper left of the trail map, which were never developed. (Courtesy of Al Traver Collection.)

For an unknown reason, the Harvard Ski team visited Sugar in 1974, and—to commemorate the occasion—Chessie MacRae and several staff members posed with the team. They are, from left to right, Sydney Gilbert, John Grogan, Kyle Roundtree, Robert Potter, Chessie MacRae, Matthew Harris, and three unidentified individuals. (Courtesy of Al Traver Collection.)

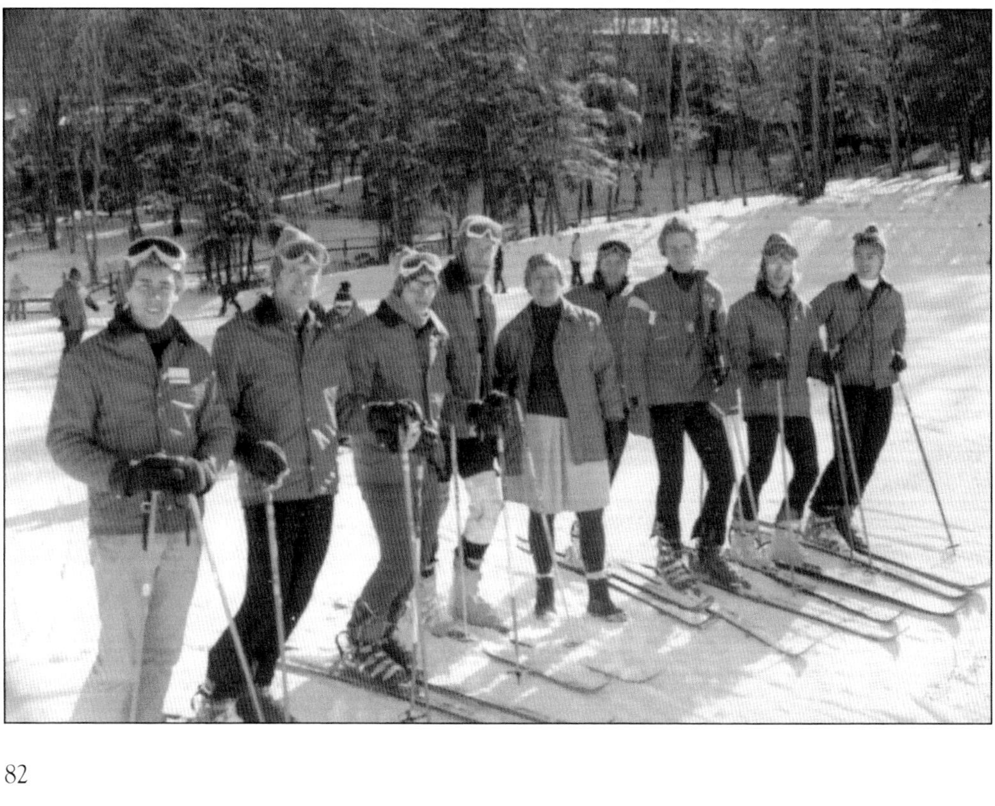

Shown here in 1974, Dedy Traver (left) and her father, Al Traver, have long been mainstays of the Sugar Mountain resort and community. Al Traver was one of the early real estate agents with the company, and his love of the mountain inspired many others to live there. Traver was the self-appointed historian for the resort, and Dedy preserves his collection as a wonderful tribute to her father and Sugar Mountain. (Courtesy of Al Traver Collection.)

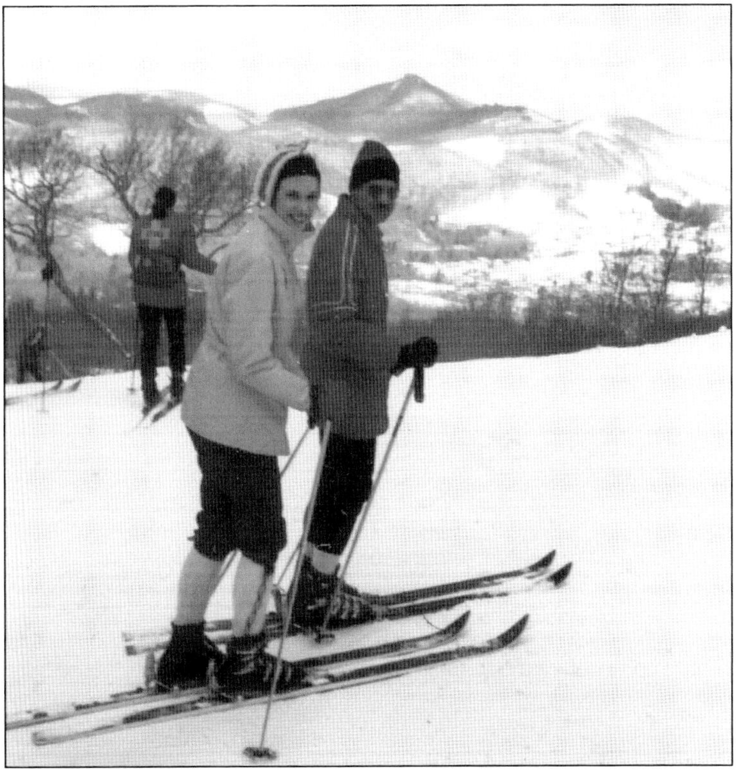

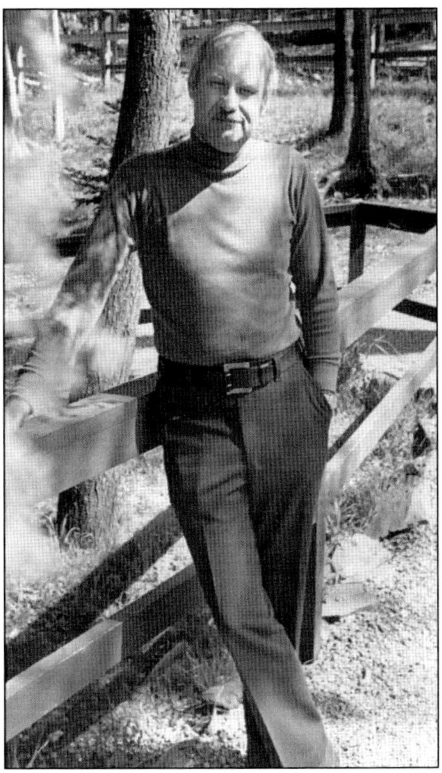

Al Traver moved from Charlotte to Sugar, where he worked as a real estate agent and became property manager for the condominiums. His deep commitment to his home was instrumental in keeping Sugar Mountain Resort successful. (Courtesy of Al Traver Collection.)

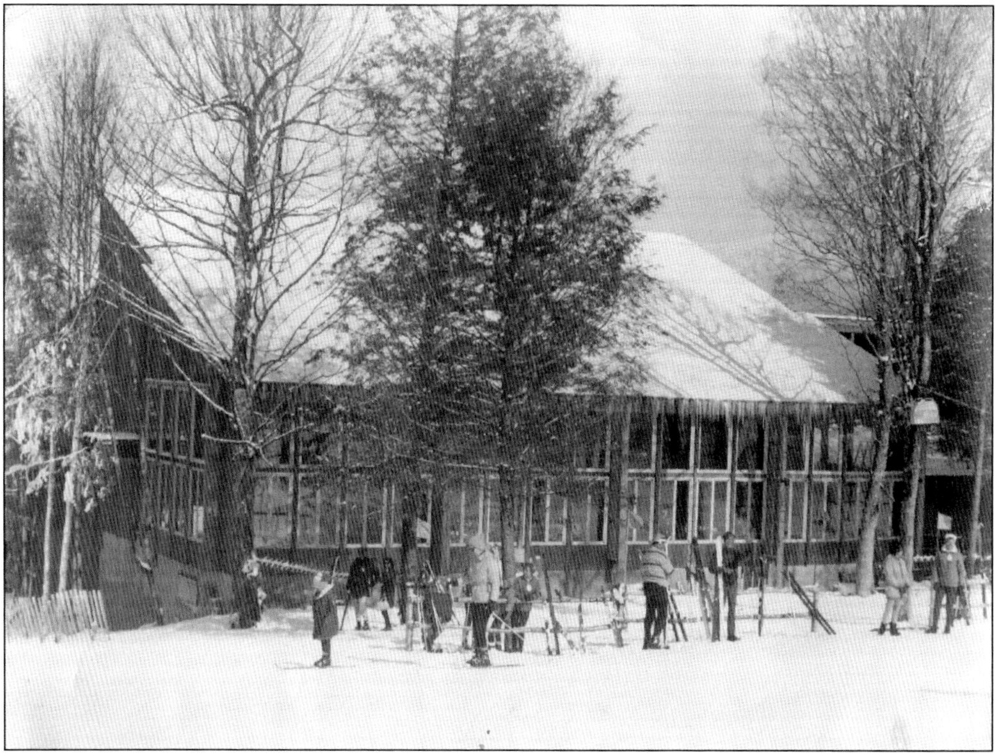

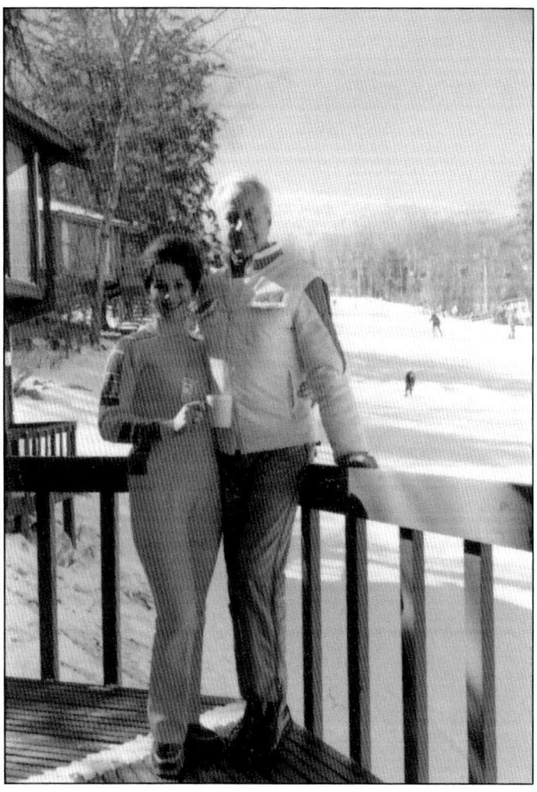

The newly constructed ski center was the hub of the ski area. It was designed with many windows to allow for viewing the slopes. The facility has since been expanded and remains a crowded spot. (Photograph by Bob Webb; courtesy of Al Traver Collection.)

Pictured here in 1976, Alex Andrews and his wife, Mari Andrews, were prime investors in the Sugar Mountain development. Having coffee on the decks of the houses overlooking the ski slopes is still a popular pastime. (Courtesy of Al Traver Collection.)

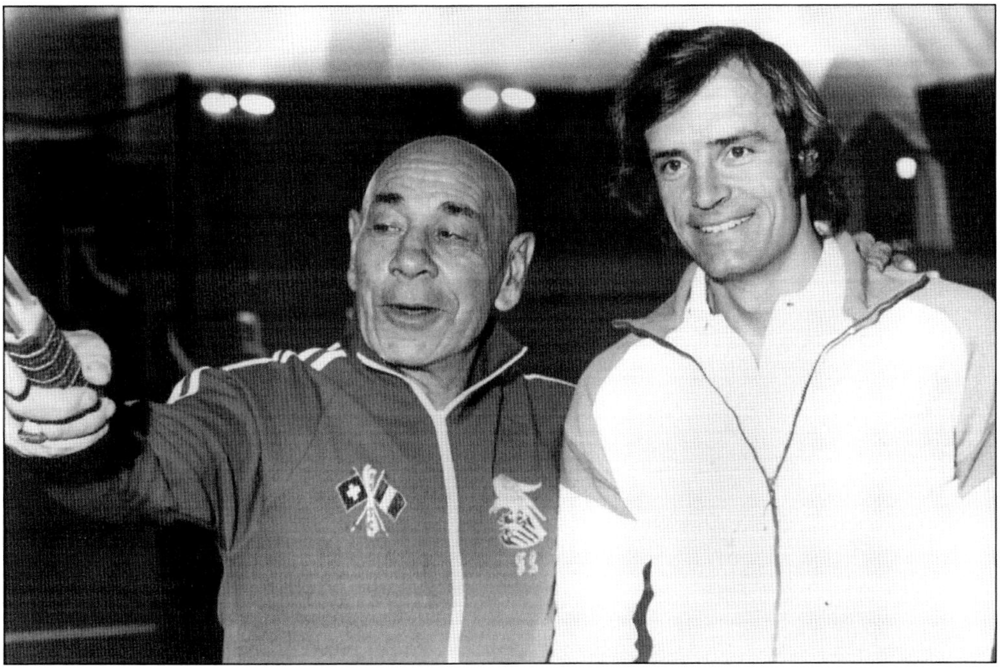

Above, Jack Lester (left), marketing director for Appalachian Ski Mountain, is pictured with Olympic skier Jean-Claude Killy. In 1972, Lester was able to convince Killy to visit the High Country ski resorts and hold the premiere of his first film, *Snow Job*, in Boone. This visit did much to put North Carolina skiing on the map, and Killy even returned in 1973 to race in North Carolina on the pro circuit. Posing in the photograph below are, from left to right, Robbie Smith, tennis pro; C.C. Hope, vice president of the First Virginia National Bank and cosponsor of Killy's visit; Jean-Claude Killy; Tom Brigham; and Eric Bindlechner, the Austrian ski instructor who brought GLM instruction to Sugar Mountain. (Courtesy of Al Traver Collection.)

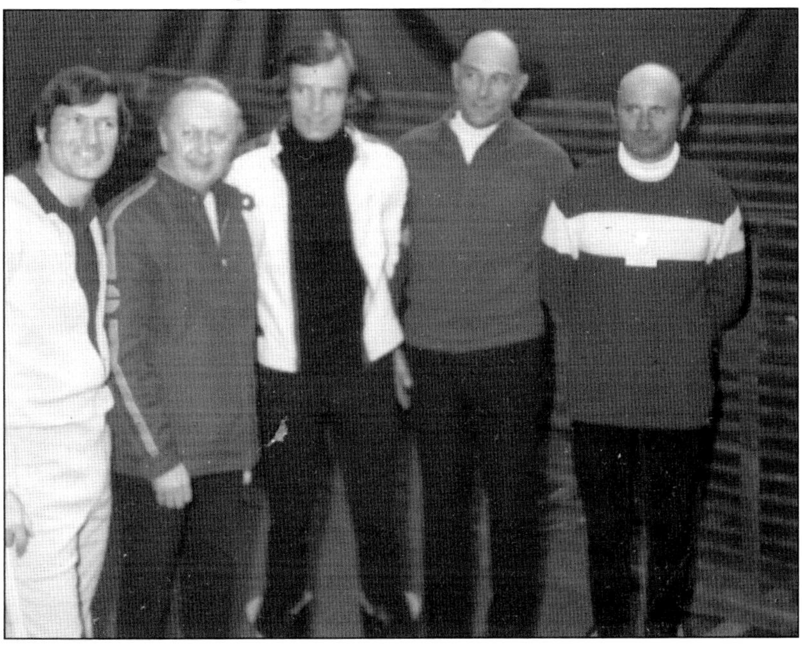

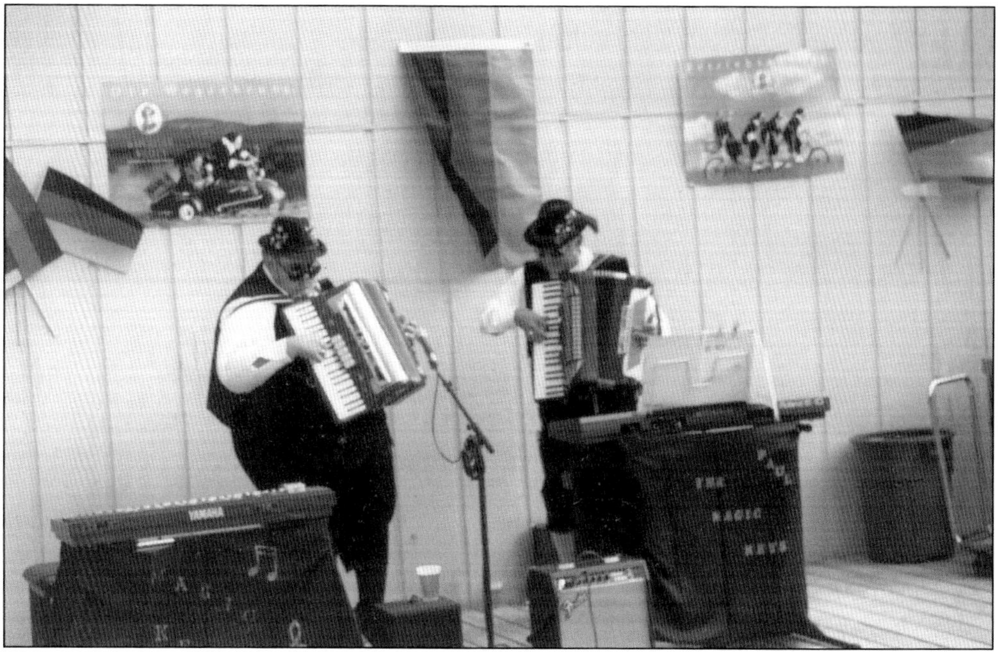

Entertainment was provided in the restaurants and lounges, including an oompah band. The Austrian ski instructors were also asked to sing and dance to provide a show for visitors. The Oktoberfest celebration, which was started in 1991, is a popular festival at Sugar during the fall and draws thousands of visitors. (Courtesy of Al Traver Collection.)

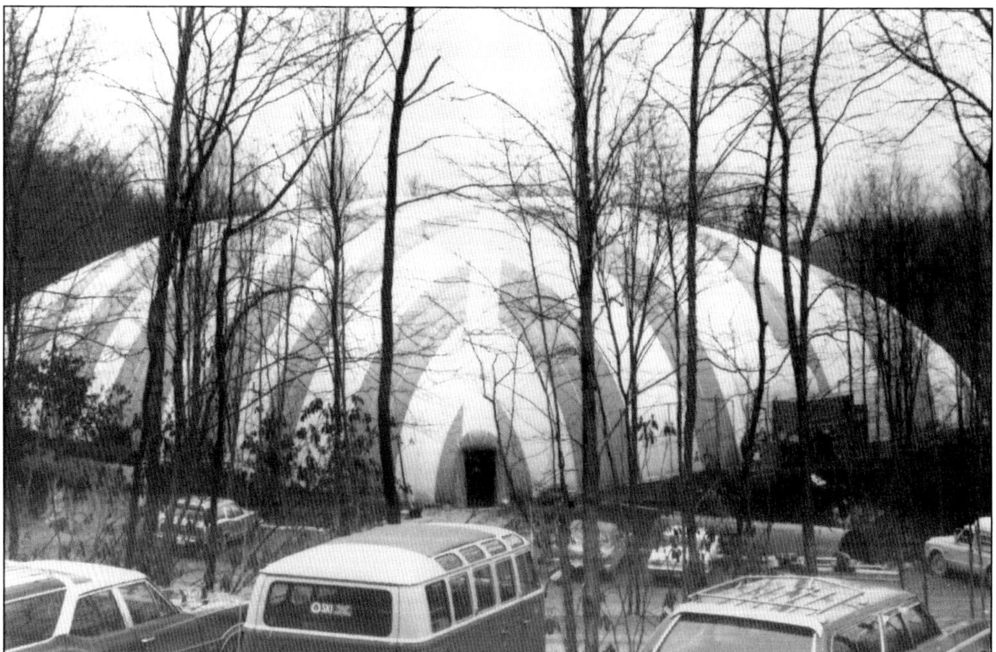

This tennis bubble was the answer to the resort's worries about providing year-round access to tennis for members and guests. It contained three tennis courts and a pro-shop and stood at the base of Sugar Mountain for many years. (Photograph by Bob Webb; courtesy of Al Traver Collection.)

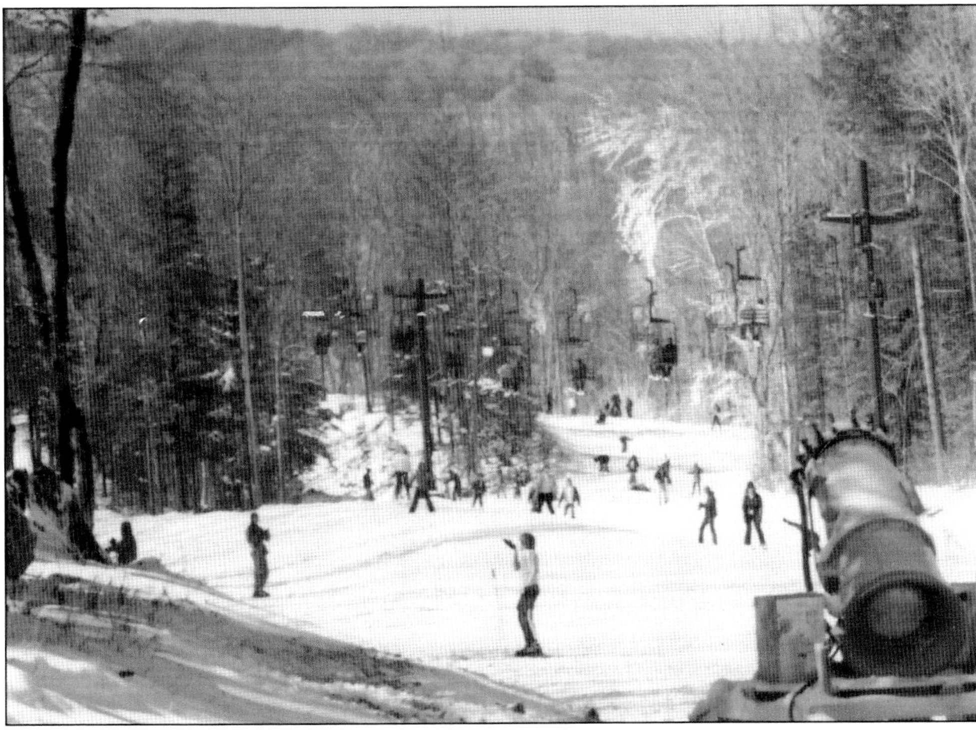

In this c. 1972 photograph, a Hedco snow gun stands ready to dust the slopes. These guns increased snowmaking capacity by 30 to 40 percent, and several were added to the slopes. Each one had a volume of 250 gallons of water per minute, which was an accomplishment at the time. (Photograph by Bob Webb; courtesy of Al Traver Collection.)

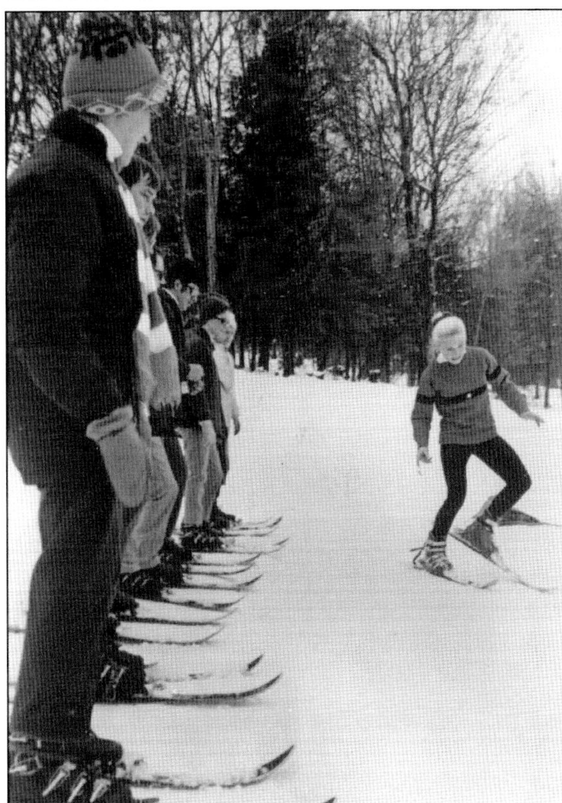

Lucy Bindlechner (right) demonstrates a parallel turn as part of the Headway Method of Graduated Learning Method (GLM) type of instruction. The technique—which originated in Killington, Vermont—was introduced to the resort by Eric Bindlechner, who was Lucy's husband and the ski school director. Skiers would begin on three-foot-long skis and progress to larger skis as they gained experience and confidence. (Photograph by Bob Webb; courtesy of Al Traver Collection.)

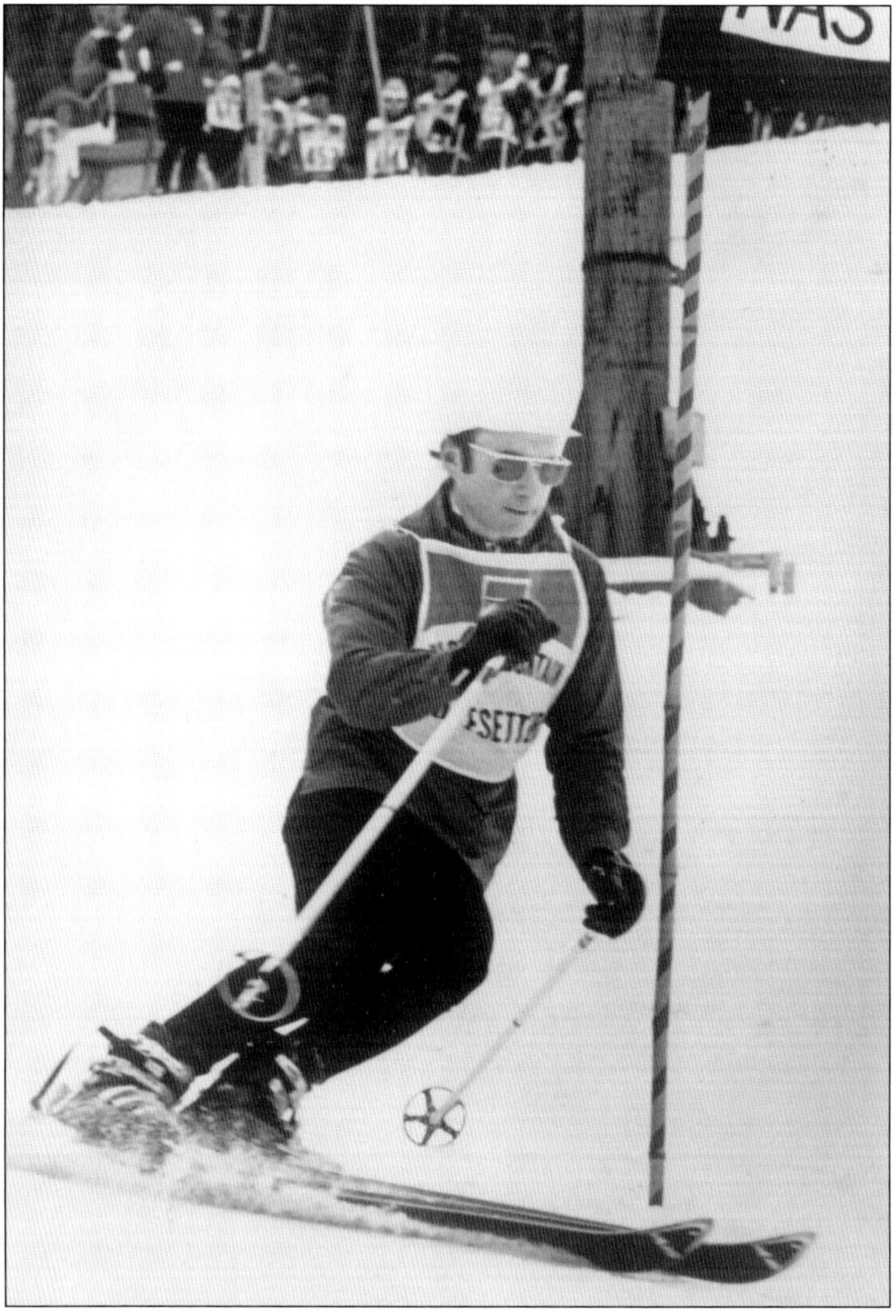

Participating in a 1974 NASTAR race, Eric Bindlechner, ski school director, speeds down Sugar's slopes in this photograph. While serving as an assistant ski school director at Killington, Vermont, Bindlechner learned Graduated Learning Method from its originator, Cliff Taylor. Bindlechner arrived at Sugar Mountain in 1969, just after Jim Cottrell's French-Swiss school had begun using GLM at Appalachian Ski Mountain. Sugar gained credibility by earning a Professional Ski Instructors Association designation for its ski school, and Eric and his wife, Lucy, made important contributions to the growth and success of Sugar Mountain's ski resort. (Photograph by Bob Webb; courtesy of Al Traver Collection.)

In this c. 1974 photograph, the double lift to Flying Mile carries passengers above running snowblowers. These snowblowers are likely the Hedco models that were popular on the mountain at that time. (Photograph by Bob Webb; courtesy of Al Traver Collection.)

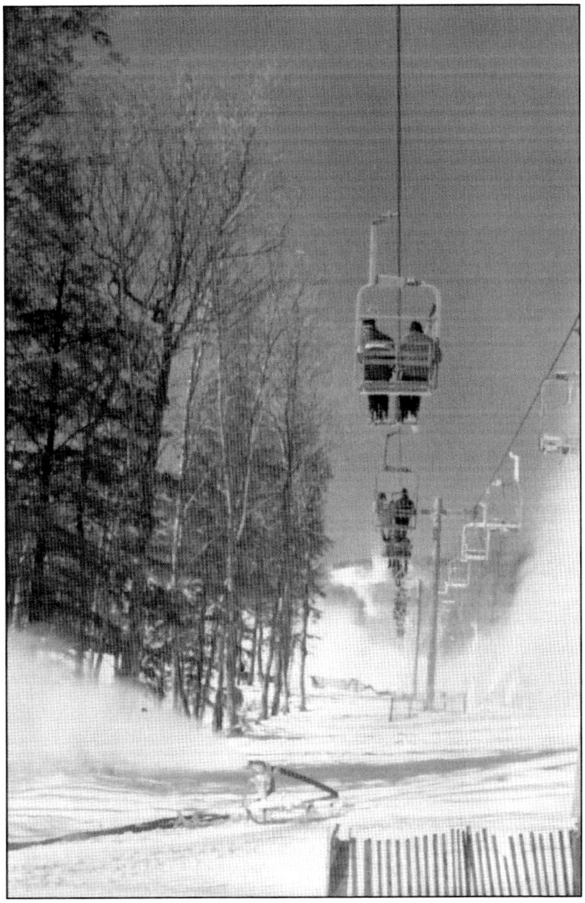

This c. 1972 postcard reads, "Schussing the Tom Terrific. Tom Terrific is no small test of the expert skier's ability at Sugar Mountain near Banner Elk, NC. Skiers who master this slope are given a patch to wear on their parkas. Sugar has 12 slopes: 5 advanced, 3 intermediate, 4 novice." (Photograph by Bob Webb; courtesy of Al Traver Collection.)

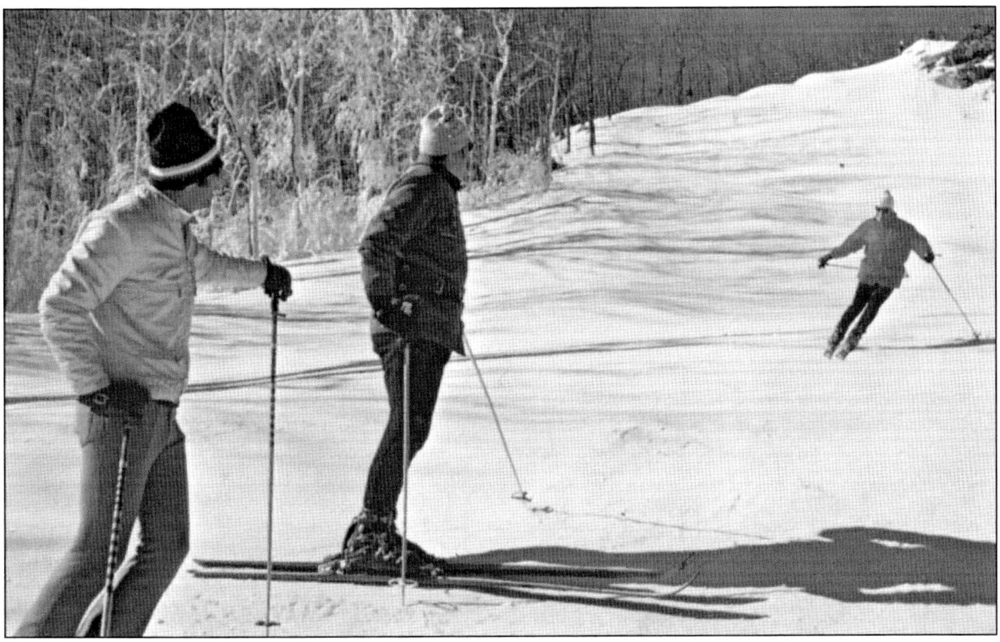

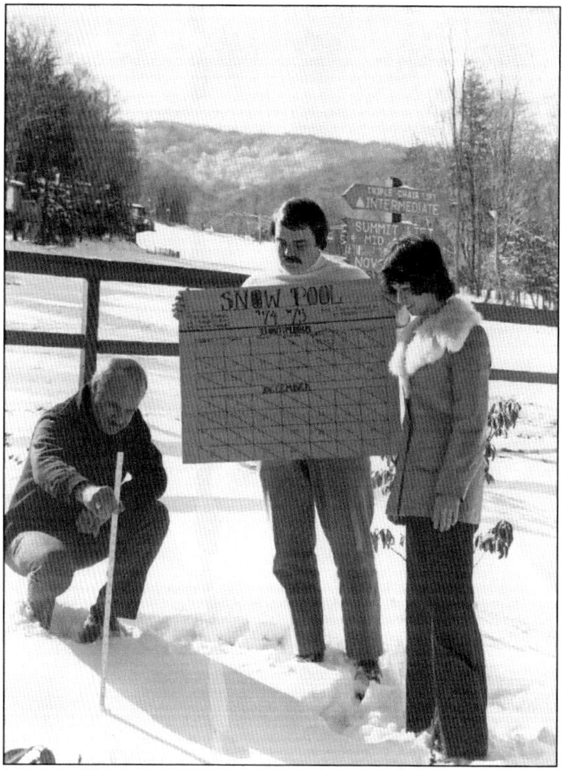

The Snow Pool was a popular event for staff in the 1970s and featured employees betting on the date and amount of the first snow. Shown here are, from left to right, Al Trever, Bill Munday, and Cecilia Strickland. (Courtesy of Al Traver Collection.)

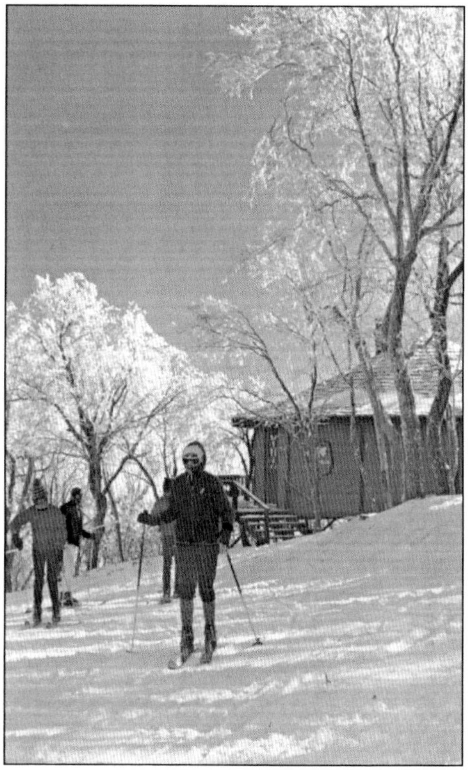

This c. 1974 postcard shows the Summit House at the top of Sugar and reads, "Summit House at Sugar Mountain: skiers head back to the slopes after a coffee break at Sugar's Summit House. An open stone fireplace inside encourages conversation and camaraderie among visitors." (Photograph by Bob Webb; courtesy of Al Traver Collection.)

One of the snowcats used to transport staff around the slopes is shown here in 1971. From left to right are Steve Campbell, Douglas MacRae, Kate MacRae, unidentified, and Bob Ash. Ash was the snowmaking manager who helped Sugar triumph over Beech and Appalachian in snowmaking capacity in the 1970s. (Courtesy of Al Traver Collection.)

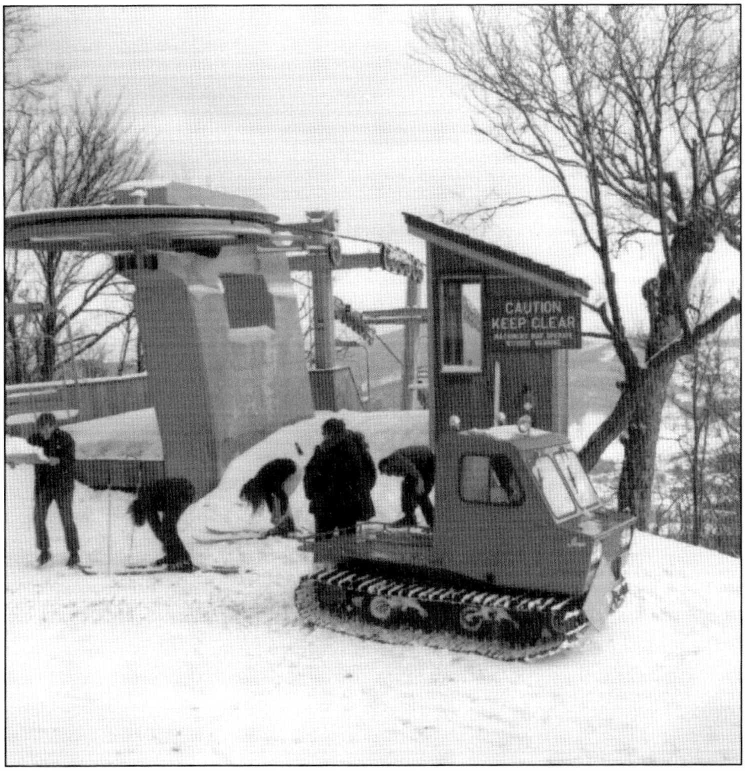

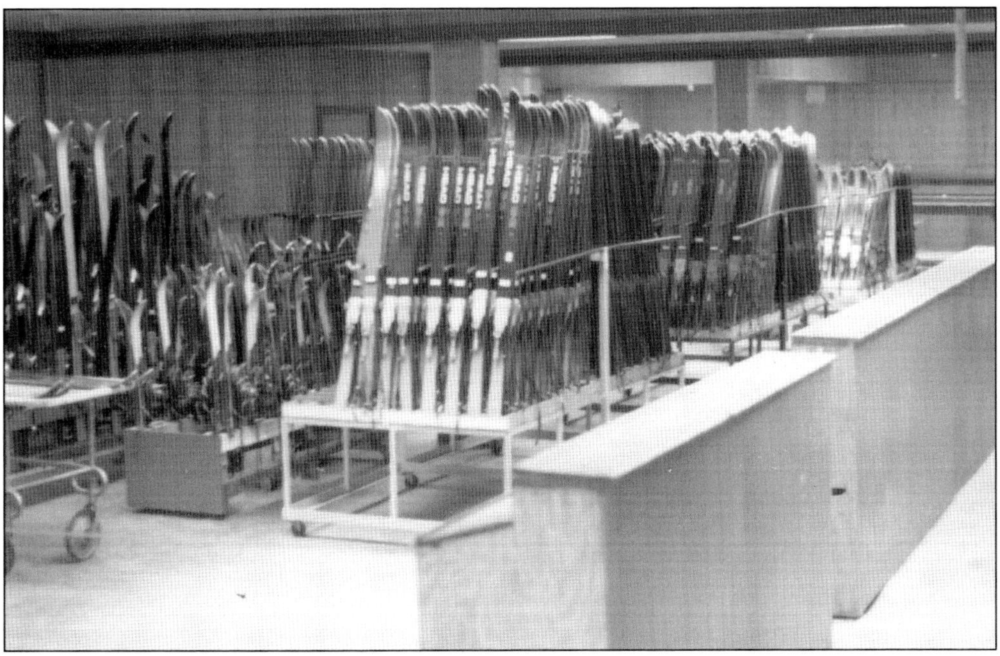

Sugar's ski school used GLM, and seen here in the rental office are some of the three-, four-, and five-foot skies available to students. Thousands of hesitant, would-be skiers conquered their fear of skiing by learning on shorter skis before progressing to longer ones. (Courtesy of Al Traver Collection.)

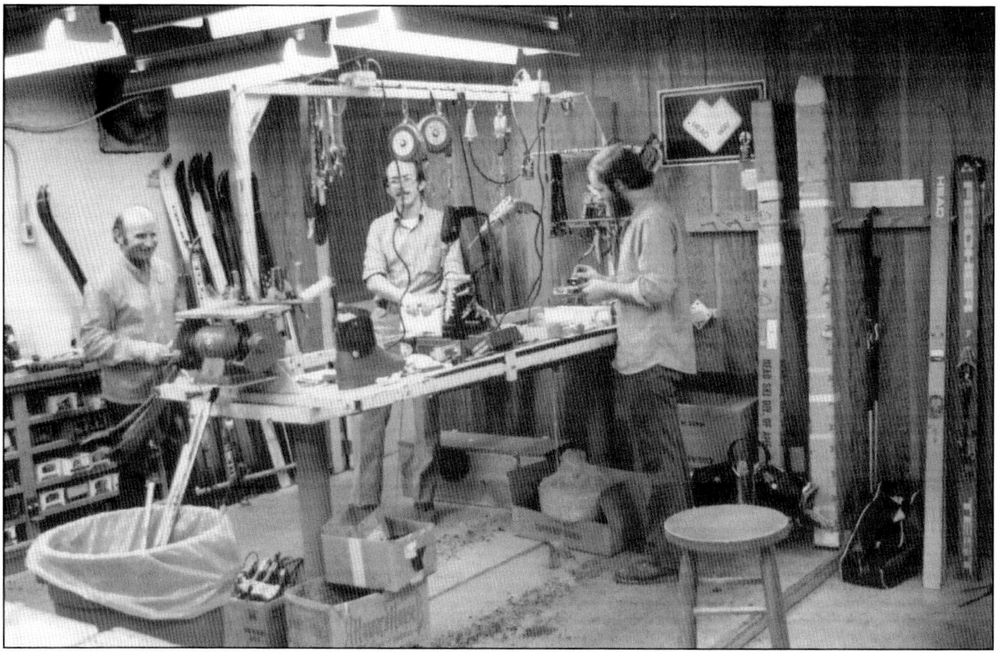

In this c. 1975 photograph, Sugar Mountain's staff wax the rental skis in the shop. Pictured from left to right are Eric Bindlechner, Carl Lyerly, and unidentified. Caring for rental skis properly helps extend the life of the skis and controls expenses for the resorts. (Courtesy of Al Traver Collection.)

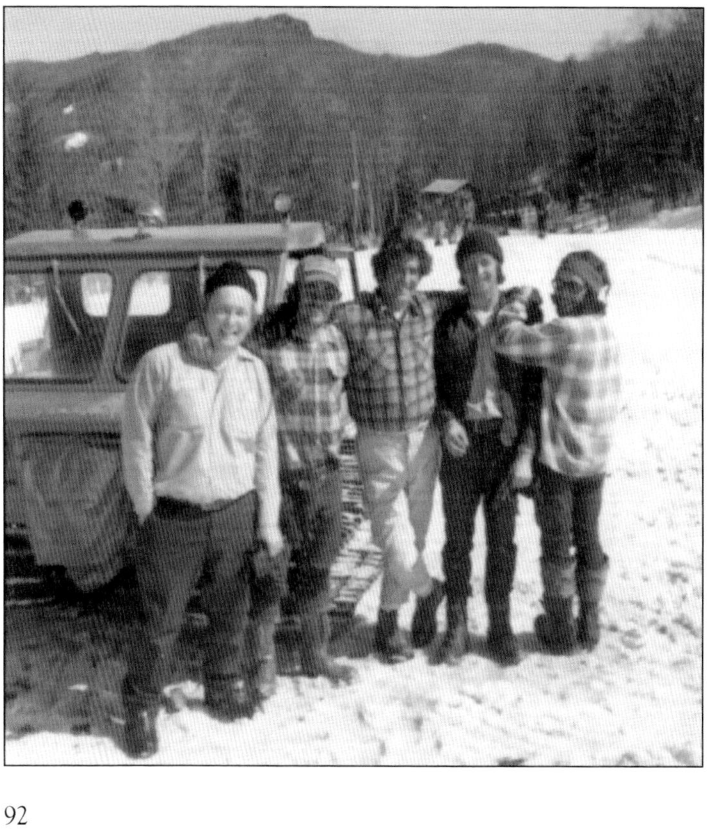

Members of the ski staff stand in front of a snowcat on a warm, sunny day on the slopes. Appalachian State University students often worked part-time at the resorts and then remained to assume more responsibilities. These resorts provide much-needed jobs for local residents. (Courtesy of Al Traver Collection.)

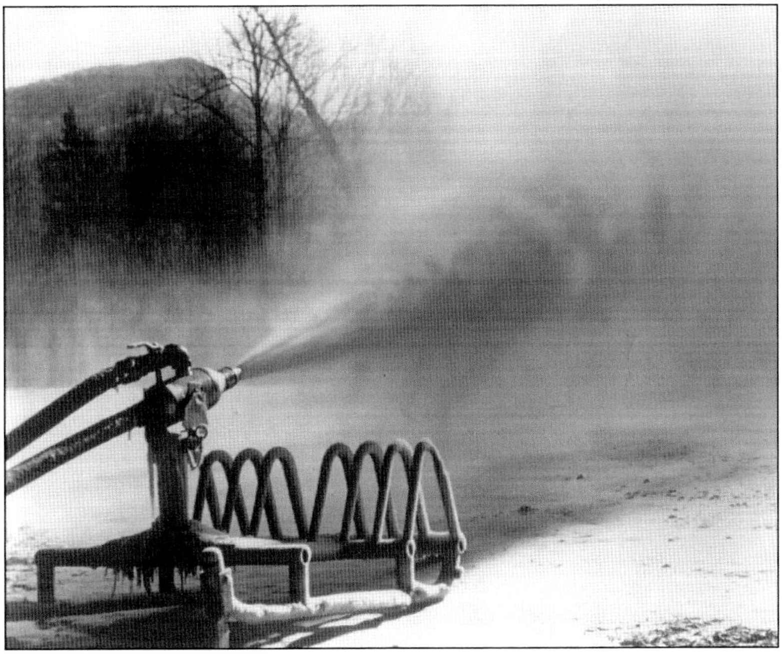

This c. 1972 photograph shows a Hedco snow gun, which was installed at Sugar to increase its snow coverage capacity and help make the most snow of all the High Country resorts. Sugar installed four of these giant Hedco cannons in the early 1970s. (Photograph by Bob Webb; courtesy of Al Traver Collection.)

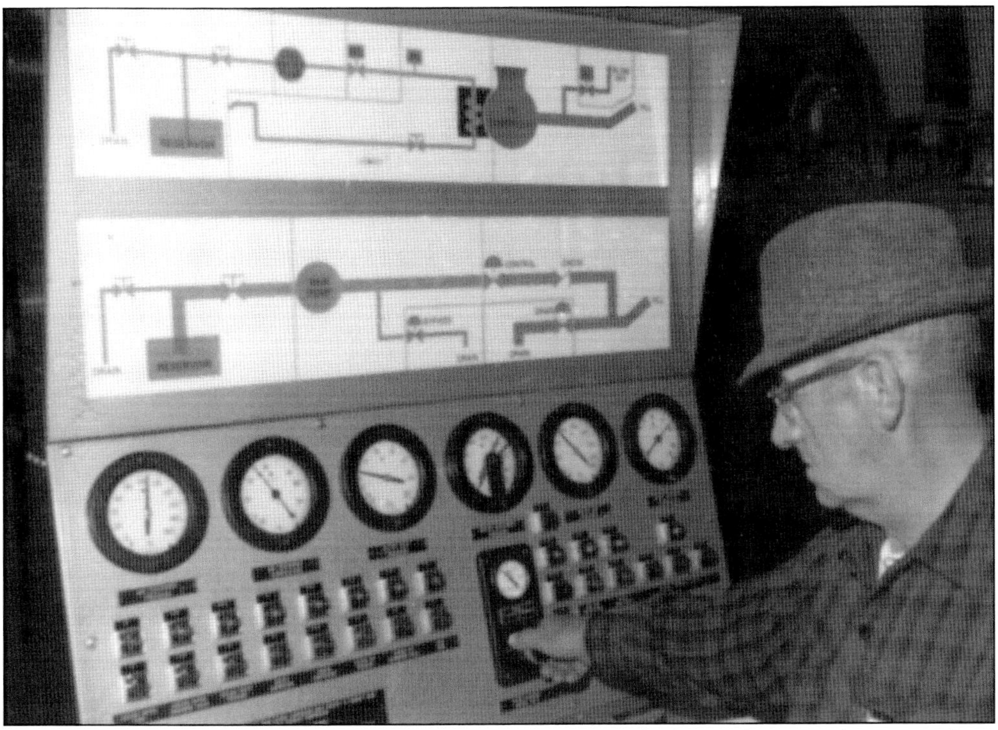

Here, Eric Tester operates equipment in the compressor house, which was the center for snowmaking in the early days. Compressed air and water were shot from large cannons to create the amount of snow necessary for skiing. (Courtesy of Al Traver Collection.)

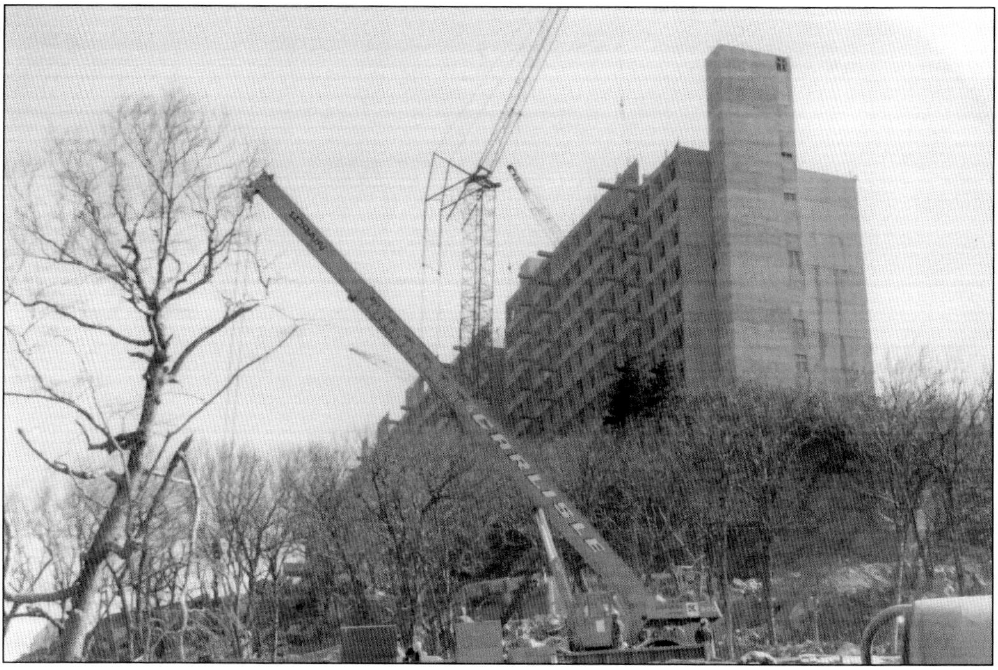

Everyone who visits the area notices this gigantic building on Sugar Mountain, which has an interesting story. Construction on Sugartop was begun in 1981 and completed in 1985, after investors purchased this property adjacent and above the ski slopes. This gigantic, 10-story condo block upset many residents, who felt that it ruined the top of the mountain. In fact, the negative feedback caused North Carolina to pass a ridge law, which restricts the height of buildings on mountaintops. High winds at this elevation have reportedly blown out windows and pushed doors open at the complex, but unit sales have continued to be steady and the views are reportedly amazing. The above photograph shows the construction, while the image below shows the finished product in its enormity. (Both, courtesy of Al Traver Collection.)

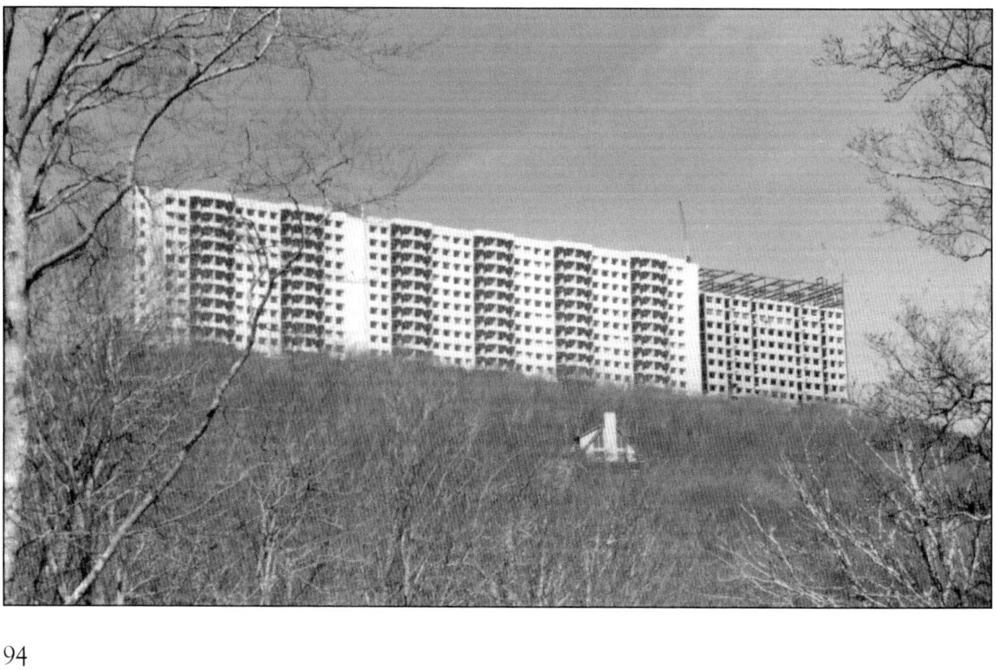

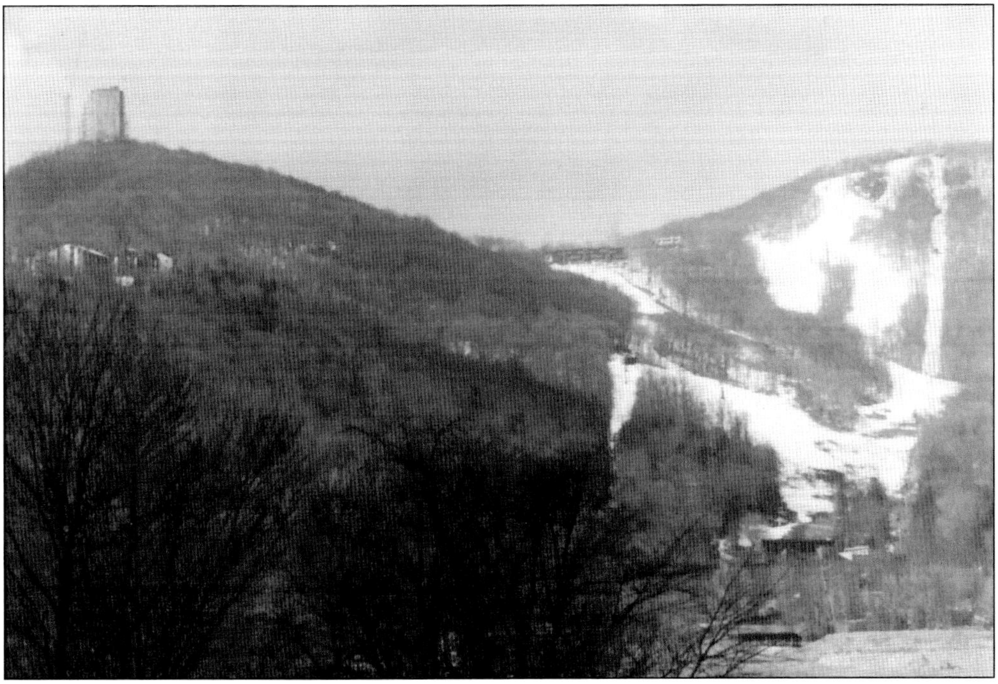

In this 1985 photograph, the ski slopes are shown in relation to Sugartop. This clearly illustrates how the building should not have been constructed on the top of the mountain. (Courtesy of Al Traver Collection.)

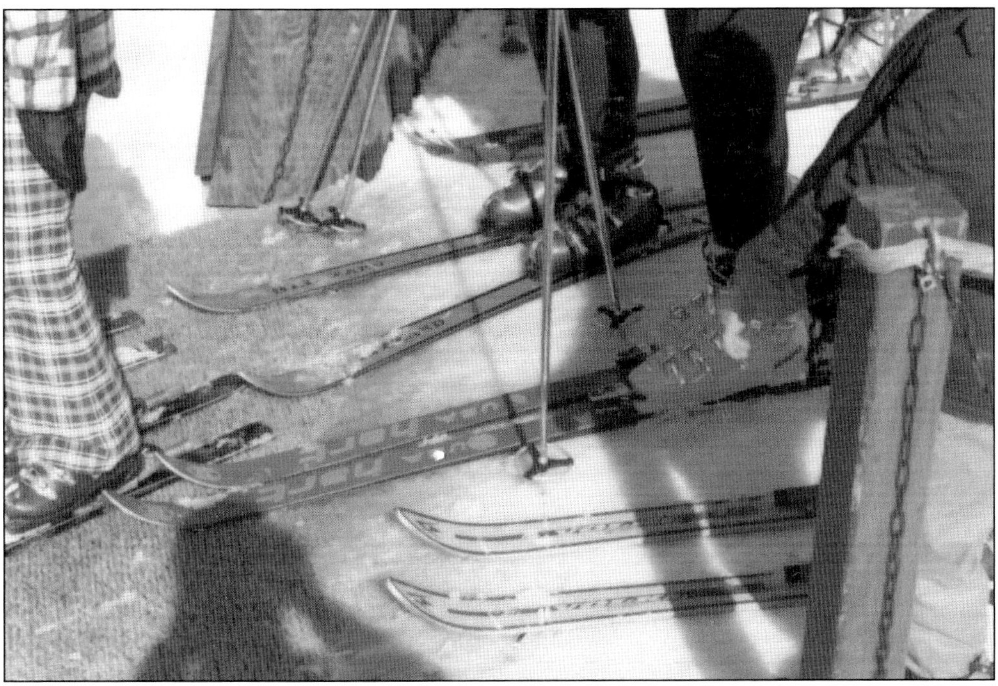

Different brands of skis from the 1970s are shown here, including the Blizzard, Hurt, and Vokel brands. Specialized ski clothing was viewed as unnecessary in the early days of skiing, but someone should have banned checked trousers from the slopes. (Courtesy of Al Traver Collection.)

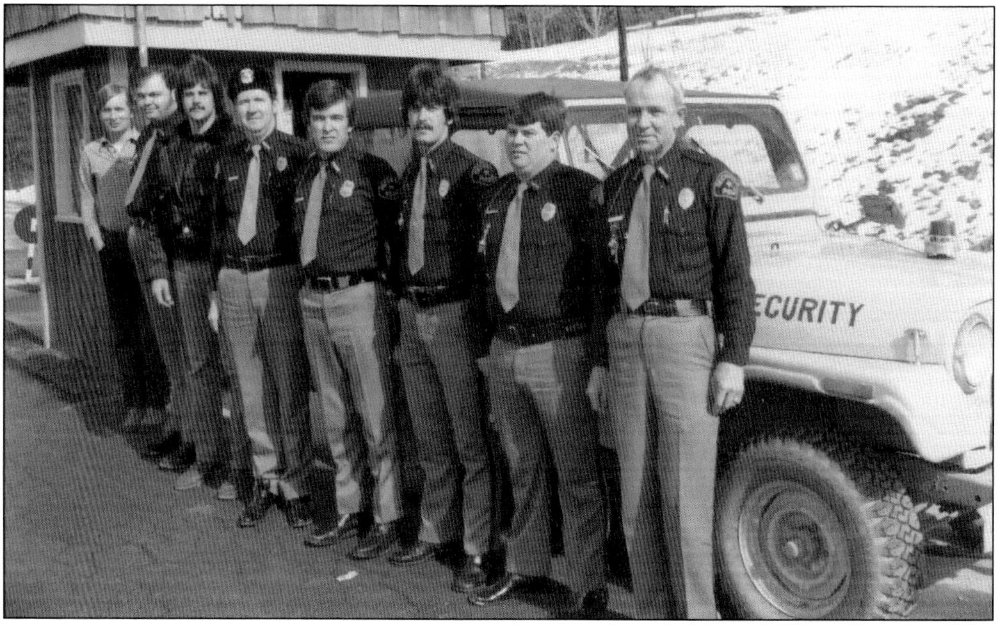

Sugar Mountain Resort's security force stands ready to protect and serve in this photograph from about 1976. Ken Ollis (far right) served as chief of security and held the position for many years. As a private resort, Sugar Mountain was required to provide its own security. Today, Sugar Mountain has been incorporated as a town and maintains a traditional police department. (Courtesy of Al Traver Collection.)

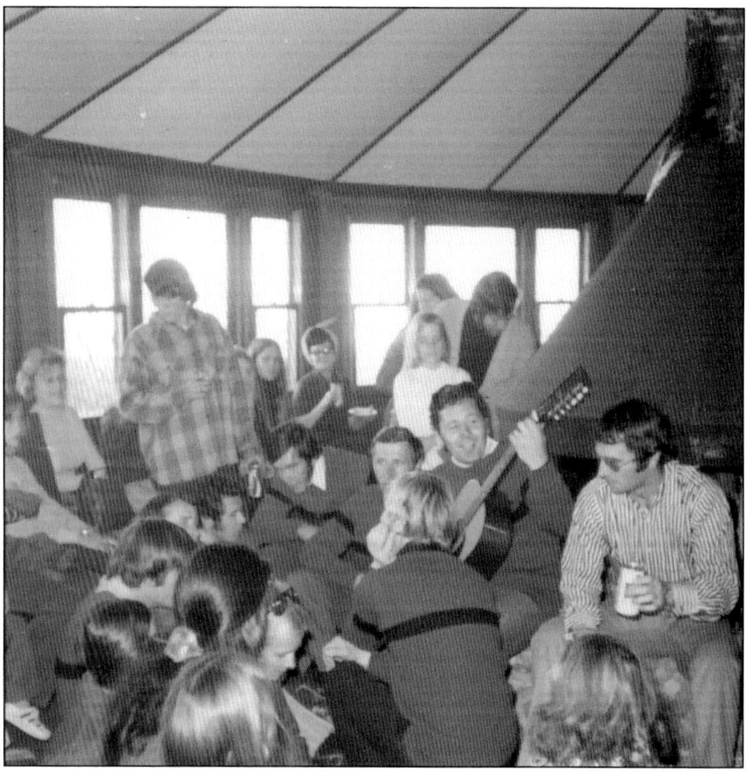

It must have been a requirement for the imported Austrian ski instructors to be musically inclined, as they were often called upon to do double duty as entertainers. Entertainment was especially needed when there was not enough snow for the slopes for skiing. Here, Poldi, a popular instructor, plays guitar for guests at Summit House. (Courtesy of Al Traver Collection.)

Nearby Appalachian State University offered skiing as a physical education course, and the Sugar Cup was a competition that the college team participated in. The identities of these students are unknown, but the coach seems to be standing at the right in this 1974 photograph. (Courtesy of Al Traver Collection.)

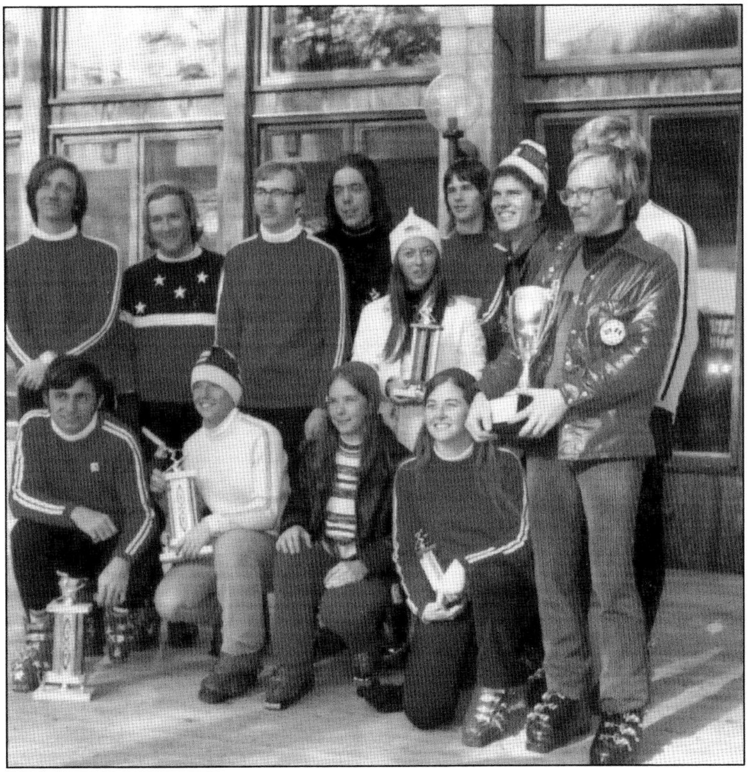

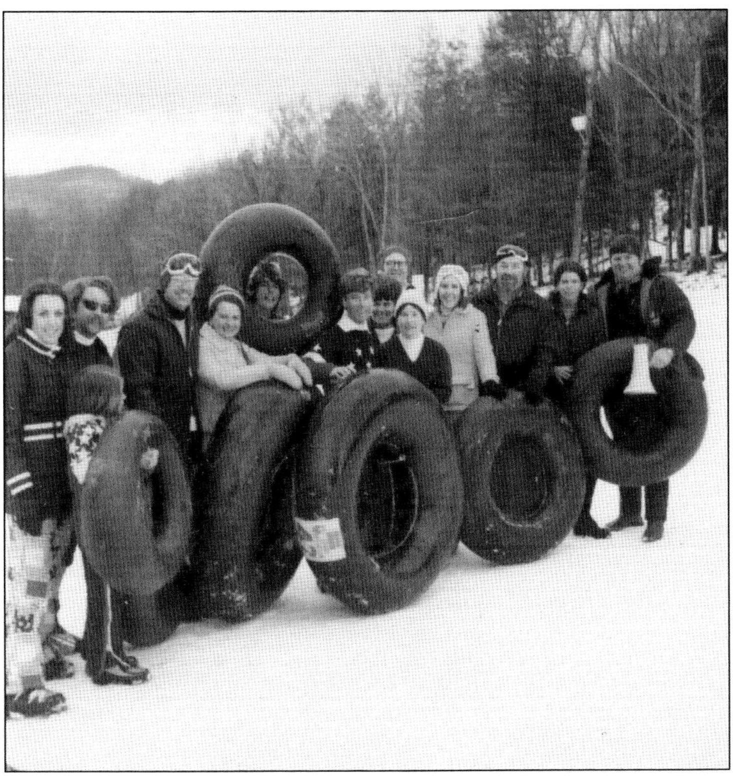

Snow tubing has always occurred on the slopes, though not always with the resort's knowledge. This crew would come onto the slopes at night, after the slopes were closed, and have great fun. Only the identity of the gentleman third from the right is known, and that is Ed Dickerson, who directed Sugar's recreation program in the 1970s. (Courtesy of Al Traver Collection.)

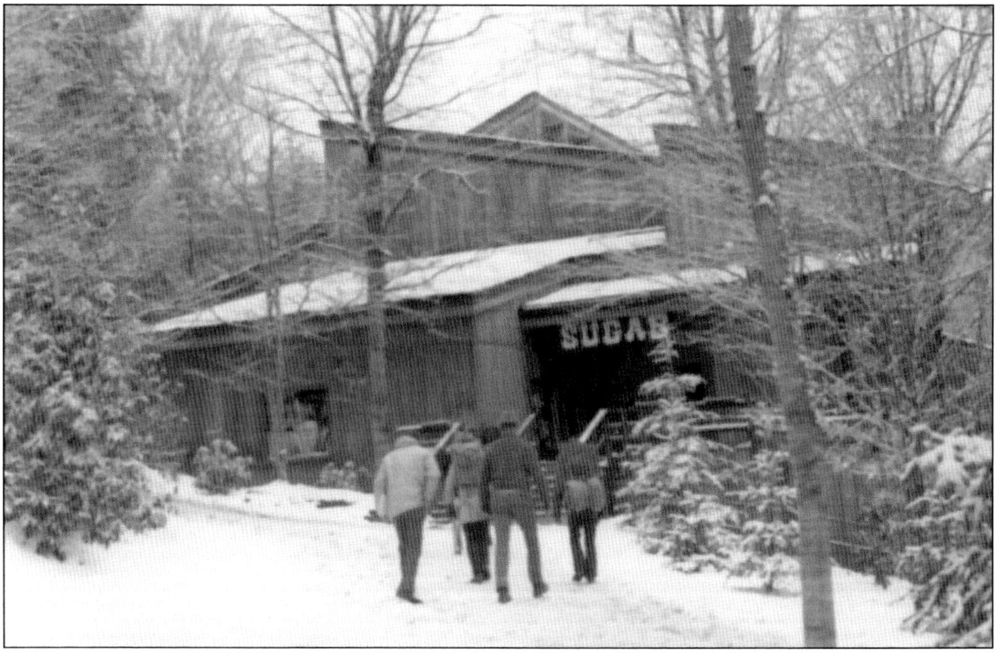

The ski center building is shown here. It housed the ski school, ski rental shop, real estate office, ski shop, and the Sugar Hollow Club. The club was a member's only affair, which met in the Maple Leaf Room on the third floor. (Courtesy of Al Traver Collection.)

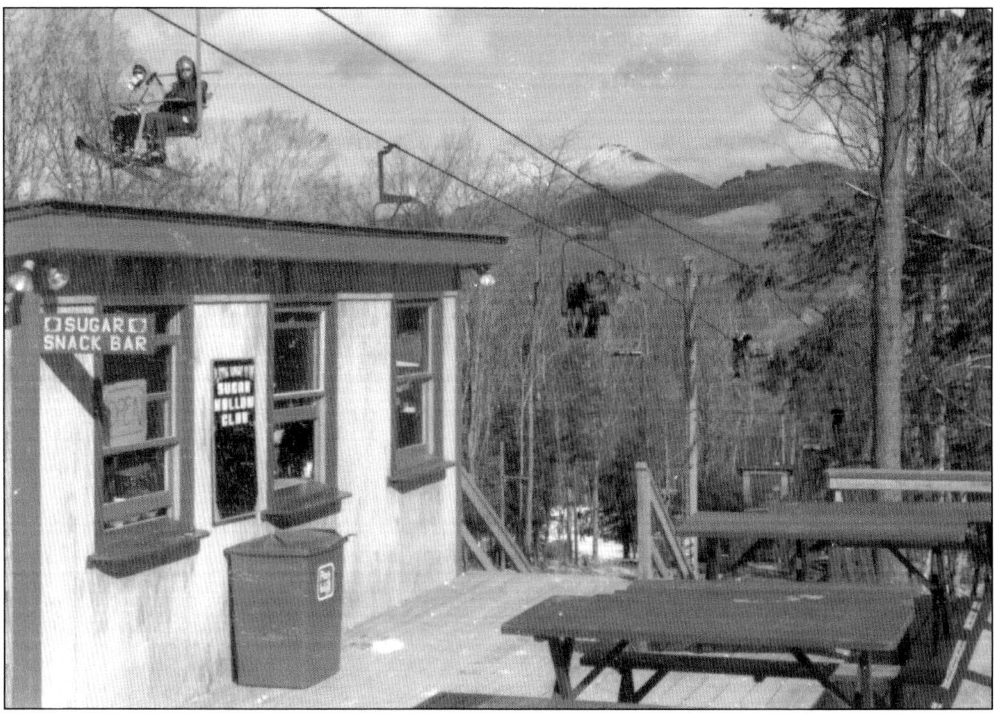

This snack bar was a popular stop in the 1970s. It was located about halfway up the Flying Mile and provided not only a resting place, but also snacks to recover and supplement a skier's energy. (Courtesy of Al Traver Collection.)

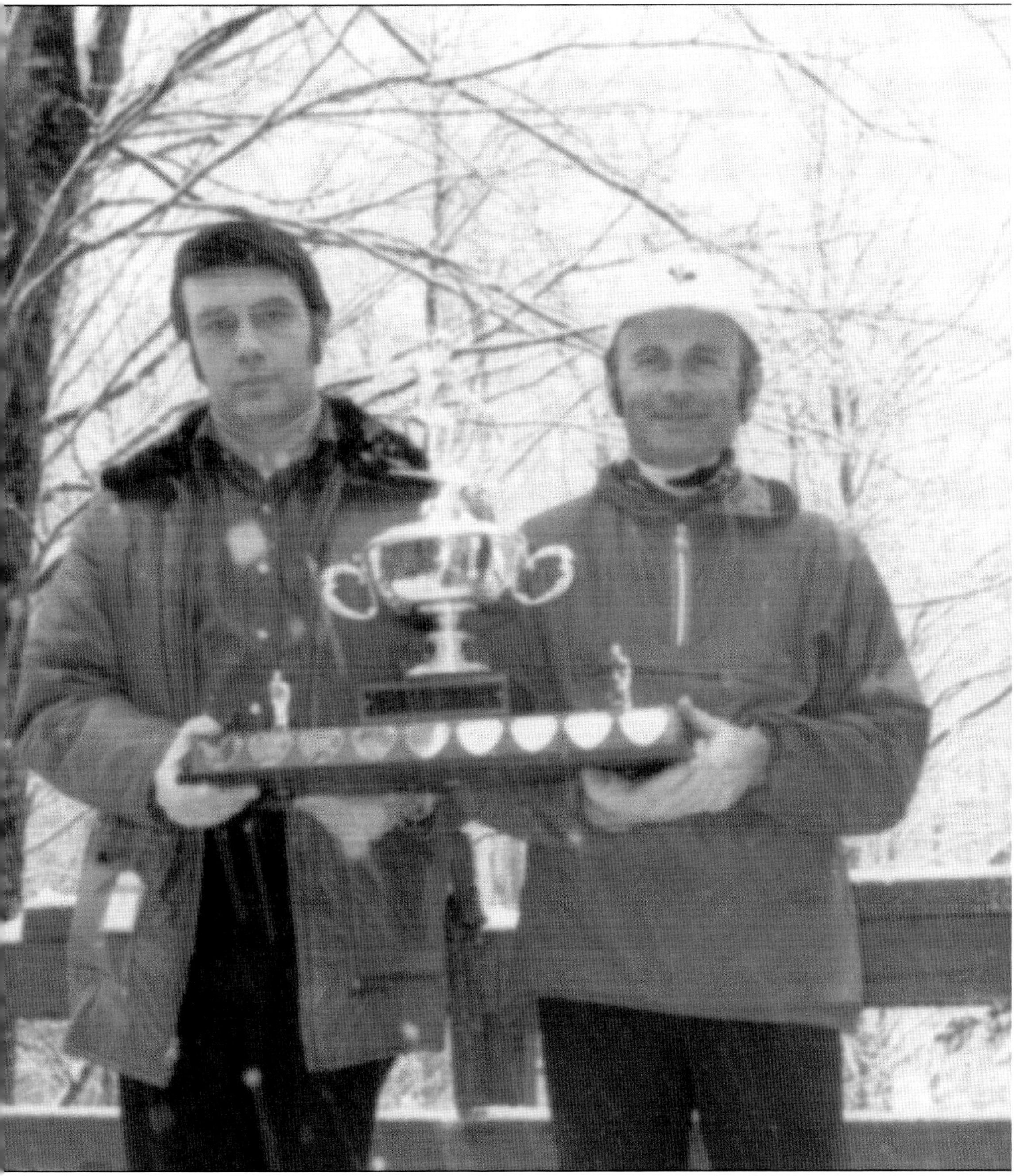

Henry Harper (left) is shown here in 1974 accepting the prestigious Metrolina Ski Award trophy from Eric Bindlechner, Sugar's ski school director. Many regional and national races were held at Sugar as it gained in popularity and reputation. (Courtesy of Al Traver Collection.)

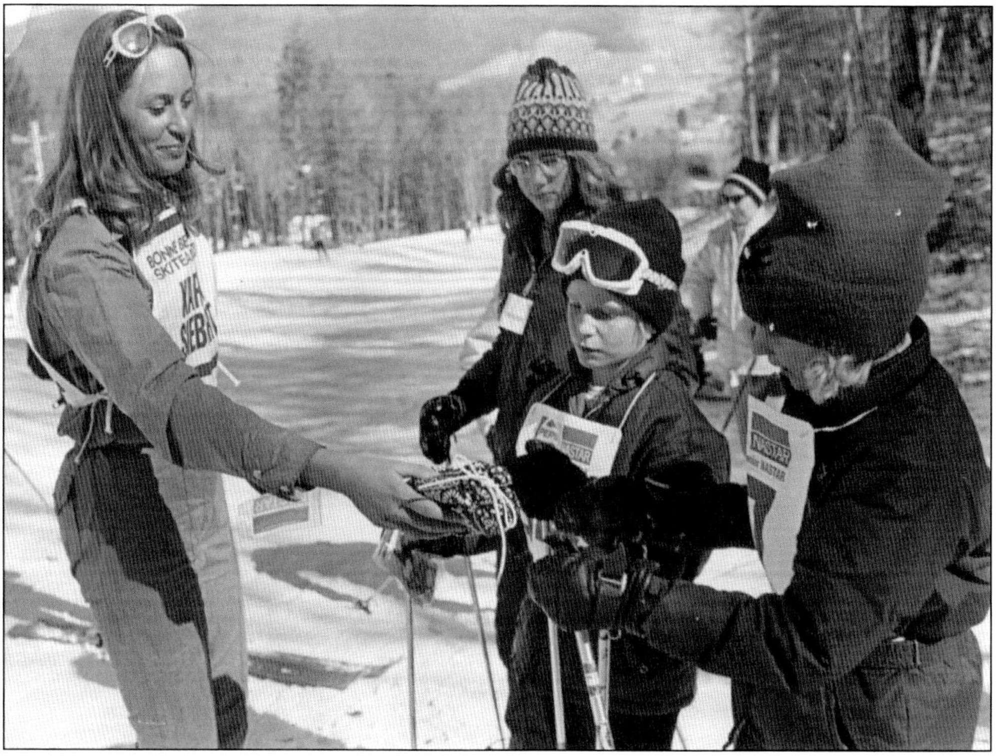

The Sunday NASTAR races drew many competitive young skiers. Here, Karen Siebert, of the Bonnie Bell ski team, is presenting an award to the winning team. (Courtesy of Al Traver Collection.)

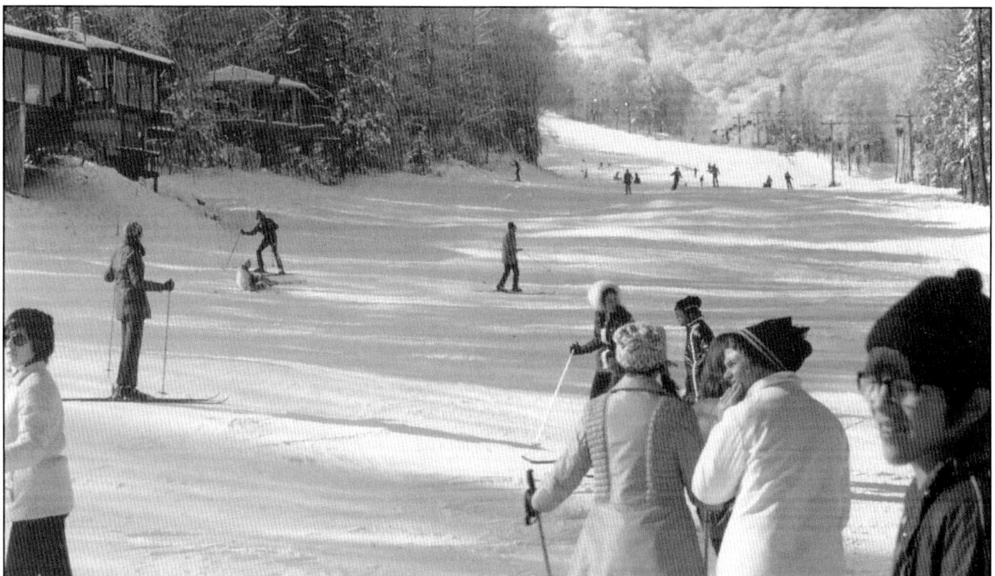

This c. 1971 photograph of the lower slopes of Flying Mile shows skiers along the slopes and the round houses (known locally as mushroom houses) that were popular in the 1970s. These houses were built at several local ski areas and resorts. (Photograph by Bob Webb; courtesy of Al Traver Collection.)

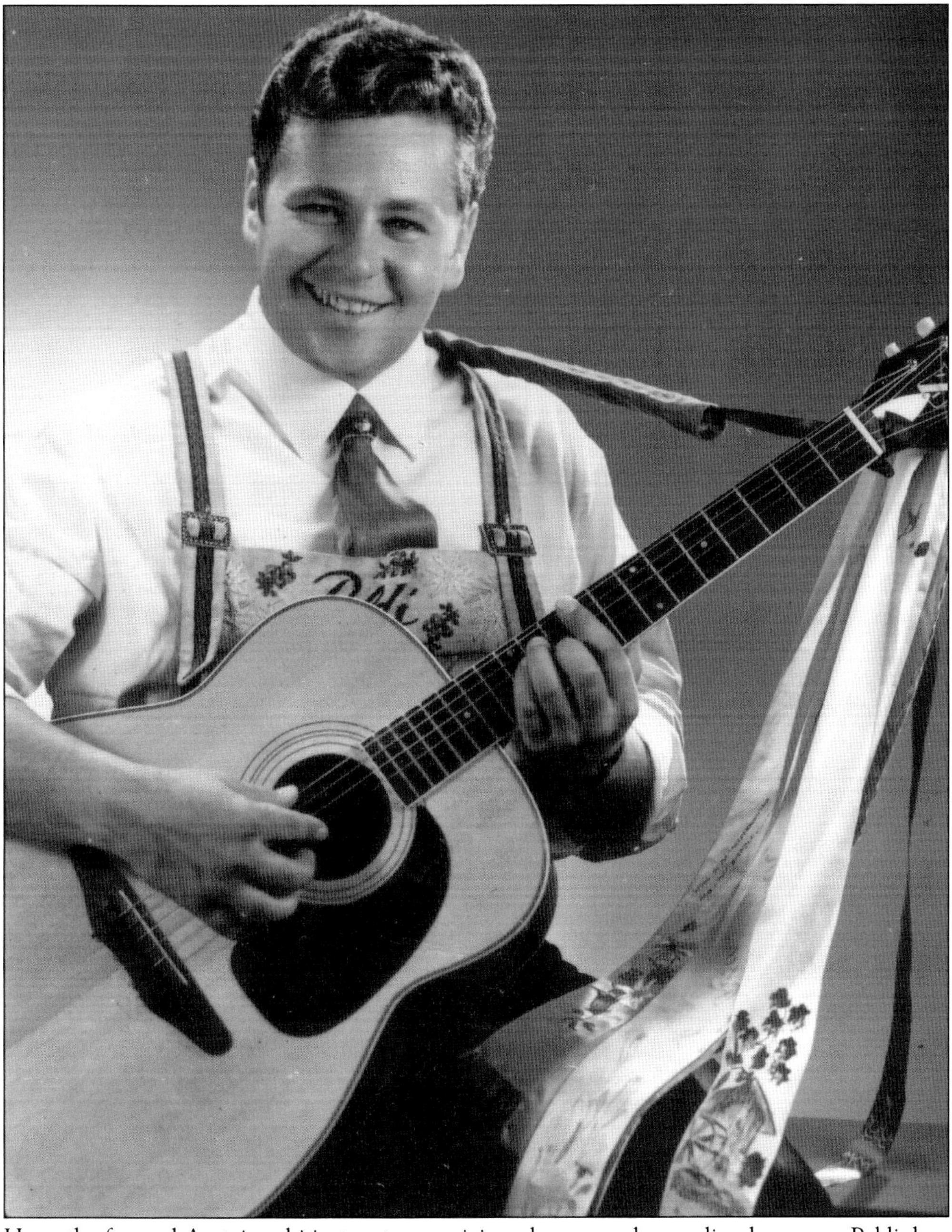

Here, the favored Austrian ski instructor, musician, dancer, and comedian known as Poldi does his second job—entertaining guests. Poldi was so popular with visitors that this photograph was made into a postcard that advertised Sugar's skiing. (Courtesy of Al Traver Collection.)

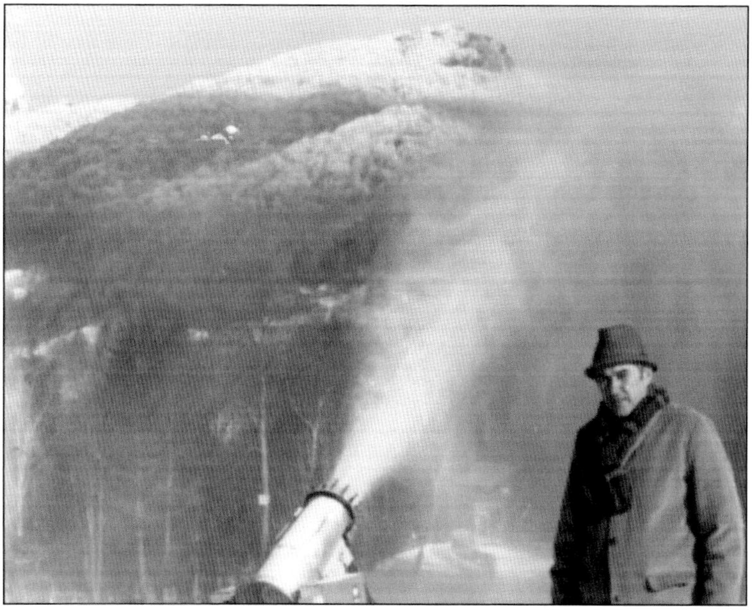

In this photograph from about 1972, Tom Brigham, one of the founders of Sugar Mountain Resort, poses next to one of the highly efficient Hedco snow cannons. These snow guns were the highest snowmaking technology of the time and helped put southern skiing on the map for skiers. (Photograph by Bob Webb; courtesy of Al Traver Collection.)

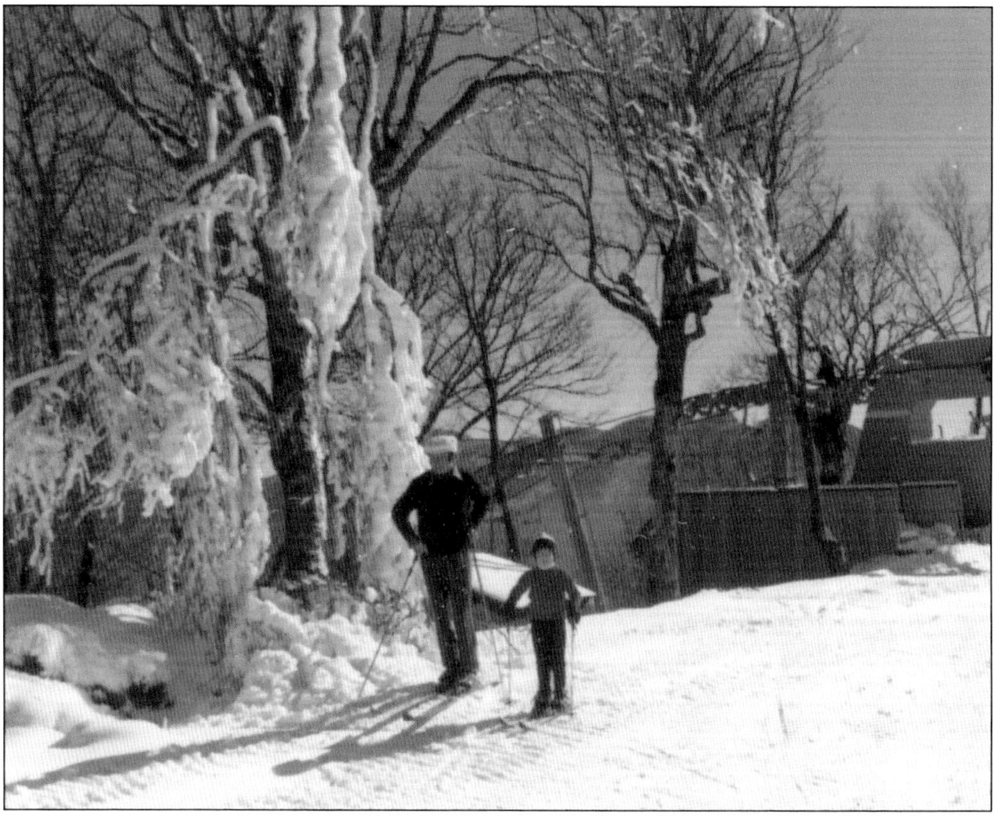

Eric Bindlechner, the well-known and talented Austrian ski school director, is seen here instructing his son Carl around 1971. There is heavy snow on the trees behind them, though it is impossible to know whether this is the result of diligent snowmaking or natural snow. (Photograph by Bob Webb; courtesy of Al Traver Collection.)

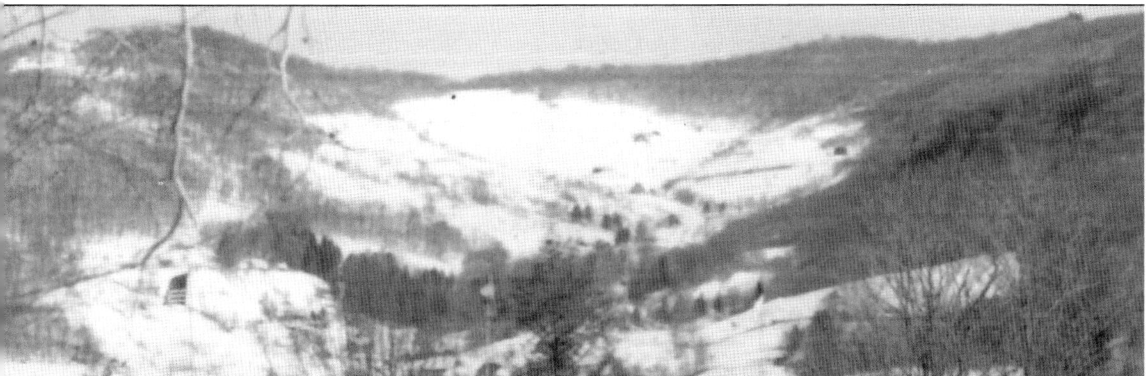

It is a crowded day on the slopes in 1975, as many students gather for lessons near the ski center. Note the lack of modern ski clothing, such as bibs and insulated pants, which is common today. The hills behind the center have some natural snow cover, but this is not necessary for Sugar, which relies on the latest in snowmaking technology. Skiing was always profitable for the resort and helped maintain the residential component during the 1970s recession, but it could not shoulder the cost of the entire resort. It is good to see that this resort—along with others in the area—was able to not just survive bankruptcy, but also flourish. (Courtesy of Al Traver Collection.)

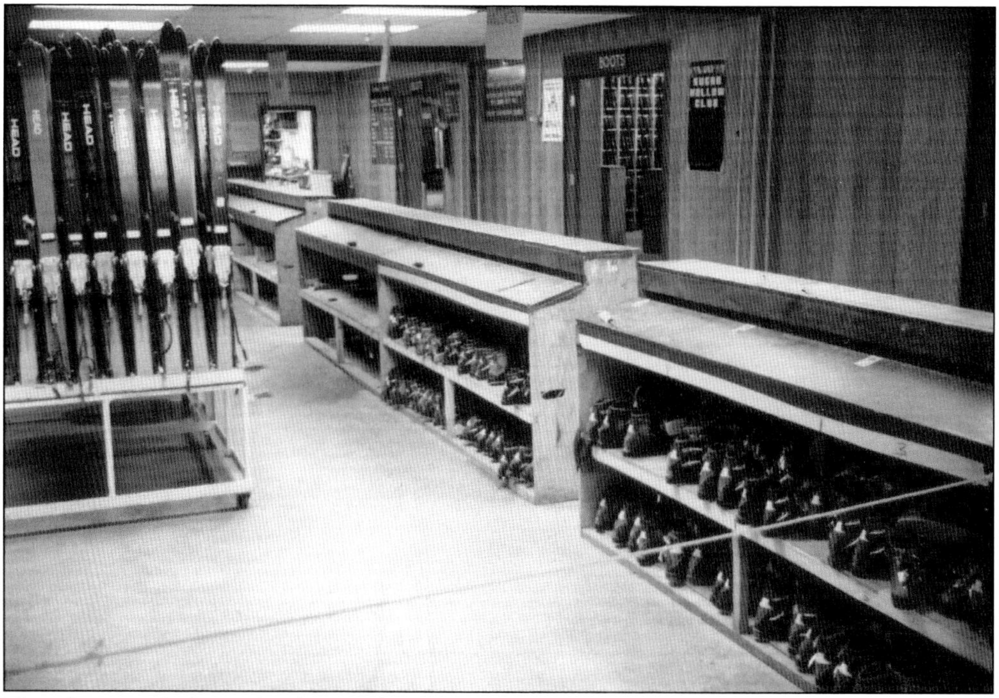

This photograph shows the ski rental center and the Head skis and boots used in the Graduated Learning Method. (Courtesy of Al Traver Collection.)

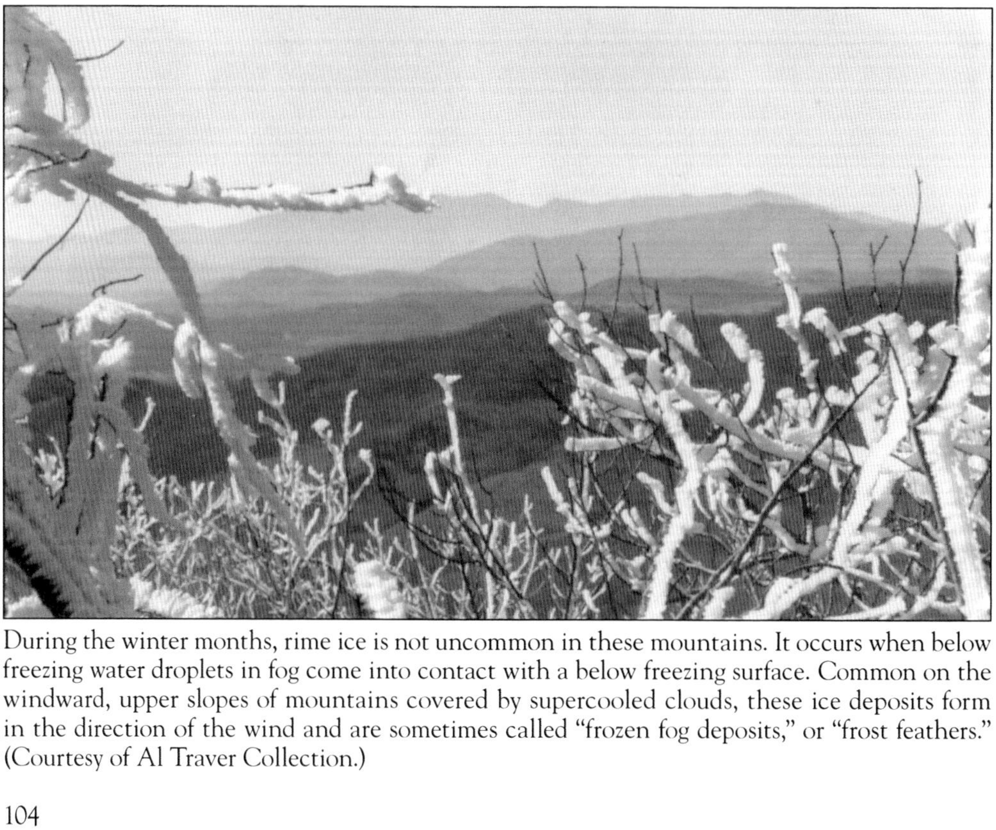

During the winter months, rime ice is not uncommon in these mountains. It occurs when below freezing water droplets in fog come into contact with a below freezing surface. Common on the windward, upper slopes of mountains covered by supercooled clouds, these ice deposits form in the direction of the wind and are sometimes called "frozen fog deposits," or "frost feathers." (Courtesy of Al Traver Collection.)

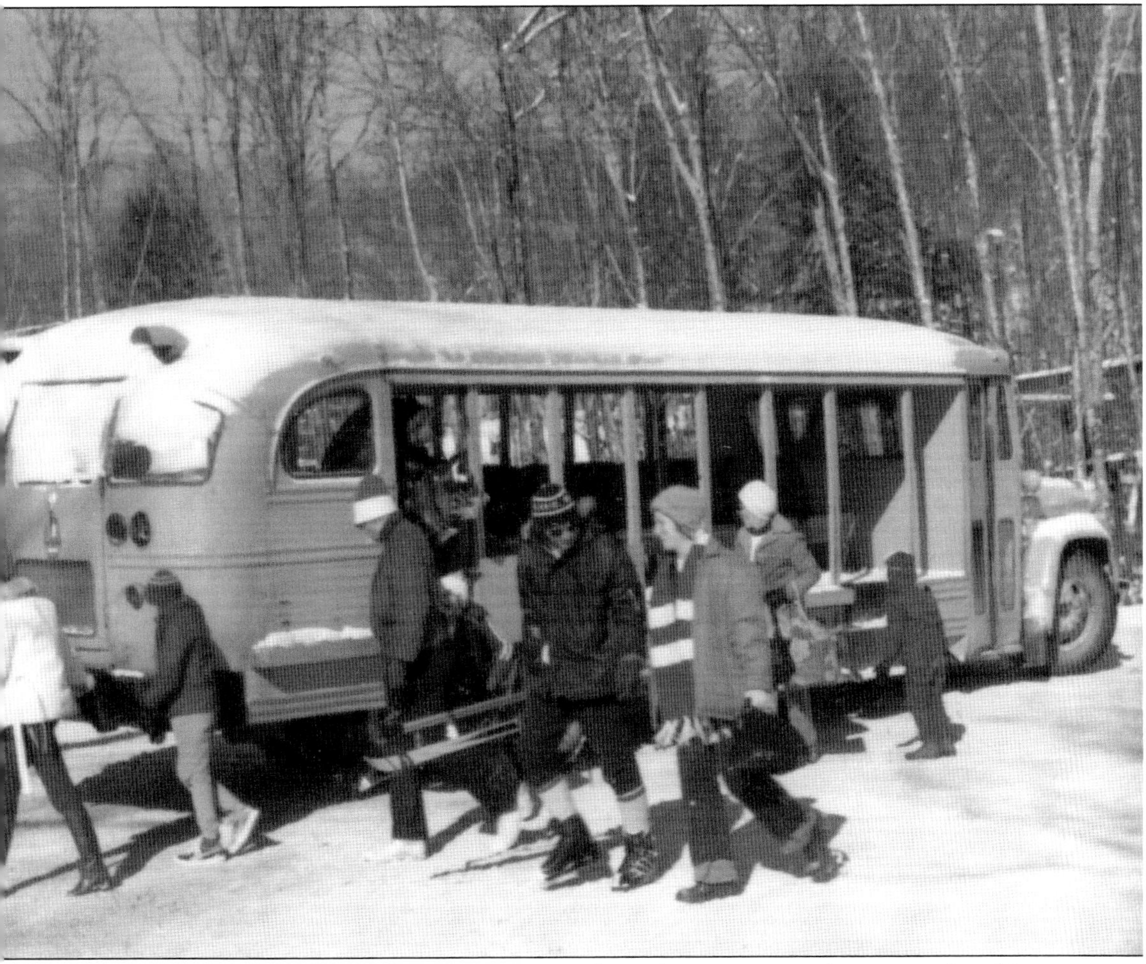

This trusty old school bus served Sugar Mountain skiers for many years. It was retrofitted by removing the doors and adding racks for ski equipment, and it was used to transport guests in from the far parking lots. (Courtesy of Al Traver Collection.)

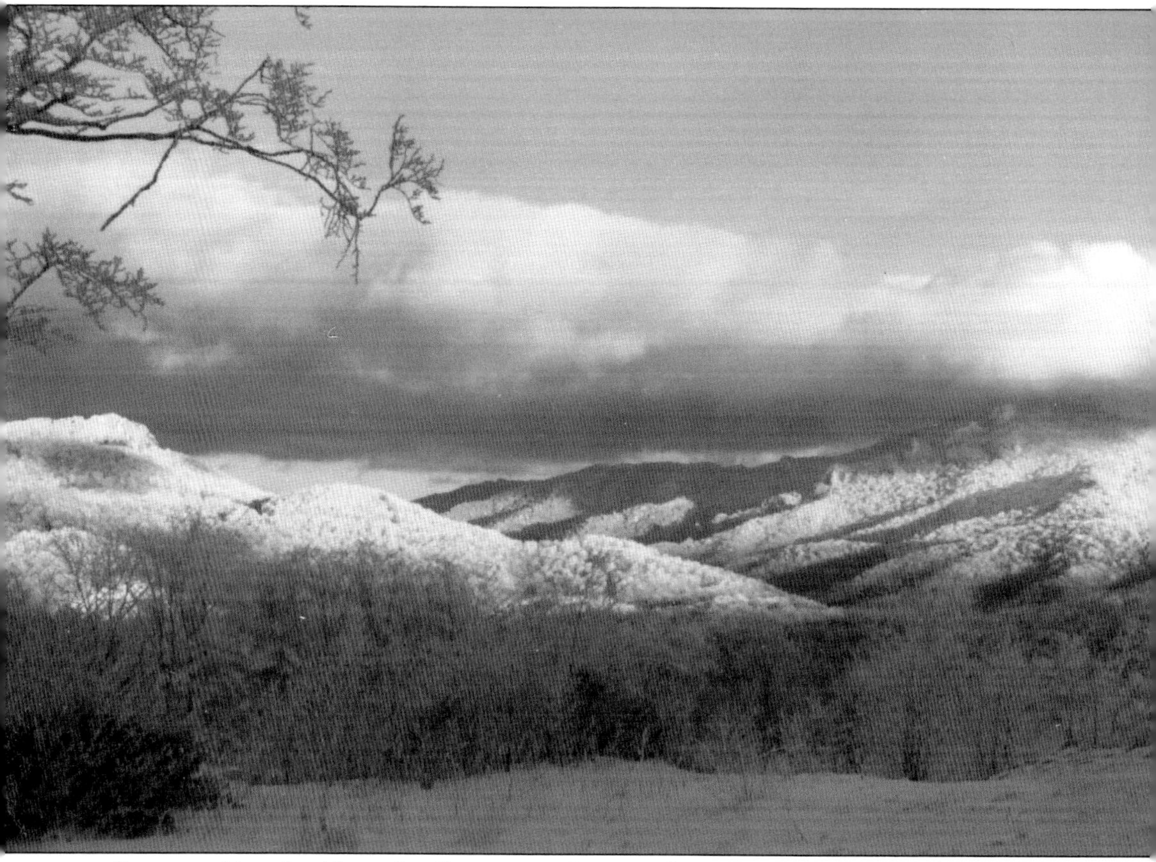

Even non-skiers should travel up Sugar to see the magnificent views. Seven Devils (now Hawksnest) can be seen in the center of this c. 1975 photograph. Sugar Mountain Resort is one of the most popular southern ski resorts and hosts festivals and activities year-round. Gunther and his wife, Kim Jochl, own and manage the resort and have improved the ski amenities. Hiking and biking trails opened on the slopes in 1993, and national mountain biking competitions are held annually. Summer lift rides are also offered to those wishing to admire the scenery. Today, the resort features a vertical drop of 1,200 feet, 20 slopes and trails on 115 acres, and 8 lifts capable of moving 8,800 guests per hour. Terrain parks, ice-skating, snowshoeing, and snow tubing are also available. Even though three excellent ski resorts call the High Country home, each has survived through financial difficulties and continues to thrive. Their economic contributions to northwestern North Carolina are significant, and thousands of visitors have had their first taste of skiing on these slopes. (Courtesy of Al Traver Collection.)

Five

Ski Sapphire Valley and Wolf Ridge Resort

Eugene M. Howerdd Sr., a lumber expert from Georgia, summered in the High Country and skied at Cataloochee before deciding to develop a ski resort in Sapphire Valley—about three miles from Cashiers, North Carolina. In 1954, he acquired about 8,500 acres, which included the Fairfield Inn and 200 acres surrounding Lake Fairfield. He developed the Sapphire Valley Inn and Golf Club, which opened in 1956. Howerdd then hired Sep Kober of West Virginia to design the ski area. Construction of the lift towers, snowmaking system, and rope tow and the renovation of an old farmhouse began soon afterwards. One of the oldest houses in Sapphire Valley became the base lodge—welcoming skiers to the area—and Austrian skiers were hired to run the ski school. Another Austrian pair, Hans and Deter, provided cocktails and music at the inn. The resort was sold in 1970, and various owners made improvements. In 1982, the growing Fairfield communities acquired the resort, but it went into bankruptcy in 1990. Today, it is owned by the Sapphire Management Company, includes 5,400 acres, and offers residents many amenities.

According to Randy Johnson, CP "Bud" Edwards begin putting together property near Mars Hill in 1965 and began work on the Big Bald development—an early recreational residential development. Edwards opened the Wolf Laurel (now Wolf Ridge) ski slopes in the winter of 1970–1971 and added snowmaking equipment during the next season. The 700-foot vertical slope included a double chairlift. The recession of the 1970s hurt the resort, and it had several owners over the next few years. Fortunately, several employees managed the resort for years—including Paul Bailey, John Goins, Col. Tom Barr, and Tim Walker—and ensured its survival. Wolf Ridge's snowmaking capabilities were expanded over the years, and in 1983, an intermediate slope was added. The resort still operates as the smallest ski area in North Carolina.

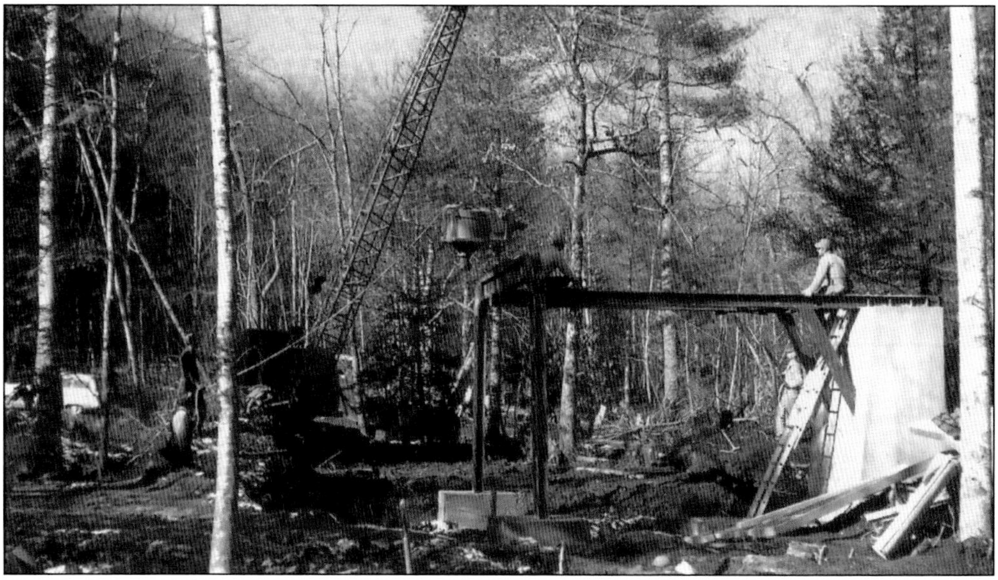

Construction of the ski area lifts is taking place in this photograph from 1965. The level of infrastructure necessary to establish a ski area is daunting, as these photographs reflect. This resort—located on US 64E—was designed by Sep Kober, who had designed several other ski areas. Eugene Howerdd believed that this area could support another ski resort after his family skied at nearby Cataloochee. Dieter Baer managed the ski area in its early years, and as a promotion, homeowners in the Hogback Lake development (established in 1964) were provided with a set of custom skis, poles, and boots, along with a free season ski pass. (Courtesy of Rick and Lisa Stargill.)

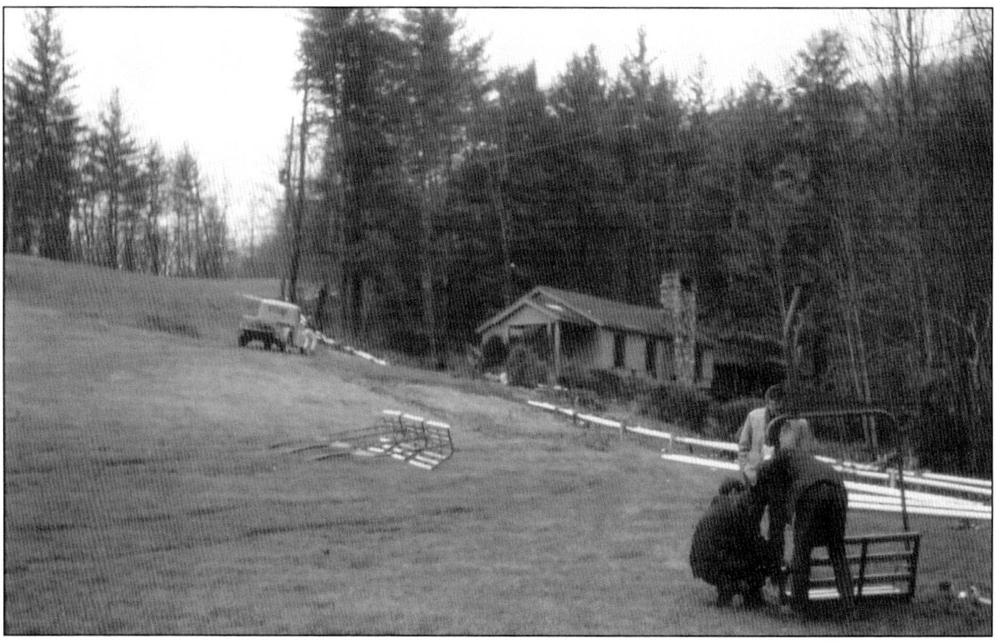

This photograph shows the construction of the lift and the snowmaking system. Providing employment for locals, especially during the winter, is a major contribution by ski resorts to the region. (Courtesy of Rick and Lisa Stargill.)

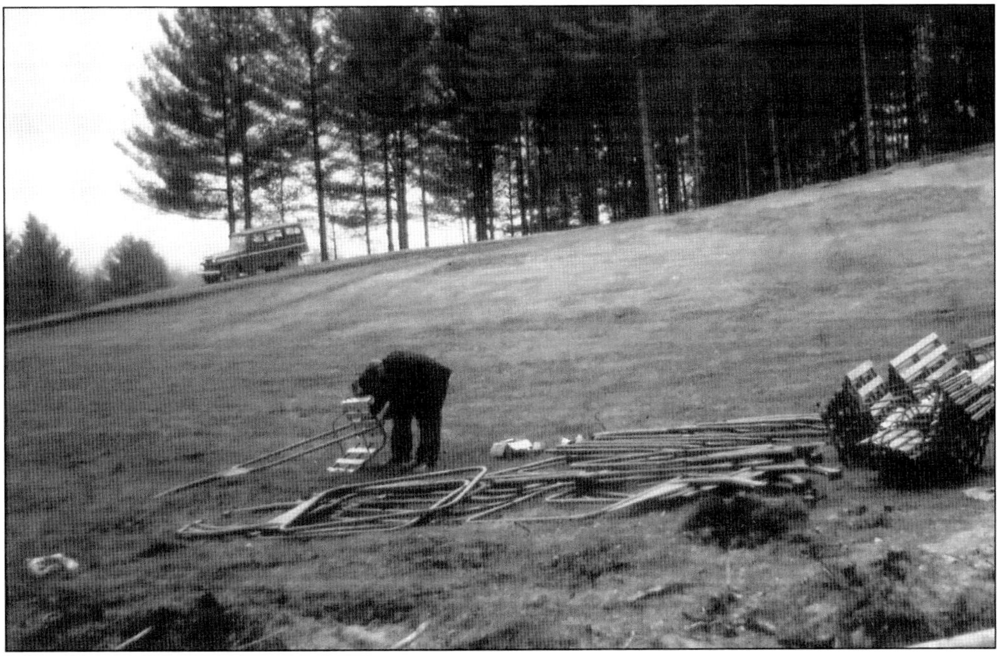

In this photograph, Sapphire employees are assembling a double chairlift for the opening of the ski area. Although smaller than the resorts in northwestern North Carolina, Sapphire provides convenient skiing for residents of Georgia and the more western regions of North and South Carolina. (Courtesy of Rick and Lisa Stargill.)

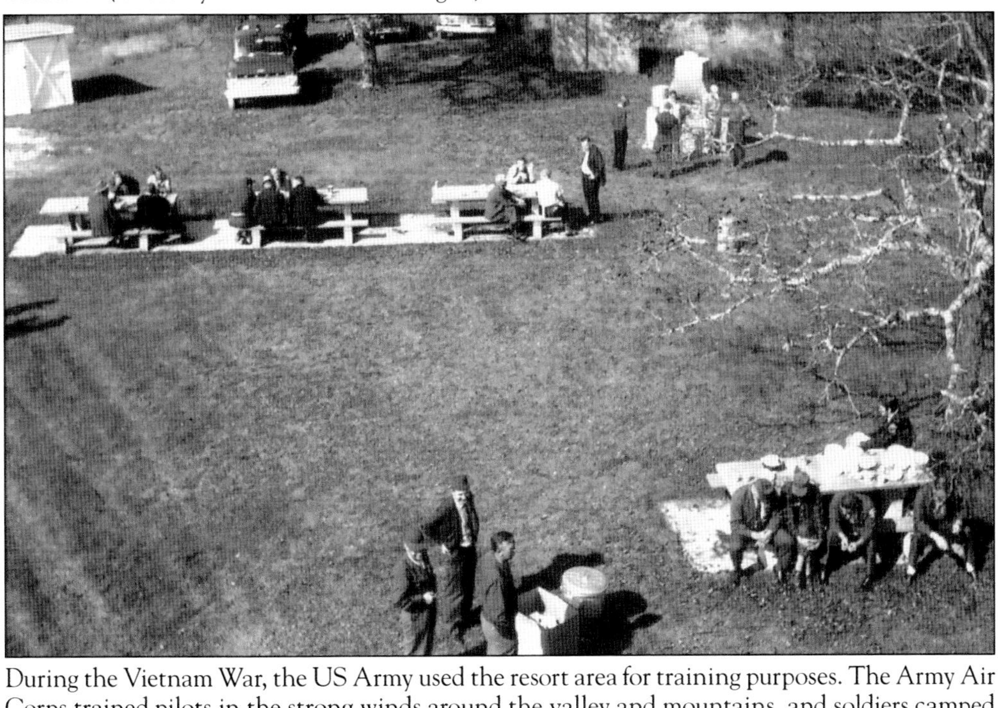

During the Vietnam War, the US Army used the resort area for training purposes. The Army Air Corps trained pilots in the strong winds around the valley and mountains, and soldiers camped in the area. Several are shown dining and relaxing in this photograph. (Courtesy of Rick and Lisa Stargill.)

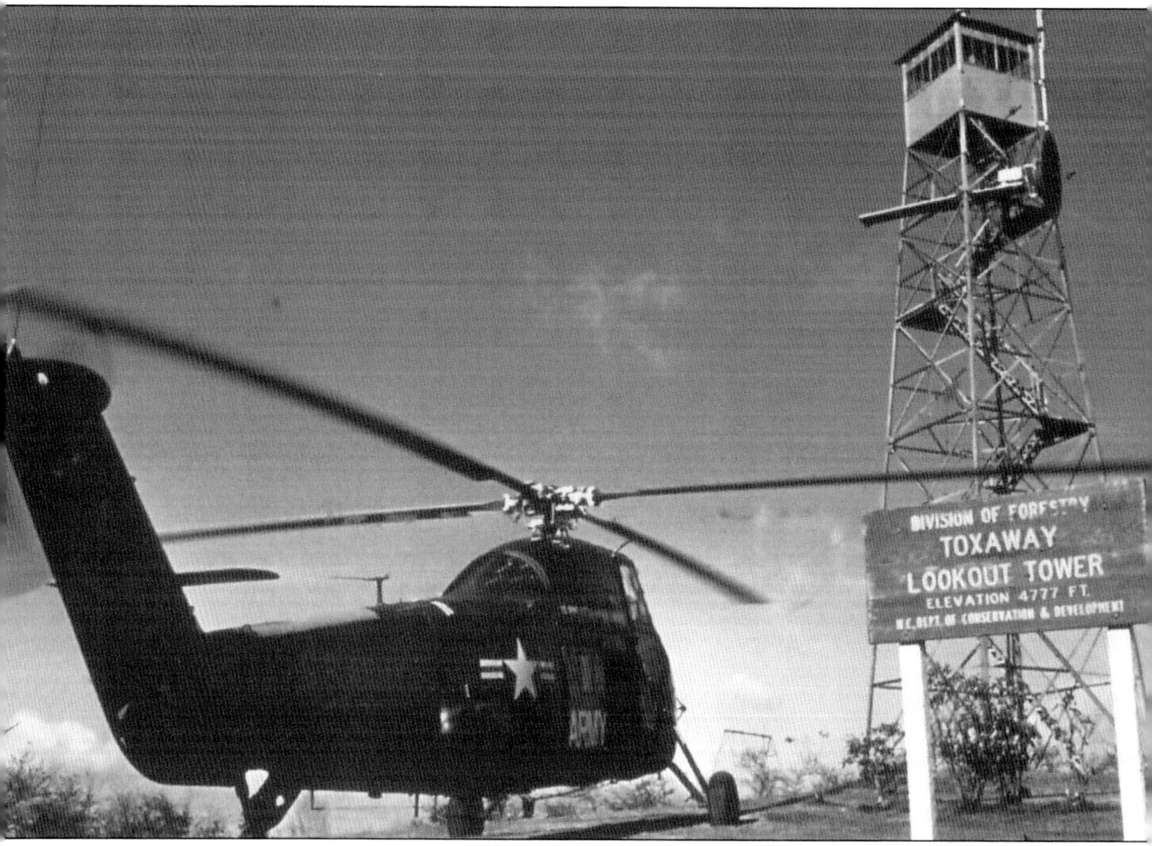

This Army helicopter is landing as part of training maneuvers taken near the resort at the Toxaway lookout tower. The Sapphire Valley resort was the home of an array of Army training maneuvers during the Vietnam War. (Courtesy of Rick and Lisa Stargill.)

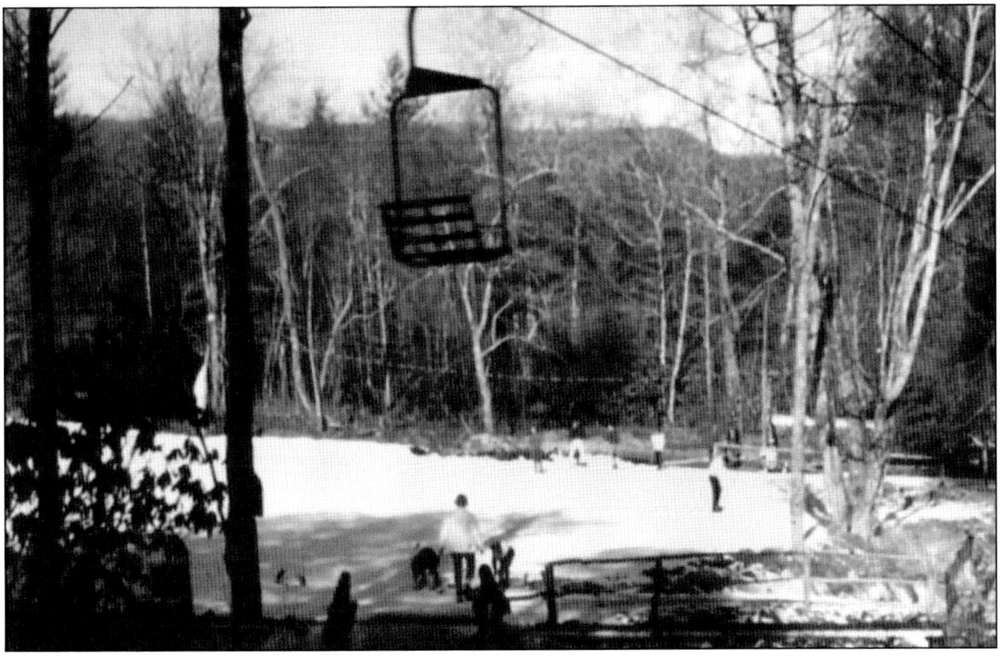

With the lifts constructed, Ski Sapphire opened in 1964 and brought in small crowds throughout the 1960s and 1970s. Many visitors prefer the smaller scale of the resort, as well as the beginner and intermediate slopes that it offers. (Courtesy of Rick and Lisa Stargill.)

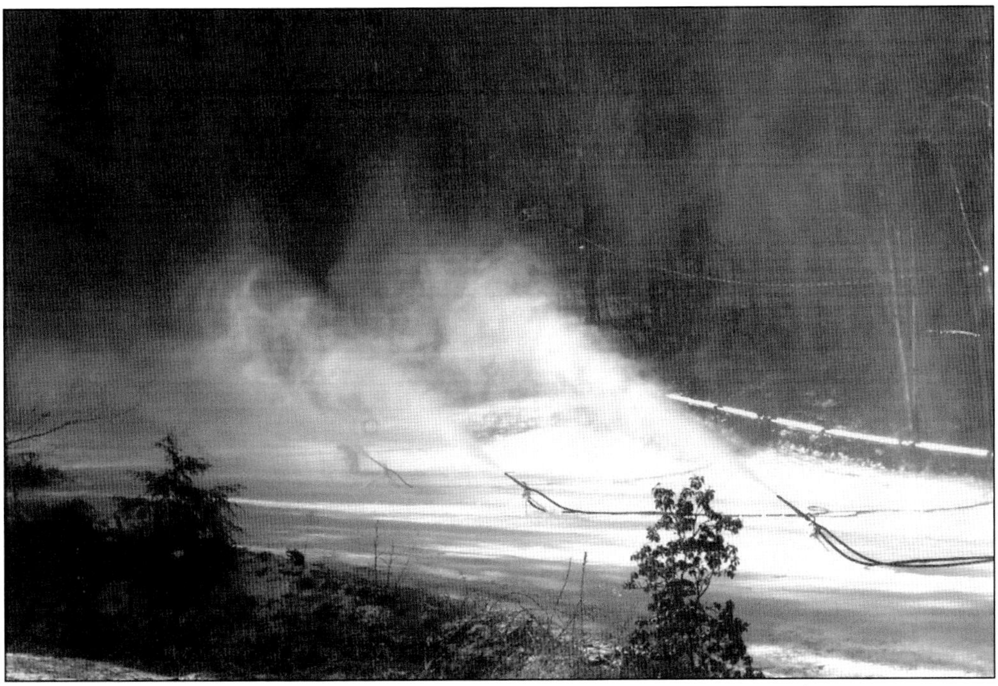

Snow guns are blasting out water and compressed air on this winter's day at Sapphire. Improvements to the resort's snowmaking capabilities took place through the years, and the system covers the current eight acres of slopes very well. (Courtesy of Rick and Lisa Stargill.)

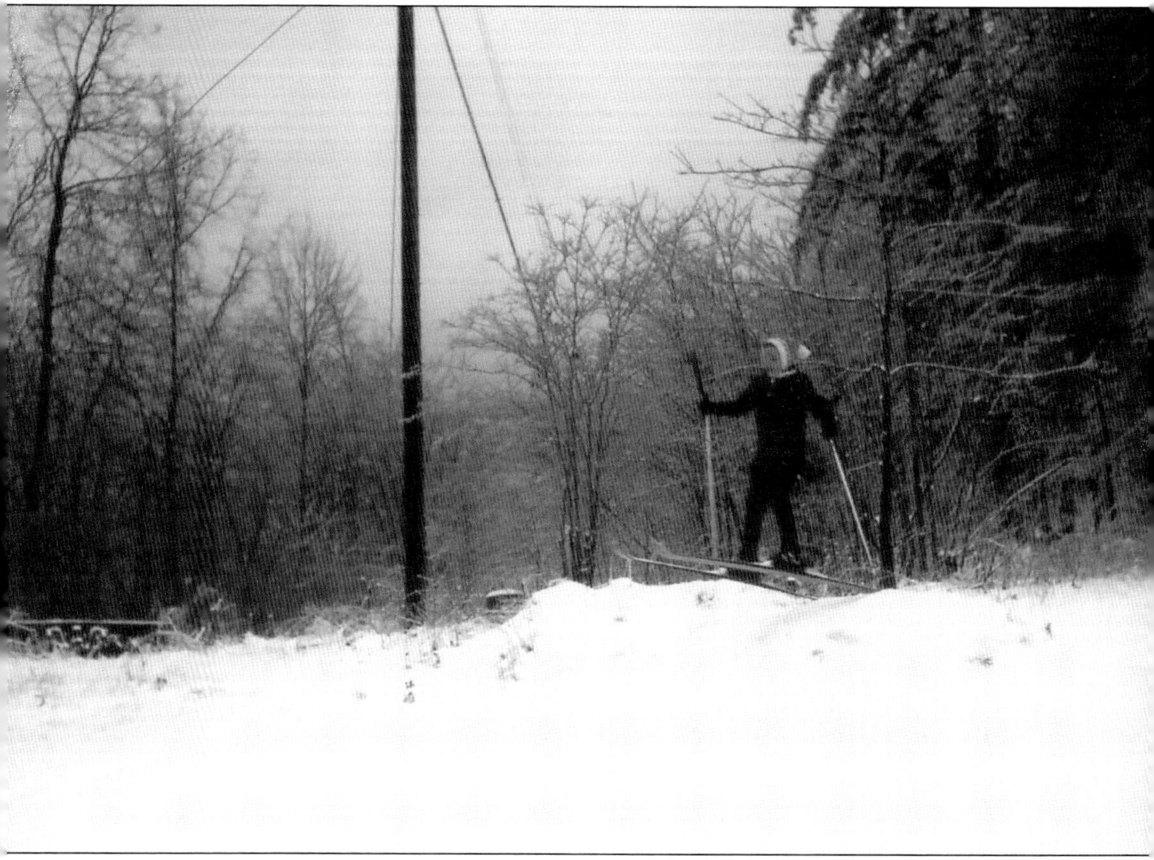

A lone skier flies down Sapphire Valley's slopes in 1970. Skiing was encouraged by the adjacent Hogback Lake real estate development, which provided buyers with free passes to the ski area, along with a set of custom skis and boots. (Courtesy History of Sapphire Valley collection.)

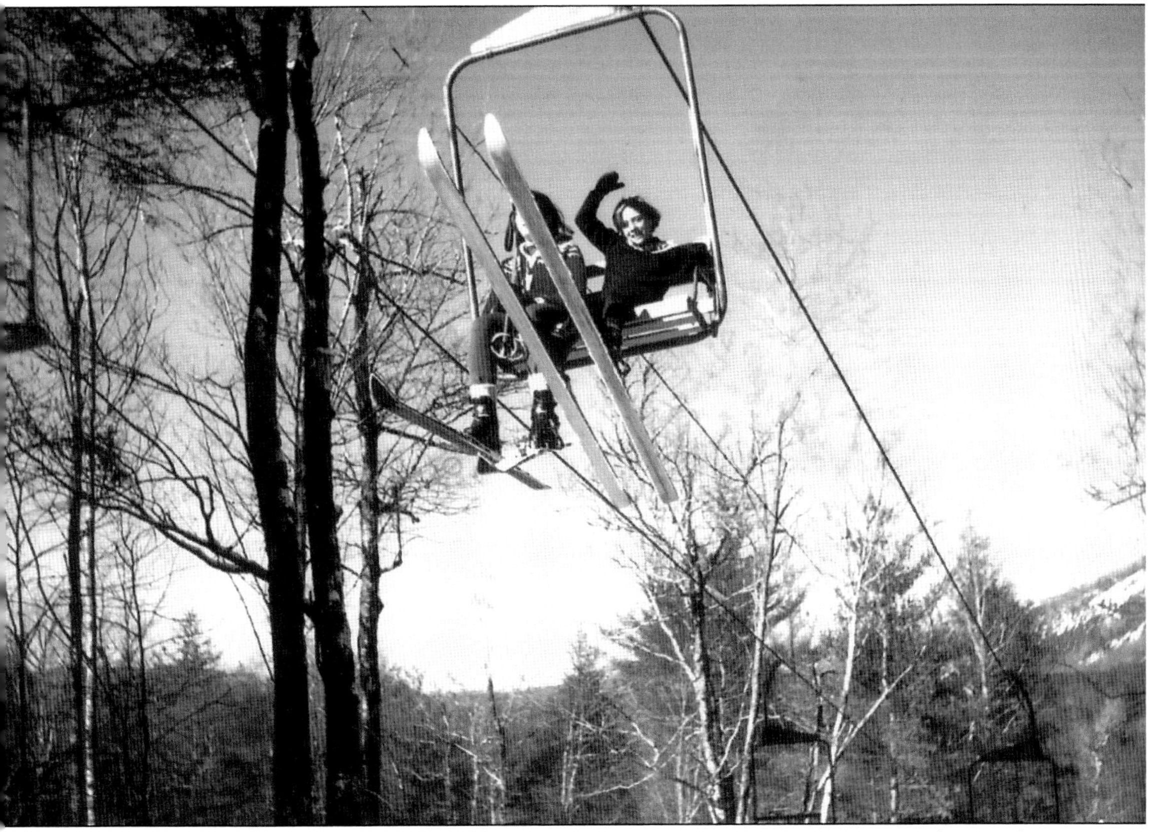

Photographed around 1975, these happy skiers wave from the chairlift on a sunny day at Ski Sapphire Valley. Note the length of the skies of the woman on the right, reflecting her expertise at skiing and the Graduated Learning Method. The other woman is wearing what seem to be shorter, more beginner-friendly skis. (Courtesy of Rick and Lisa Stargill.)

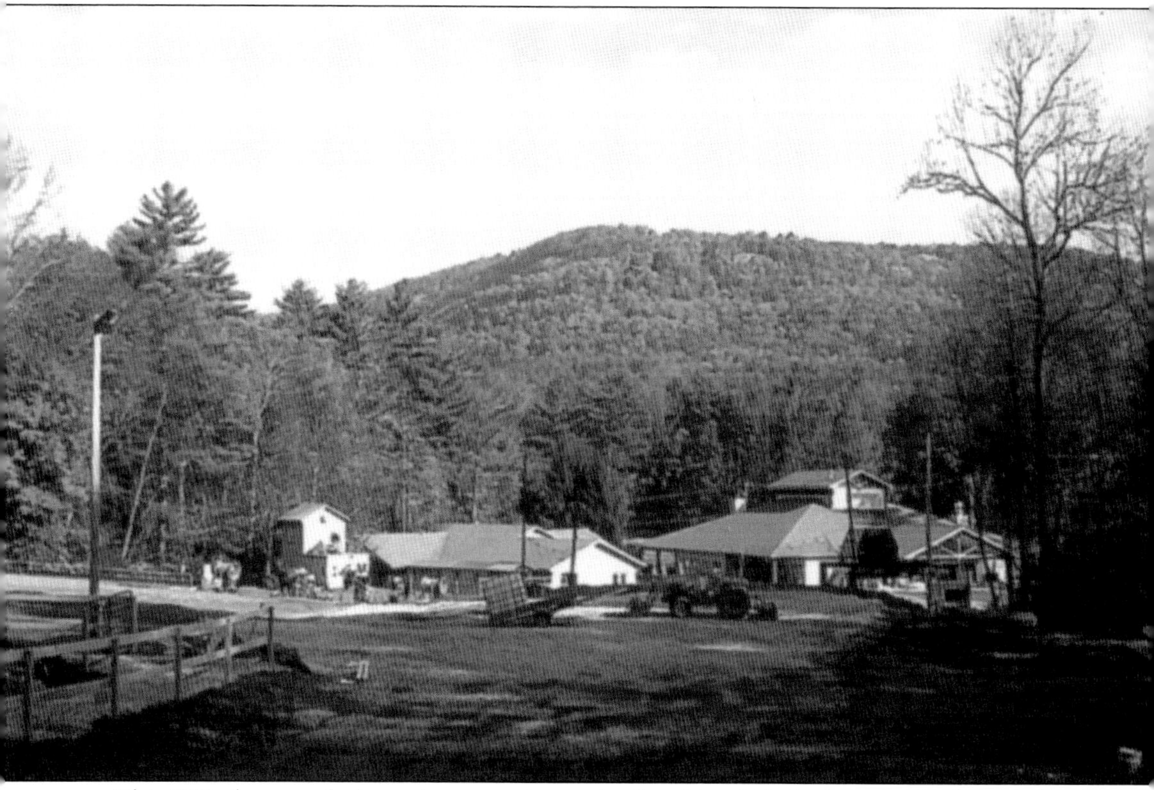

This 1980 photograph shows the expansion to the Sapphire ski lodge, which added needed space to the hub of the resort. Originally, the oldest house in the valley served as the base lodge and provided a place for families and friends to enjoy beverages, fondue, and snacks in front of the large, rustic fireplace. Sadly, the house was demolished, but the original fireplace was salvaged and plans are under way to restore it. The current owners plan to continue expansion and upgrade the resort. With a 1,600-foot main run, Ski Sapphire Valley offers a quad-lift, snow tubing and sled runs, and a new moving carpet that moves skiers back to the top for more runs. (Courtesy of Rick and Lisa Stargill.)

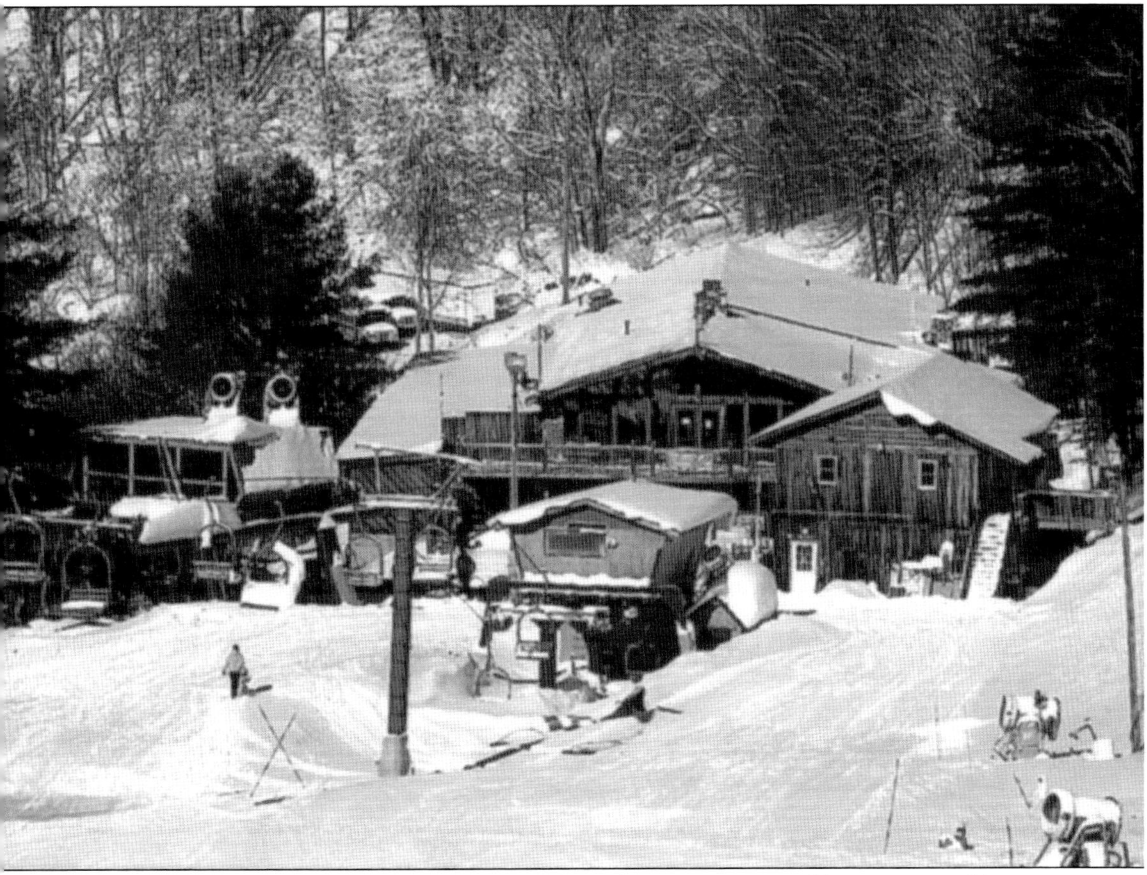

The Wolf Ridge lodge is pictured here in 1970 after a heavy snow. Snowblowers are visible on the lower right of the image, while the chairlift leads through the center. The Wolf Laurel ski area opened in the winter of 1970–1971 and provided skiing to the parts of North Carolina closer to Mars Hill. Various owners have overseen an increase in snowmaking capacity and the installation of an intermediate slope in 1983. Today, the resort features a vertical drop of 700 feet, 5 lifts with a capacity of 5,500 guests per hour, and 20 slopes and trails on 82 skiable acres. (Courtesy of Wolf Ridge website.)

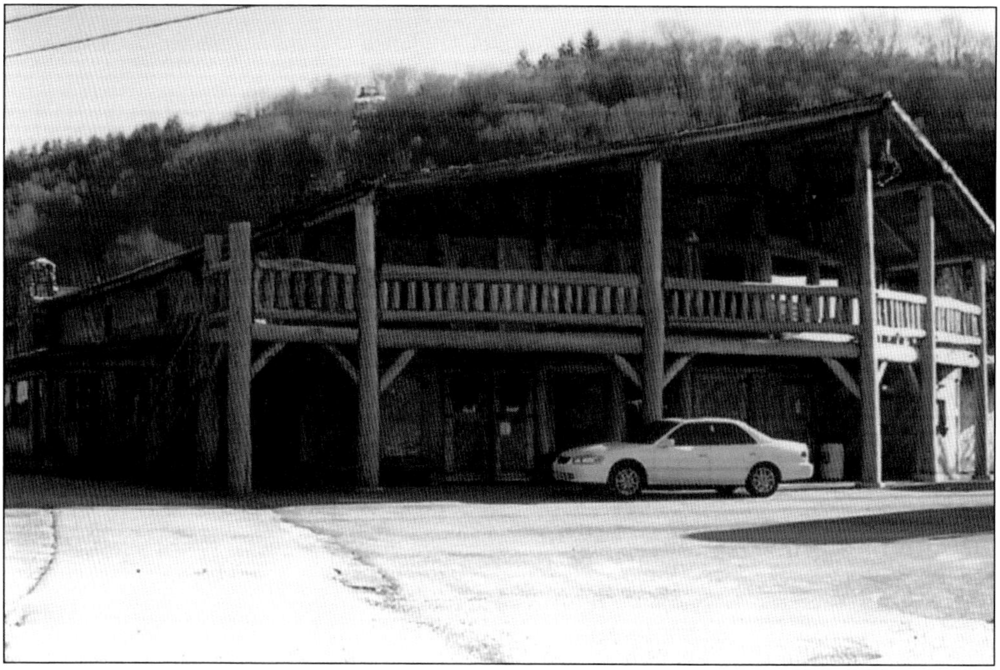

The lodge at Wolf Ridge is built of large timbers and logs, which lend a rustic, rural atmosphere to the resort. The ski slopes are located behind the lodge building. (Courtesy of Wolf Ridge website.)

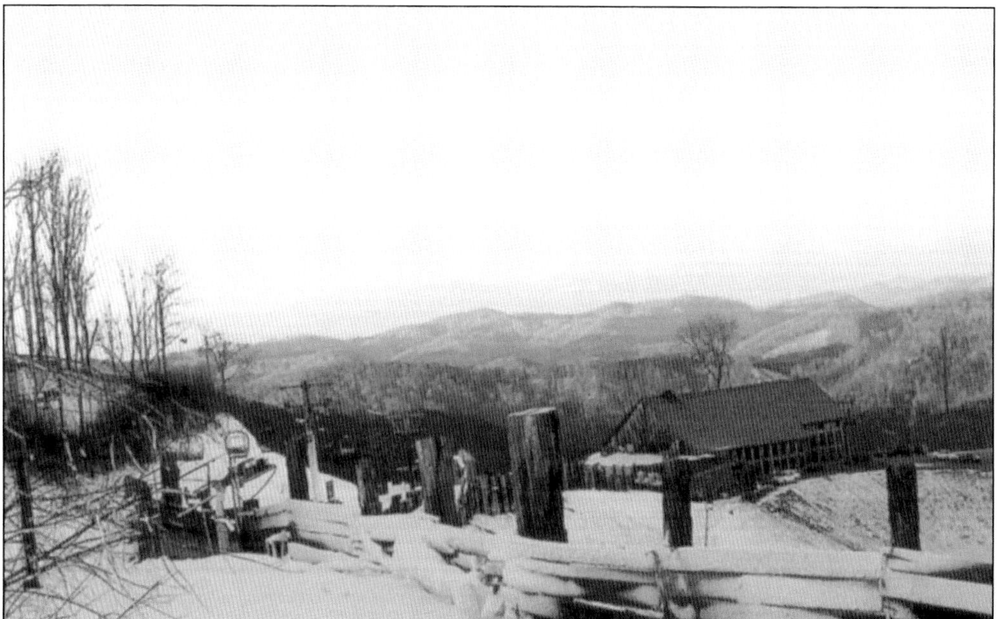

This photograph shows the incredible long-range views available at Wolf Ridge. The lodge building is located along the right of the photograph, and a lift is visible on the left. (Courtesy of Wolf Ridge website.)

Six

Lost Ski Areas

Even as North Carolina became the prominent location for skiing in the South, many ski resorts ultimately failed and have since faded into memory. Among the reasons for their demise are financial issues and the 1970s recession. Lost ski areas in North Carolina include Hound Ears, High Meadows, Mill Ridge, and Hawksnest. Hound Ears was developed by Grover and Harry Robbins in 1964 and was one of the northwestern region's first second-home developments. High Meadows opened in 1966 near Roaring Gap in Allegheny County, North Carolina. Mill Ridge was opened in 1970–1971 in Foscoe—near Boone—by Buck Smith and the Mill Ridge developers. The slope for Mill Ridge only measured 3,200 feet, and author Randy Johnson has called it "the South's biggest little slope." The Mill Ridge park was popular with telemark skiers and families and included a modern lodge. It passed through several owners before closing. The slopes at Hawksnest—or Seven Devils, as it was first named—were graded in 1966, and the resort opened that winter. It was developed by Herb Reynolds.

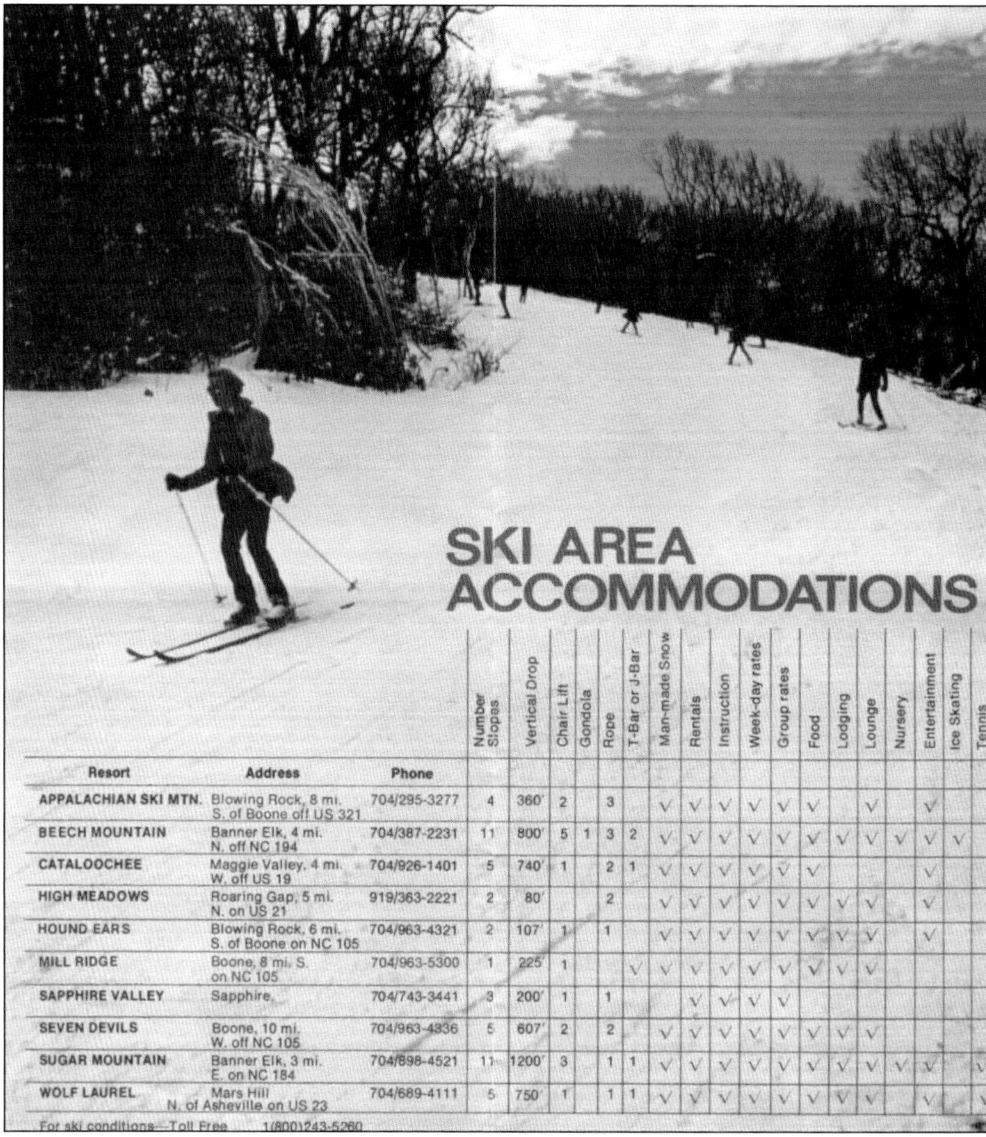

SKI AREA ACCOMMODATIONS

Resort	Address	Phone	Number Slopes	Vertical Drop	Chair Lift	Gondola	Rope	T-Bar or J-Bar	Man-made Snow	Rentals	Instruction	Week-day rates	Group rates	Food	Lodging	Lounge	Nursery	Entertainment	Ice Skating	Tennis
APPALACHIAN SKI MTN.	Blowing Rock, 8 mi. S. of Boone off US 321	704/295-3277	4	360′	2		3		√	√	√	√	√	√		√		√		
BEECH MOUNTAIN	Banner Elk, 4 mi. N. off NC 194	704/387-2231	11	800′	5	1	3	2	√	√	√	√	√	√	√	√	√	√	√	
CATALOOCHEE	Maggie Valley, 4 mi. W. off US 19	704/926-1401	5	740′	1		2	1	√	√	√	√	√	√				√		
HIGH MEADOWS	Roaring Gap, 5 mi. N. on US 21	919/363-2221	2	80′			2		√	√	√	√	√	√	√	√		√		
HOUND EARS	Blowing Rock, 6 mi. S. of Boone on NC 105	704/963-4321	2	107′	1		1		√	√	√	√	√	√	√	√		√		
MILL RIDGE	Boone, 8 mi. S. on NC 105	704/963-5300	1	225′	1			√	√	√	√	√	√	√	√	√				
SAPPHIRE VALLEY	Sapphire,	704/743-3441	3	200′	1		1			√	√	√	√							
SEVEN DEVILS	Boone, 10 mi. W. off NC 105	704/963-4336	5	607′	2		2		√	√	√	√	√	√	√	√				
SUGAR MOUNTAIN	Banner Elk, 3 mi. E. on NC 184	704/898-4521	11	1200′	3		1	1	√	√	√	√	√	√	√	√	√	√		√
WOLF LAUREL	Mars Hill N. of Asheville on US 23	704/689-4111	5	750′	1		1	1	√	√	√	√	√	√	√	√		√		√

For ski conditions—Toll Free 1(800)243-5260

This early North Carolina skiing brochure shows the 10 ski resorts operating at the time: Appalachian Ski Mountain, Beech Mountain, Cataloochee, High Meadows, Hound Ears, Mill Ridge, Sapphire Valley, Seven Devils, Sugar Mountain, and Wolf Laurel. These intrepid southern ski resorts knew that marketing this new sport to Southerners would be key to their survival and that cooperation among them was of paramount importance. The newly created North Carolina ski areas succeeded by setting up college classes, offering group skiing, welcoming tour buses, developing package deals at local hotels, holding ski shows on the road, sponsoring special events, hosting famous skiers, and sending out press releases. Business leaders in these resorts' communities supported and welcomed the development of winter sports, as it augmented their tourism industries and added to their economic vitality. (Courtesy of Appalachian Ski Mountain Collection.)

High Meadows Inn

ROARING GAP, NORTH CAROLINA

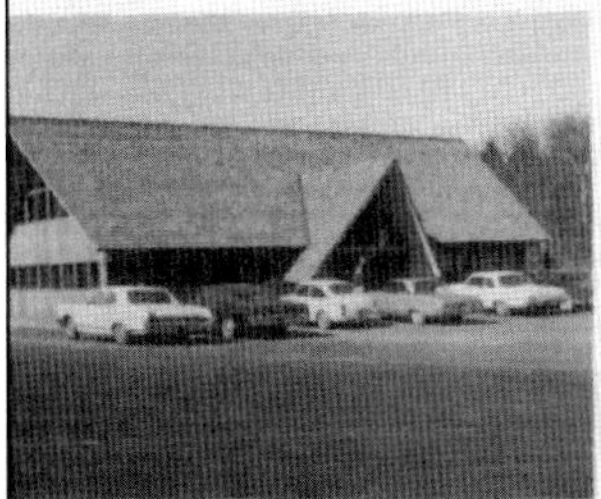

DAILY RATES

June 1st thru Oct. 31st
Single (one person) $15.00
Double (2 people) $20.00

November 1st thru May 31st
Single (one person) $12.00
Double (2 people) $16.00
$2.00 extra each additional person
Meetings rooms available
Inquire about group rates

High Meadows Ski Lodge

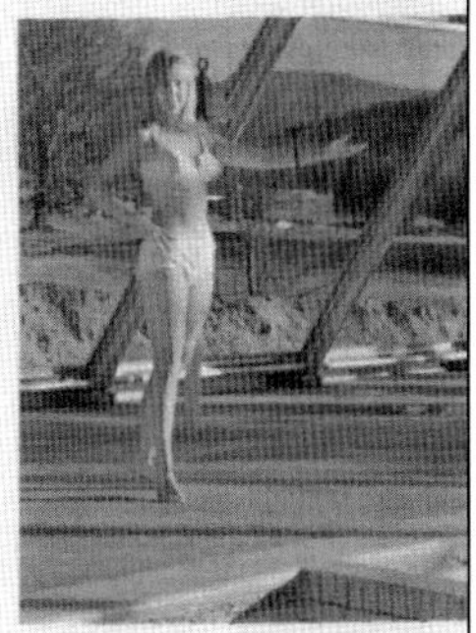

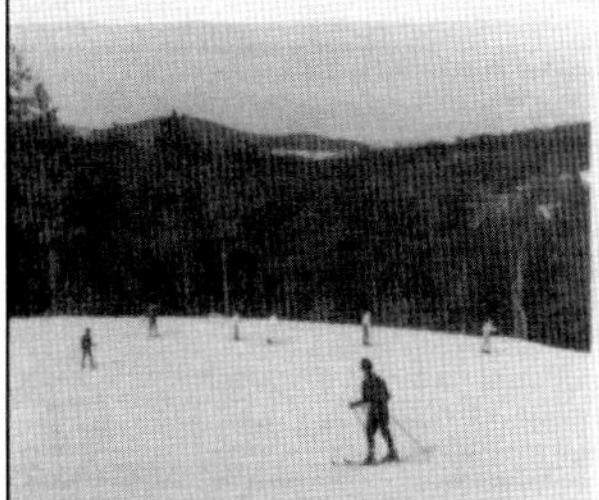

DAILY RATES

Tuesday thru Friday 1 pm to 10 pm
Adults—Equipment Rental
$4.00 Tow $4.00
6 pm to 10 pm. $3.00 Tow $3.00
Children under 12—Equip. Rental
$3.00 Tow $3.00
6 pm to 10 pm $2.00 Tow $2.00

Weekends 9:00 am to 4:30 pm
Adults—Equipment Rental
$5.00 Tow $5.00
Children under 12—Equip. Rental
$3.00 Tow $3.00
Saturday Night—Equip. Rental
6-10 pm
Adult - $3.00 Tow $3.00
Children - Rental $2.00 Tow $2.00
Closed Mondays

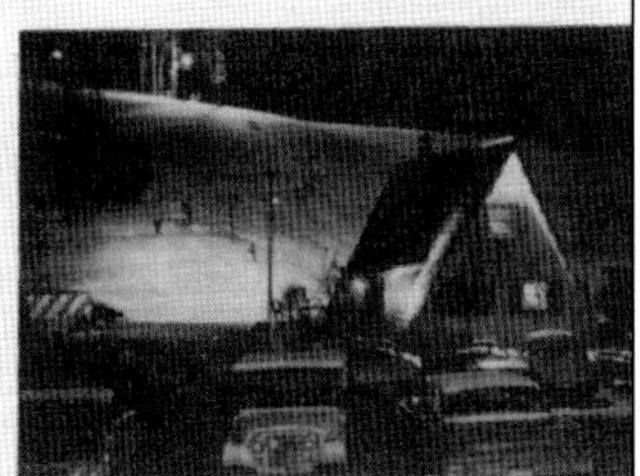

Ski & Pool Membership
1 person .... $75.00 per year
Each additional person $25.00
SPECIAL GROUP RATES

Here is a brochure for the High Meadows Ski Lodge, located at Roaring Gap. Clyde Reavis, Charles Swift, and C.B. Hughes opened the resort in 1966, which had a 1,100-foot intermediate slope, restaurant, hotel and motel, convention center, pool, and golf course. In its day, the resort drew many visitors, and even though the ski slope is no longer operating, it continues to provide recreation for locals and visitors to the area. (Courtesy of Appalachian Ski Mountain Collection.)

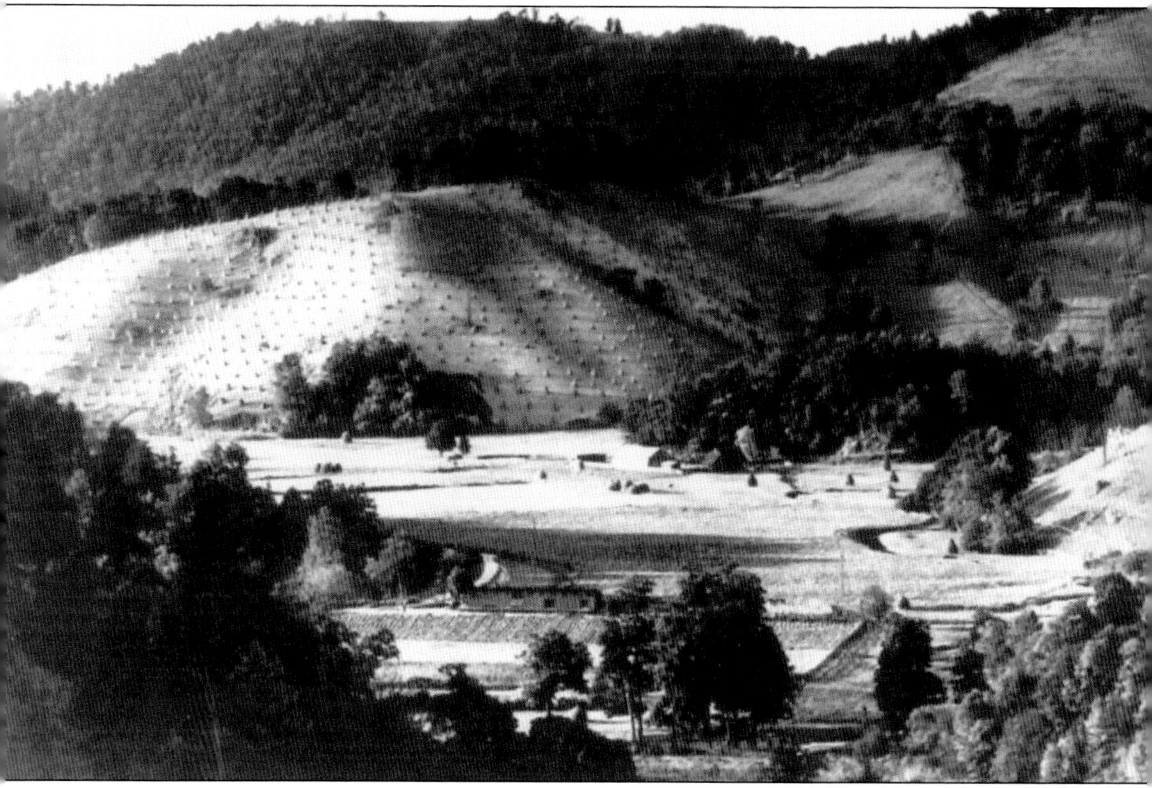

In 1964, Grover and Harry Robbins founded Hound Ears, the first upscale second-home community in the High Country. It included a golf course, a beautiful clubhouse, and a small ski area. With an elevation of only 3,000 feet, the two slopes mainly provided skiing for beginners and cross-country skiers. Telemark skiing clinics were held regularly, and the resort earned Mobil's four-star rating. Although the ski resort is closed now, the residential development, clubhouse, and golf course remain popular for residents. In 2014, Hound Ears is celebrating its 50th anniversary and planning many celebrations. The above photograph dates to about 1920, showing the fields and cleared hillsides where the resort was to be built. (Courtesy of Hound Ears Club Collection.)

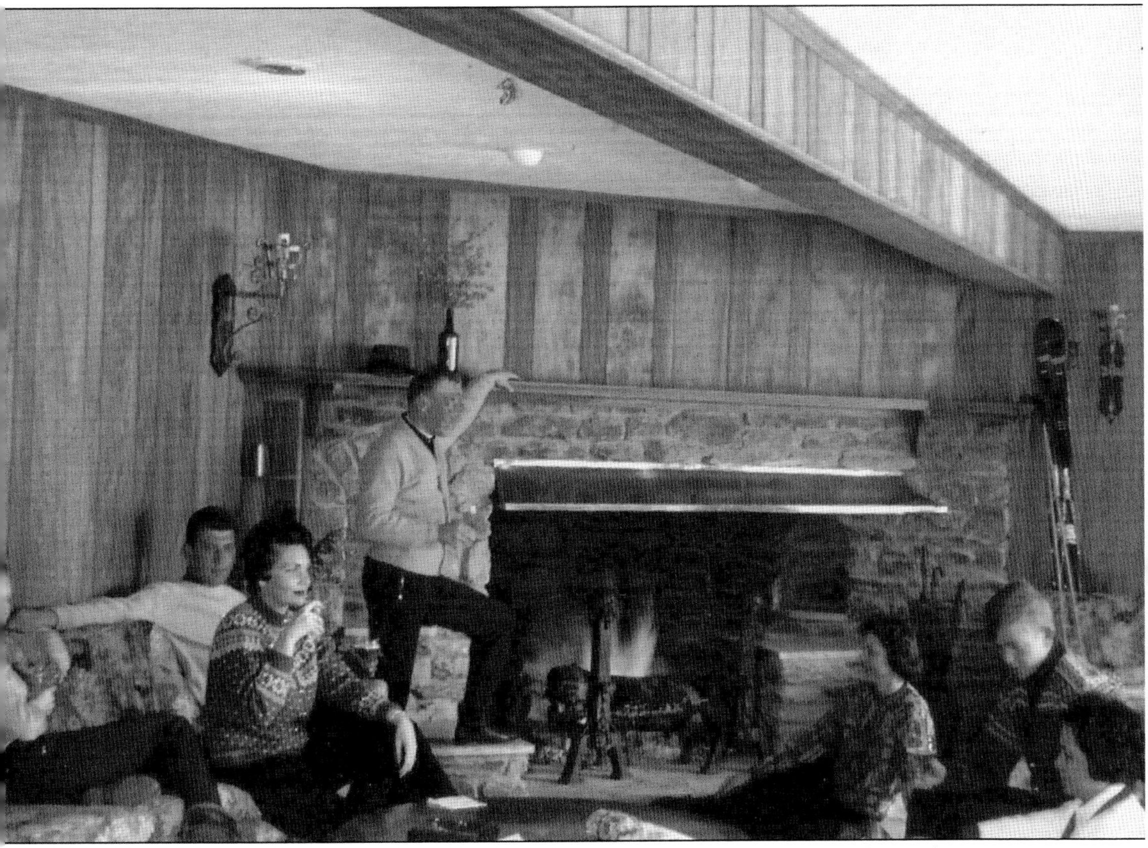

Hound Ears can boast of being the earliest high-end second-home community in the High Country region, and today, many of the original houses from the 1960s and 1970s blend in well with newer vacation homes. Designed by nationally acclaimed architect Claus Moberg, the clubhouse has a luxurious and welcoming atmosphere, with paneled wall and a large stone fireplace, and has been well preserved and is still being used today. Here is the upscale clubhouse around 1964, where guests could relax and enjoy food and drink in front of the attractive stone fireplace. (Courtesy of Hound Ears Club Collection.)

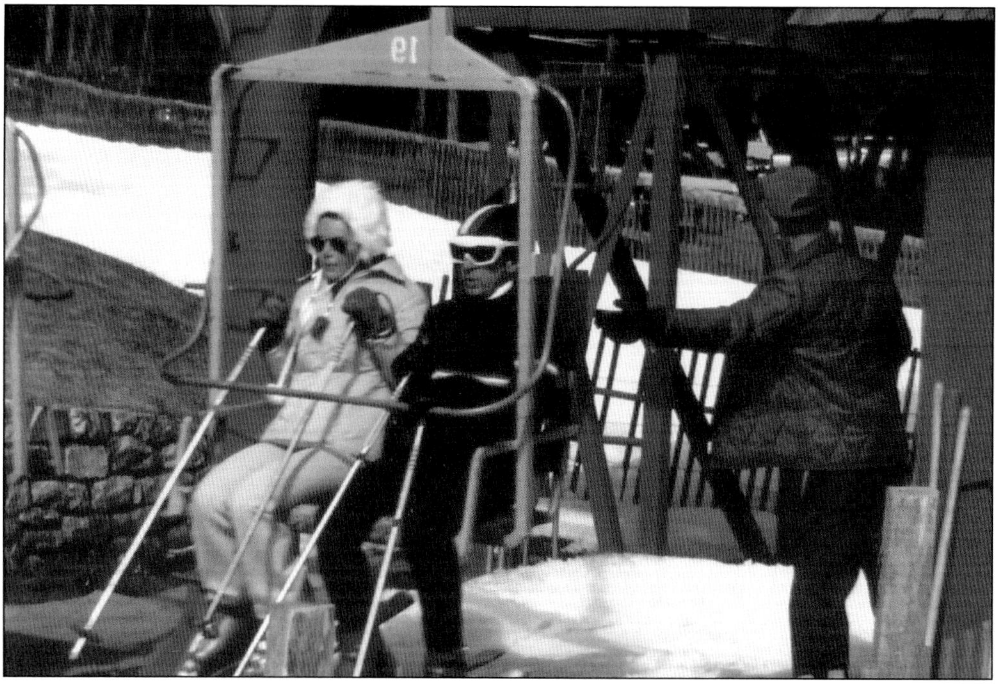

In the c. 1970 photograph above, two warmly dressed skiers at Hound Ears have just boarded the double lift on their way up to the slopes. Although it was a small ski area, Hound Ears served as an excellent place to learn to ski and was well liked by cross-country skiers. Below, two skiers are in line at the lift shack and are ready to board the chairlift. (Both, courtesy of Hound Ears Club Collection.)

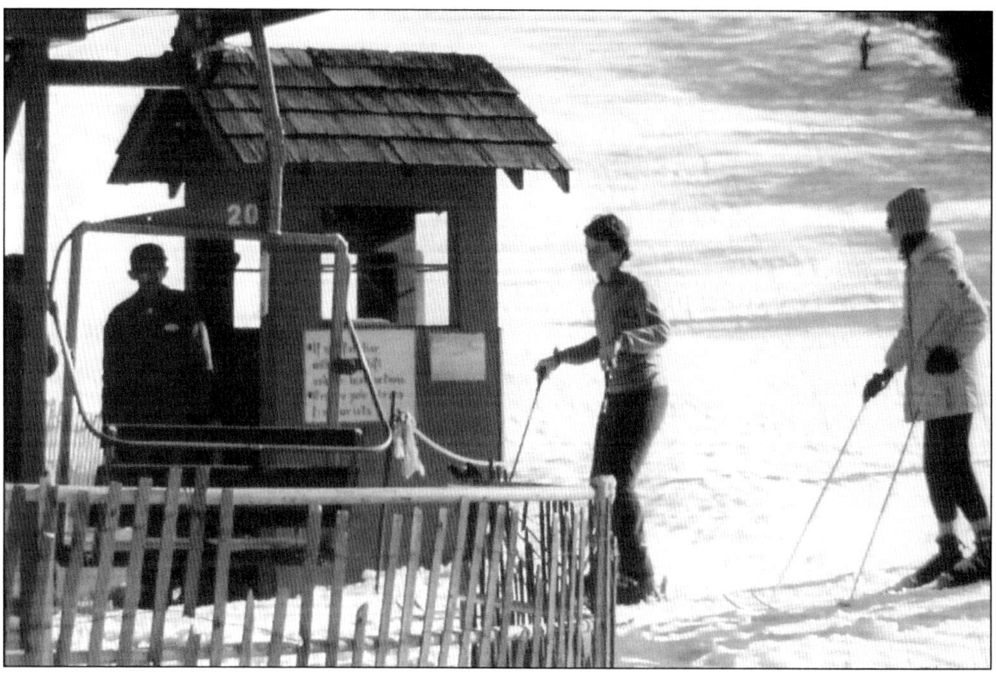

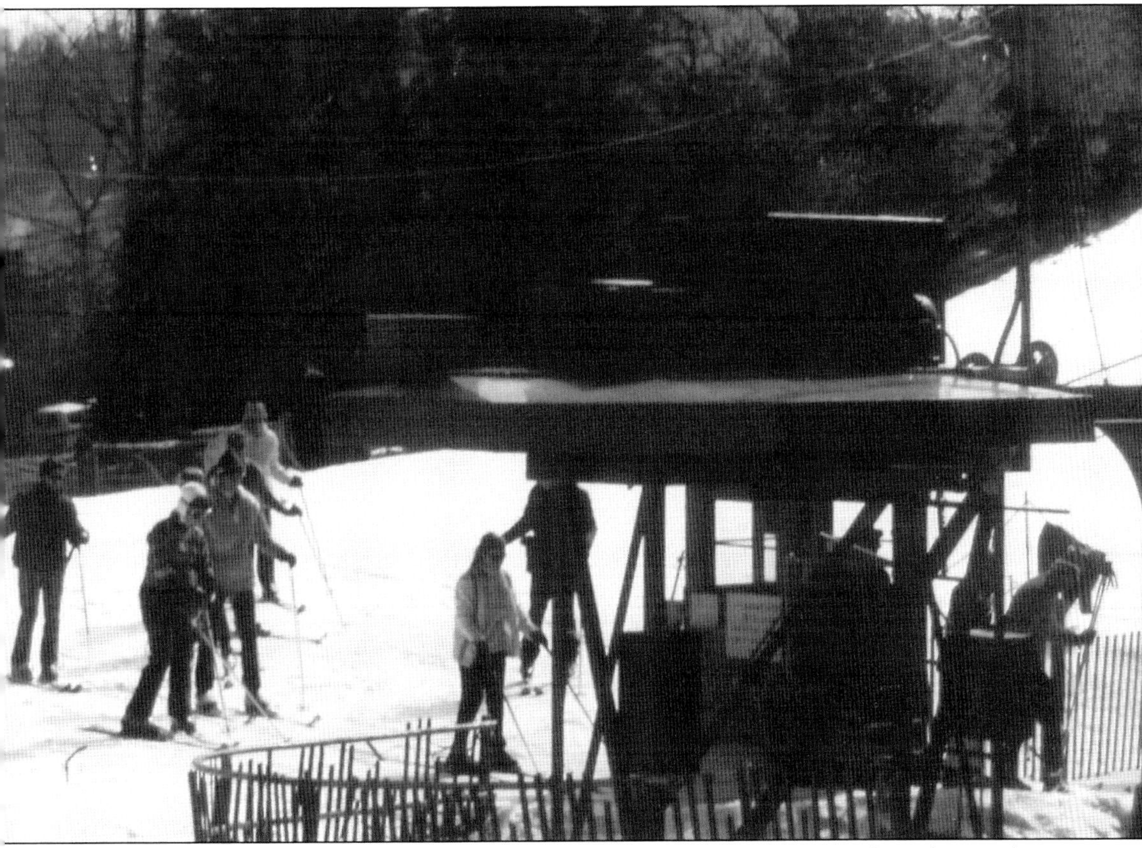

These skiers are waiting on the double lift to go up to the beginner and intermediate slopes. The resort was usually never crowded, and it provided a less-steep environment for many Southerners to learn to ski. (Courtesy of Hound Ears Club Collection.)

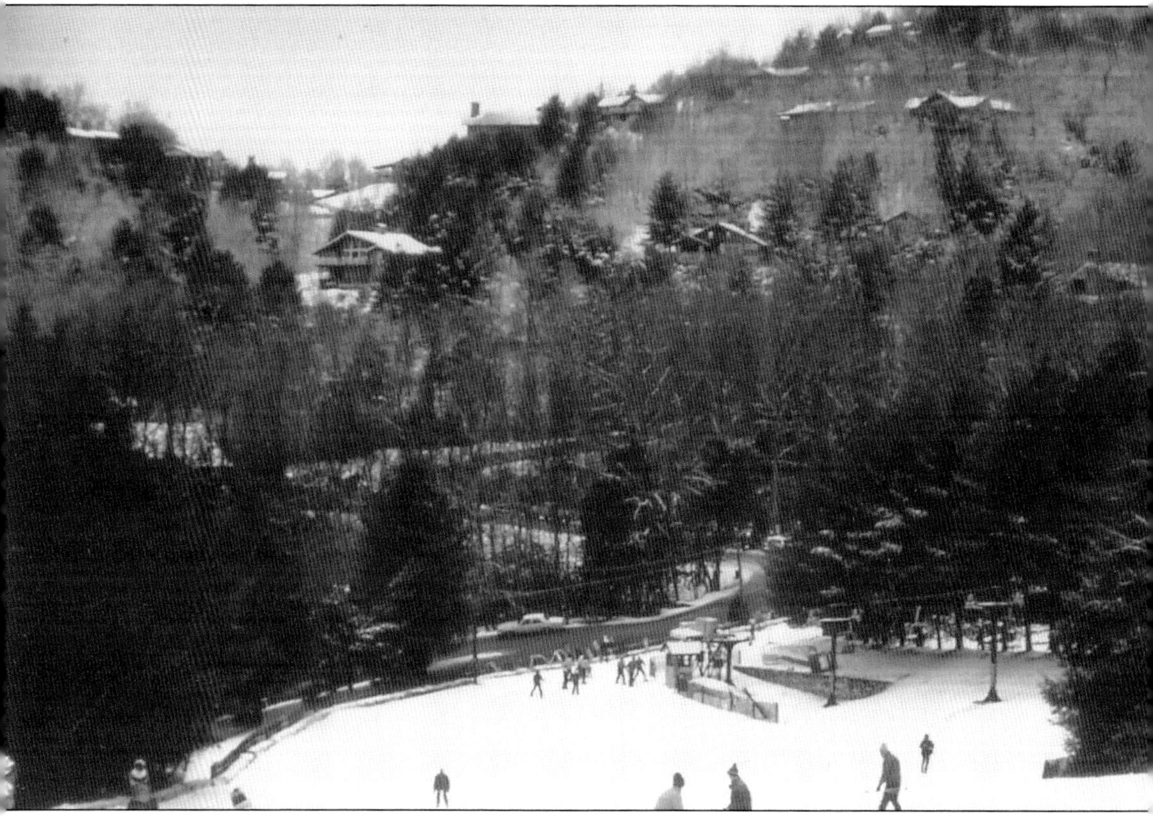

Here is another look at the Hound Ears Club ski slopes, showing the luxury homes built on the hills that surround the recreational amenities. Although popular with the club's members, the ski area was expensive to maintain and the members decided to cease operations. Some residents still long for their own private ski area, but it is not likely to be reopened. Interestingly, the resort's golf course has also served a second purpose as a landing strip for members' small private planes. The resort was originally named for the resemblance of the surrounding hills to a hound's ears. (Courtesy of Hound Ears Club Collection.)

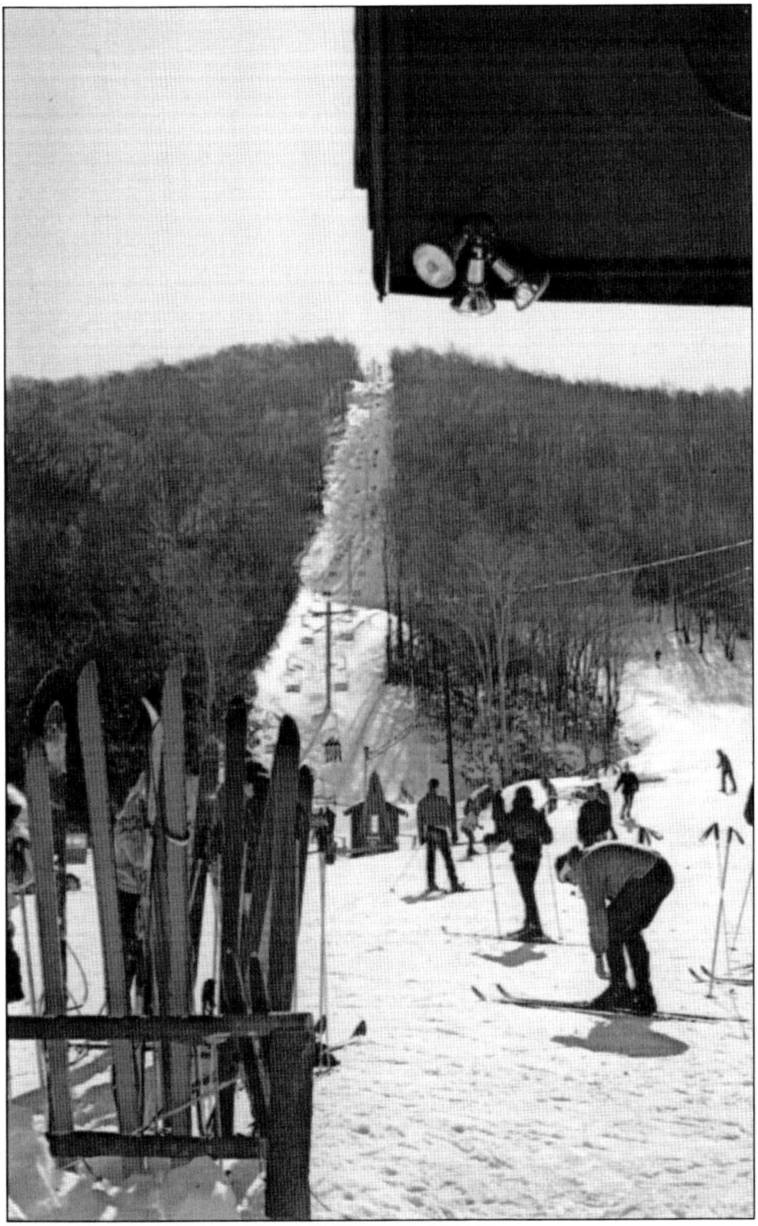

Known first as Seven Devils Ski Area and later as Ski Hawksnest, this ski resort opened as part of a larger residential area between 1966 and 1967. It was designed for more intermediate skiers and featured 7 slopes, 20 acres of skiing trails, and a vertical drop of 619 feet. The views of Grandfather Mountain were a favorite for skiers, and the popular lodge featured fireplaces, gathering places, a cafeteria, a ski shop, a rental office, and the main office. The ski area was closed several years ago, and today, it exists as the Hawksnest Tubing Park. It claims to be the largest snow-tubing park on the East Coast, with 20 lanes for tubing. Hawksnest also features zip lines and claims to be the longest zip-line tour on the East Coast, with 20 lines. Four of those lines are mega or super zips, with four lines measuring over 1,500 feet in length. A total of four miles of zip-line riding comprise the course, ranging up to 200 feet and providing speeds of up to 50 miles per hour. (Courtesy of Hawsknest Snowtubing and Zipline.)

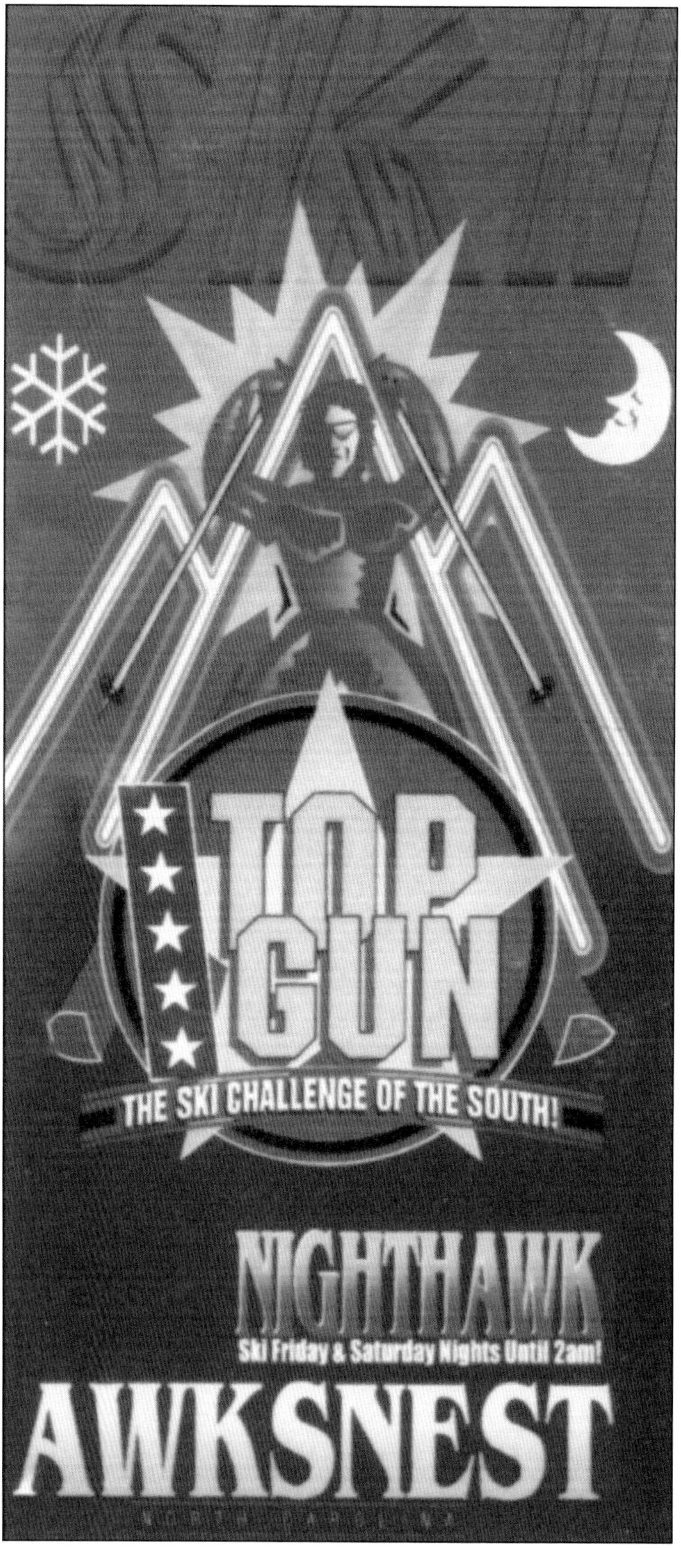

This ski brochure summarizes the atmosphere of Ski Hawksnest, showing its sponsorship of the Top Gun, "the ski challenge of the South." Herb Reynolds developed the resort with assistance from Gardner Gidley. After several owners made improvements to the slopes, lodge, and snowmaking equipment, the ski area was purchased by the Cottom family. They continue to operate the zip-line and tubing park today. According to Randy Johnson, the Nordic segment of the Southeastern Winter Special Olympics was held on these slopes. The town of Seven Devils incorporated in 1981. (Courtesy of Hawksnest Snowtubing and Zipline.)

BIBLIOGRAPHY

Alexander, Tom. *Mountain Fever.* Fairview, NC: Bright Mountain Book, Inc., 1995.
Belin, Dave. "NC Ski Areas Association Economic Impact Study." RRC Associates, Boulder, Colorado, September 2010.
Calhoun, Sam. "Dream On Sugar Mountain." *High Country Magazine* 5 (February 2010).
Cottrell, Jim. *Skiing Everyone.* Winston-Salem, NC: Hunter Textbooks, Inc., 2011.
Johnson, Randy. "A Half-Century of High Country Skiing." *High Country Magazine* 7 (December 2011): 16–34.
———. "A Half-Century of High Country Skiing." *High Country Magazine* 6 (March 2011): 53–56.
———. *Southern Snow: The Winter Guide to Dixie.* Boston: Appalachian Mountain Club, 1987.
The Beech Mountain Historical Society. *Beech Mountain.* Charleston, SC: Arcadia Publishing, 2009.
Warmuth, Donna Akers. *Boone.* Charleston, SC: Arcadia Publishing, 2003.
———. *Blowing Rock.* Charleston, SC: Arcadia Publishing, 2004.